TeeBox

COMPREHENSIVE GOLF COURSE GUIDES

™

TM

TeeBox
ARIZONA
GOLF GUIDE

Comming Soon
Hawaii Golf Guide - Nov.
California Golf Guide - Jan.
Florida Golf Guide - Feb.

BY

STEPHAN K. HARPER

 **TeeBox**
COMPREHENSIVE GOLF COURSE GUIDES
TM

COMPREHENSIVE GOLF COURSE GUIDES

Author	*Art Director*	*Technical Director*	*Project Assistants*
STEPHAN HARPER	STEPHAN HARPER	ROBERT HAMEL	KENT HARPER
			ROBERT HAMEL
			RAY GILBREATH

Published by
TeeBox
3241 E. SHEA BLVD. SUITE #7
PHOENIX, AZ 85028

Printed by
PATTERSON PRINTING
1550 TERRITORIAL RD.
BENTON HARBOR, MI 49022

TM

TO MY WIFE KAREN, WHO GAVE UP EVERYTHING EXCEPT HER FAITH IN ME.

TO EVERYONE WHO LOVES THE GAME OF GOLF.

TM

ACKNOWLEDGMENTS

TEEBOX: THE ARIZONA GOLF GUIDE contains a collection of information that is unsurpassed on any level of sports information currently available to the general pubic. TeeBox wishes to thank those who made this book possible:

ALL THE GOLF COURSES
> in the state of Arizona that responded to our inquires.

MY WIFE KAREN
> for her continued support and patience.

ROBERT HAMEL
> for providing uncompromised technical direction that resulted in a new data compilation technique and for helping to establish the POGA.

MY FAMILY
> who believed in my dream.

RAY GILBREATH
> for bringing his insight and encouragement to the office everyday and also a devoted POGA member.

VINCE BLASKO PHD.
> for helping to forge new creativity.

JAMES HAMEL
> who gave TeeBox a home.

TM

INTRODUCTION

I love to play golf. In fact, I think I could play golf every day of my entire life and never get tired of it. Get up early, go to the driving range and hit a large bucket, then scamper around the putting green and listen for my name to be called while I'm working on my 3 footers and my 60 footers (the two putts I can never seem to sink), Then I'll go shoot somewhere between an 82 and a 95 and be happy with some shots and disgusted with others. There is just something that stirs the soul when you pit yourself against the mighty forces of mother nature all rolled up into 18 holes. No matter how good or bad you play, you're always anxious to get back and try again. **The question though is not when to play again, but where. That's where TeeBox steps in.**

TeeBox came about because "I" didn't know where to play. I was on vacation in an unfamiliar city. I had told my wife that I was at least going to play every other day. Then I went on an unforgettable voyage through phone books, newspapers, bookstores, relatives, and anything else that I could get my hands on to tell me anything about the golf courses in that area. Nothing! All I had were phone numbers to every course within that metropolitan area. I finally resorted to playing 2 courses...the one I saw while driving into town and the only one my wife's uncle could remember. He hadn't played there in 5 years because of poor health. I played each course twice and had a great time. I even shot a 79 one day. **If I could have had this book on my vacation, there would have been no mystery about finding a golf course that week. I would have easily found the type of courses I like to play, where they were, how to get there, and strategy on how to conquer it.** That's why you bought this book, isn't it.

There are three (3) parts to this guide: The Courses, The Ultimate Course Index, and The Locator Map. The Courses section is set up so that you can look at the box under the course title and quickly determine whether that course interests you. When you find one you like, then read the descriptions that follow. Next, **The Ultimate Course Index** lists courses alphabetically by these separate categories: name, city, access, layout, architect, resorts, toughness, length, cost, tournaments & honors. For example, if you want to play a desert layout, look up all the courses listed under "Desert Layouts" and then look that course up in "The Courses" section. Lastly, **The Locator Map** is the last thing in the book. It folds out to show you where the courses are, and what type of access they allow. All in a glance. It's that easy. No trudging through phone books and long lost relatives. Just look in The TeeBox Arizona Golf Guide.

DESCRIPTION KEY

Type of Layout is marked with a "Black Circle"

DESERT ○   **TRADITIONAL** ●   **LINKS** ○

TERRAIN   **TREES**   **WATER**

Terrain	Trees	Water
Flat	No trees	No water
Gentle	some trees	Some water
Average	Average	Average
Hilly	More trees	More water
Mountains	Forest	A lot of water

 **COURSE FAVORS A...** Draw — Draw, Fade, or Neither

 WIDTH OF FAIRWAYS Tight — Tight, Average, or Forgiving

 **AMT. OF BUNKERS** Many — None, Average, or Many

TM

CONTENTS

THE COURSES

THE ULTIMATE COURSE INDEX

THE LOCATOR MAP

™

THE COURSES

49ERS GOLF AND C.C.

HOTEL GUEST PRIORITY   18 HOLES

12000 E. Tanque Verde Rd.   Tucson, AZ 85749   602-749-4212

DESERT ○   TRADITIONAL ●   LINKS ○

| TERRAIN | TREES | WATER |

GREENS	Bent	COURSE FAVORS A...	Draw
FAIRWAYS	Bermuda	WIDTH OF FAIRWAYS	Normal
BUNKERS	Regular	AMT. OF BUNKERS	Many

PAR	YARDS	RATING	SLOPE	1992 GREEN FEES $
72	6681	71.9	116	HIGH $35
72	6147	69.2	113	LOW $35
72	5687	72	119	SPECIALS None

THE COURSE COMMENTARY

The course has narrow fairways and a lot of out-of-bounds. Accuracy is at a premium. The signature hole is the 533 yard par-5 15th. It's a dogleg left playing to a shallow green guarded by 4 bunkers.

TOUGHEST HOLE THE 405 YARD PAR-4 1ST HOLE IS NARROW WITH A BLIND APPROACH TO THE GREEN.

BIRDIE HOLE THE 472 YARD PAR-5 7TH HOLE PLAYS STRAIGHT AWAY AND HAS A VERY FORGIVING FAIRWAY.

WATER IN PLAY ON... 3 HOLES

OVERALL STRATEGY KEEP THE BALL IN THE FAIRWAY OR YOU'LL RUN INTO TROUBLE WITH THE TREES IN THE ROUGH.

CART REQUIRED? No

PRACTICE FACILITIES? DRIVING RANGE   PUTTING GREEN   CHIPPING GREEN

COURSE IS OPEN... YES

OVERSEEDING OCTOBER FOR 2 WEEKS. TEES, GREENS, AND RANGE.

RESTAURANT? RESTAURANT AND LOUNGE

ACCOMMODATIONS? NONE

DON'T FORGET YOUR.. N/A

COURSE DESIGNER N/A

 # OF ROUNDS ANNUALLY 25,000

DIRECTIONS TAKE THE SPEEDWAY TO TANQUE VERDE RD., THEN GO EAST 8 MILES.

2

COURSE LAYOUT

HOLE	1	2	3	4	5	6	7	8	9	10	11	12	13	14	15	16	17	18
CHAMP	405	352	194	378	415	383	472	176	526	153	530	396	364	379	533	419	423	183
MENS	381	326	166	358	388	334	457	147	507	133	486	371	300	352	510	393	400	138
LADIES	353	303	142	321	362	299	444	121	493	108	460	344	270	328	490	373	376	101
PAR	4	4	3	4	4	4	5	3	5	3	5	4	4	4	5	4	4	3
M.HCP	7	13	15	11	3	5	9	17	1	16	4	10	14	12	2	6	8	18
L.HCP	5	13	15	11	7	9	3	17	1	16	6	10	14	12	2	4	8	18

500 CLUB

PUBLIC   18 HOLES

4707 W. Pinnacle Peak Rd.   Phoenix, AZ 85310   *602-492-9500*

DESERT ● TRADITIONAL ○ LINKS ○

TERRAIN	TREES	WATER
	🌲🌲🌲	〰️〰️〰️

	GREENS	Other	COURSE FAVORS A...	Fade
	FAIRWAYS	Other	WIDTH OF FAIRWAYS	Normal
	BUNKERS	Regular	AMT. OF BUNKERS	Many

	PAR	YARDS	RATING	SLOPE	1992 GREEN FEES $	
	72	6700	70.3	115	HIGH	$35
	72	6300	68.2	109	LOW	$16
	73	5600	70.3	113	SPECIALS	$10 after noon

THE COURSE COMMENTARY   *The greens and fairways are tiff grass and are in excellent condition. Tom Sneva, winner of the Indianapolis 500, is the co-owner of the course. It is also home to the worlds fastest golf cart. Driving range is lighted Monday thru Friday.*

TOUGHEST HOLE	THE 164 YARD PAR-3 11TH HOLE IS A BLIND, UPHILL TEE SHOT WITH O.B. LEFT AND RIGHT.
BIRDIE HOLE	THE 321 YARD PAR-4 15TH HOLE IS STRAIGHT AWAY WITH NO TROUBLE.
WATER IN PLAY ON...	6 HOLES
OVERALL STRATEGY	STAY OUT OF THE DESERT.
CART REQUIRED?	NO
PRACTICE FACILITIES?	DRIVING RANGE PUTTING GREEN CHIPPING GREEN
COURSE IS OPEN...	YES
OVERSEEDING	OCTOBER FOR 1 WEEK. TEES AND GREENS.
RESTAURANT?	RESTAURANT, SNACK BAR ON THE COURSE, AND BEVERAGE CART.
ACCOMMODATIONS?	CLOSE TO HOTELS ON I-17
DON'T FORGET YOUR..	ROCK IRON
COURSE DESIGNER	BRIAN WHITCOMB & STUART BRUENING
#OF ROUNDS ANNUALLY	70,000
DIRECTIONS	3 MILES WEST OF I-17 ON PINNACLE PEAK RD.

HOLE	1	2	3	4	5	6	7	8	9	10	11	12	13	14	15	16	17	18
CHAMP	389	573	400	375	203	382	404	196	511	492	164	355	186	410	321	335	422	512
MENS	376	543	341	357	158	362	378	184	489	475	139	334	157	344	300	315	409	487
LADIES	353	475	326	338	115	338	350	168	463	450	121	299	126	306	280	270	375	404
PAR	4	5	4	4	3	4	4	3	5	5	3	4	3	4	4	4	4	5
M.HCP	8	2	18	4	14	16	6	12	10	11	5	3	13	7	15	17	1	9
L.HCP	4	6	14	10	18	12	2	16	8	1	17	5	3	7	15	9	13	11

AHWATUKEE C.C.

SEMI PRIVATE   18 HOLES

12432 S. 48th St.   Phoenix, AZ 85044   602-893-1161

DESERT ○   **TRADITIONAL** ●   **LINKS** ○

TERRAIN	**TREES**	**WATER**
	🌲🌲🌲🌲	〰️〰️〰️

GREENS	Bermuda	**COURSE FAVORS A...**	Mix
FAIRWAYS	Bermuda	**WIDTH OF FAIRWAYS**	Normal
BUNKERS	Regular	**AMT. OF BUNKERS**	Minimal

PAR	YARDS	RATING	SLOPE	1992 GREEN FEES $	
72	6698	71.5	124	**HIGH**	$60
72	6073	68.5	116	**LOW**	$33
72	5506	70.3	118	**SPECIALS**	Inquire

THE COURSE COMMENTARY

The signature hole is the par-3 14th that plays to a 16 handicap. Your tee shot is over water with a spectacular mountain view that links the course through a housing development.

TOUGHEST HOLE	THE 406 YARD PAR-4 6TH HOLE. YOU MUST LAY UP OFF THE TEE WITH A MIDDLE TO LONG IRON TO HAVE A SHOT AT THE GREEN.
BIRDIE HOLE	THE 391 YARD PAR-4 7TH HOLE. THIS IS A SHORT PAR-4 BUT THE GREEN CAN BE VERY DECEPTIVE.
WATER IN PLAY ON...	5 HOLES
OVERALL STRATEGY	HIT IT STRAIGHT OFF THE TEE BECAUSE THERE IS O.B. ON EVERY HOLE ON EVERY SIDE.
CART REQUIRED?	YES
PRACTICE FACILITIES?	DRIVING RANGE CHIPPING GREEN
COURSE IS OPEN...	YES
OVERSEEDING	OCTOBER FOR 2 WEEKS. TEES, GREENS, AND FAIRWAYS.
RESTAURANT?	RESTAURANT AND LOUNGE
ACCOMMODATIONS?	NEARBY HOTELS INCLUDE: BEST WESTERN, HILTON, WESCORT AT THE BUTTES, AND POINT SOUTH MOUNTAIN.
DON'T FORGET YOUR..	STRAIGHTEST DRIVER.
COURSE DESIGNER	N\A
# OF ROUNDS ANNUALLY	70,000
DIRECTIONS	TAKE THE ELLIOT RD. EXIT WEST FROM I-10. THEN GO SOUTH ON 48TH ST. FOR 2 MILES.

COURSE LAYOUT NOT AVAILABLE

HOLE	1	2	3	4	5	6	7	8	9	10	11	12	13	14	15	16	17	18
CHAMP	397	549	396	184	400	406	391	220	514	382	517	186	386	192	297	386	388	507
MENS	382	520	367	157	377	354	310	186	480	356	473	171	336	144	267	354	361	478
LADIES	356	487	328	126	338	308	274	164	438	329	437	147	307	106	235	334	336	456
PAR	4	5	4	3	4	4	4	3	5	4	5	3	4	3	4	4	4	5
M.HCP	5	9	13	11	3	1	17	7	15	6	12	10	8	16	14	2	4	18
L.HCP	5	3	11	13	9	1	17	15	7	10	6	14	12	18	16	2	4	8

AHWATUKEE LAKES G.C.

PUBLIC   18 HOLES

13431 S. 44th St. Phoenix, AZ 85044   *602-893-3004*

DESERT ○   TRADITIONAL ●   LINKS ○

TERRAIN   **TREES**   **WATER**

GREENS *Bermuda*	**COURSE FAVORS A...** *Mix*	
FAIRWAYS *Bermuda*	**WIDTH OF FAIRWAYS** *Normal*	
BUNKERS *Regular*	**AMT. OF BUNKERS** *Average*	

PAR	YARDS	RATING	SLOPE	1992 GREEN FEES $	
60	4019	59.1	97	**HIGH**	*$20*
60	3660	57.4	93	**LOW**	
60	3177	59.3	95	**SPECIALS**	*Call*

THE COURSE COMMENTARY

This is an 18 hole executive course with a lot of water...12 holes to be exact.

TOUGHEST HOLE	THE 398 YARD PAR-4 9TH HOLE IS STRAIGHTAWAY AND LONG WITH WATER OFF THE TEE TO THE RIGHT.
BIRDIE HOLE	THE 262 YARD PAR-4 10TH IS REACHABLE OFF THE TEE WITH A LONG DRIVE. DON'T GO LEFT.
WATER IN PLAY ON...	12 HOLES
OVERALL STRATEGY	SHOOT FOR THE PIN
CART REQUIRED?	NO
PRACTICE FACILITIES?	DRIVING RANGE PUTTING GREEN CHIPPING GREEN
COURSE IS OPEN...	YES
OVERSEEDING	OCTOBER FOR 2 WEEKS. TEES, GREENS, AND FAIRWAYS.
RESTAURANT?	SNACK BAR
ACCOMMODATIONS?	NO
DON'T FORGET YOUR..	FAVORITE PUTTER
COURSE DESIGNER	N/A
# OF ROUNDS ANNUALLY	N/A
DIRECTIONS	TAKE THE WARNER RD. OFF I-10, GO WEST, THEN SOUTH AT 44TH ST. FOR 1 MILE.

COURSE LAYOUT

HOLE	1	2	3	4	5	6	7	8	9	10	11	12	13	14	15	16	17	18
CHAMP	148	148	305	189	95	369	170	213	398	262	168	356	137	163	188	163	369	178
MENS	133	136	285	165	82	355	141	140	377	244	155	338	124	130	170	151	357	177
LADIES	115	121	265	147	67	298	118	124	290	225	140	285	109	114	106	139	344	170
PAR	3	3	4	3	3	4	3	3	4	4	3	4	3	3	3	3	4	3
M.HCP	13	15	11	9	17	5	7	3	1	18	16	2	14	10	4	12	6	8
L.HCP	15	13	5	7	17	3	9	11	1	6	12	4	18	16	10	14	2	8

ANTELOPE HILLS NORTH G.C.

PUBLIC   18 HOLES

19 Clubhouse Dr. Prescott, AZ 86301   602-445-0583

DESERT ◯   **TRADITIONAL** ●   **LINKS** ◯

TERRAIN	TREES	WATER

GREENS	Bent	COURSE FAVORS A...	Fade
FAIRWAYS	Bent	WIDTH OF FAIRWAYS	Tight
BUNKERS	Regular	AMT. OF BUNKERS	Average

	PAR	YARDS	RATING	SLOPE	1992 GREEN FEES $	
	72	6778	71.4	131	HIGH	$25
	72	6539	69.5	121	LOW	$15
	74	6087	74.3	126	SPECIALS	Afternoon rates

THE COURSE COMMENTARY

The signature hole is the 160 yard par-3 15th over water. The course is tree lined and very scenic. Annual tournaments include The AGA Father-Son, The AGA Northern Arizona Amateur, The JGAA State Championship, and the Smoki Amateur.

TOUGHEST HOLE	THE 459 YARD PAR-4 16TH IS AN UPHILL CLIMB TO A 2-TIERED GREEN.
BIRDIE HOLE	THE 541 YARD PAR-5 17TH IS DOWNHILL AND VERY REACHABLE IN TWO SHOTS.
WATER IN PLAY ON...	5 HOLES
OVERALL STRATEGY	KEEP YOUR BALL IN THE FAIRWAY AND STAY BELOW THE HOLE.
CART REQUIRED?	NO
PRACTICE FACILITIES?	DRIVING RANGE PUTTING GREEN CHIPPING GREEN
COURSE IS OPEN...	YES
OVERSEEDING	AIRIFY COURSE IN APRIL & AUGUST FOR 1 WEEK.
RESTAURANT?	COFFEE SHOP AND RESTAURANT - BANQUET FACILITIES
ACCOMMODATIONS?	BEST WESTERN AND SHERATON ARE 7 MILES FROM GOLF COURSE.
DON'T FORGET YOUR...	SUNSCREEN
COURSE DESIGNER	LAWRENCE HUGHES
# OF ROUNDS ANNUALLY	50,000
DIRECTIONS	7 MILES NORTH OF PRESCOTT ON US 89, NEXT TO THE PRESCOTT AIRPORT.

COURSE LAYOUT

HOLE	1	2	3	4	5	6	7	8	9	10	11	12	13	14	15	16	17	18
CHAMP	406	408	213	395	132	490	407	380	509	461	411	493	171	398	160	459	480	405
MENS	386	397	205	385	126	478	392	374	499	455	400	484	160	388	144	424	447	395
LADIES	376	380	168	337	114	455	375	354	452	416	392	451	153	366	84	420	418	380
PAR	4	4	3	4	3	5	4	4	5	4	4	5	3	4	3	4	5	4
M.HCP	7	3	9	15	17	1	11	13	5	4	14	6	16	10	18	2	8	12
L.HCP	11	7	15	13	17	1	5	9	3	4	12	2	16	10	18	6	8	14

ANTELOPE HILLS SOUTH G.C.

PUBLIC   18 HOLES

19 Clubhouse Dr. Prescott, AZ 86301   *602-445-0583*

DESERT ●   TRADITIONAL ○   LINKS ○

TERRAIN	TREES	WATER

GREENS	*Bent*	**COURSE FAVORS A...**	*Draw*
FAIRWAYS	*Bent*	**WIDTH OF FAIRWAYS**	*Normal*
BUNKERS	*Regular*	**AMT. OF BUNKERS**	*Many*

PAR	YARDS	RATING	SLOPE	1992 GREEN FEES $	
72	7014	67.8	114	**HIGH**	*$25*
72	6423	68.5	117	**LOW**	*$15*
72	5560	71.0	113	**SPECIALS**	*Afternoon rates*

THE COURSE COMMENTARY

The signature hole is the 209 yard par-3 11th with a long carry over water. Annual events include 2 major Arizona amateur events and the state father & son tournament.

TOUGHEST HOLE	THE 209 YARD PAR-3 11TH OVER A LAKE WITH BUNKERS GUARDING THE FRONT OF THE GREEN.
BIRDIE HOLE	THE 521 YARD PAR-5 1ST HOLE IS EASILY REACHABLE IN 2 SHOTS.
WATER IN PLAY ON...	5 HOLES
OVERALL STRATEGY	HIT THE BALL HARD AND LONG; THERE'S NOT MANY TREES.
CART REQUIRED?	NO
PRACTICE FACILITIES?	DRIVING RANGE PUTTING GREEN CHIPPING GREEN
COURSE IS OPEN...	YES
OVERSEEDING	AUGUST FOR 1 WEEK
RESTAURANT?	COFFEE SHOP AND RESTAURANT. BANQUET FACILITIES AVAILABLE.
ACCOMMODATIONS?	BEST WESTERN AND SHERATON ARE 7 MILES FROM GOLF COURSE.
DON'T FORGET YOUR..	L-WEDGE
COURSE DESIGNER	GARY PANKS
# OF ROUNDS ANNUALLY	50,000
DIRECTIONS	7 MILES NORTH OF PRESCOTT ON US 89, NEXT TO THE PRESCOTT AIRPORT.

COURSE LAYOUT

HOLE	1	2	3	4	5	6	7	8	9	10	11	12	13	14	15	16	17	18
CHAMP	521	396	526	309	170	467	359	213	456	429	209	590	437	368	151	403	541	469
MENS	482	356	484	275	141	430	328	176	417	417	179	544	419	318	136	366	517	438
LADIES	405	310	404	238	107	376	298	139	381	375	123	500	369	301	102	319	438	375
PAR	5	4	5	4	3	4	4	3	4	4	3	5	4	4	3	4	5	4
M.HCP	7	11	5	15	17	1	13	9	3	10	12	6	8	16	18	14	4	2
L.HCP	7	9	5	15	17	1	11	13	3	10	116	2	8	14	18	12	6	4

APACHE SUN G.C.

PUBLIC   9 HOLES

919 E. Pima Rd.   Queen Creek, AZ 85242

602-987-9065

DESERT ○   **TRADITIONAL** ●   **LINKS** ○

TERRAIN	TREES	WATER

GREENS	Bermuda		COURSE FAVORS A...	Mix
FAIRWAYS	Bermuda		WIDTH OF FAIRWAYS	Forgiving
BUNKERS	Regular		AMT. OF BUNKERS	Minimal

	PAR	YARDS	RATING	SLOPE	1992 GREEN FEES $	
	34	2661	31.3	N/A	HIGH	$10
	34	2530	30.3	N/A	LOW	$8
	34	2284	30.4	N/A	SPECIALS	None

THE COURSE COMMENTARY

This course is fairly wide open and is in great condition.

TOUGHEST HOLE	THE 500 YARD PAR-5 1ST HOLE IS LONG AND PLAYS TO A LARGE GREEN. HIT IT BIG OFF THE TEE.
BIRDIE HOLE	THE 118 YARD PAR-3 9TH HOLE PLAYS TO A LARGE GREEN. DON'T BE SHORT OF THE GREEN.
WATER IN PLAY ON...	3 HOLES
OVERALL STRATEGY	SHOOT FOR THE PIN BECAUSE THE GREENS ARE GOOD SIZED.
CART REQUIRED?	No
PRACTICE FACILITIES?	N/A
COURSE IS OPEN...	YES
OVERSEEDING	OCTOBER FOR 2 WEEKS.
RESTAURANT?	SNACK BAR
ACCOMMODATIONS?	No
DON'T FORGET YOUR..	1 IRON
COURSE DESIGNER	N/A
# OF ROUNDS ANNUALLY	N/A
DIRECTIONS	GO NORTH OF OCOTILLO RD. & VINYARD. TURN RIGHT ON PIMA RD.

COURSE LAYOUT NOT AVAILABLE

HOLE	1	2	3	4	5	6	7	8	9	10	11	12	13	14	15	16	17	18
CHAMP	500	281	375	342	173	320	186	366	118									
MENS	488	268	365	336	167	310	125	360	111									
LADIES	458	185	344	315	157	272	115	333	105									
PAR	5	4	4	4	3	4	3	4	3									
M.HCP	1	11	3	7	13	9	15	5	17									
L.HCP	2	12	4	8	14	10	16	6	18									

APACHE WELLS C.C.

SEMI PRIVATE 18 HOLES

5601 E. Hermosa Vista Dr. Mesa, AZ 85205   602-830-4725

DESERT ○   TRADITIONAL ●   LINKS ○

| TERRAIN | TREES | WATER |

GREENS	Bermuda		COURSE FAVORS A...	Draw
FAIRWAYS	Bermuda		WIDTH OF FAIRWAYS	Tight
BUNKERS	Regular		AMT. OF BUNKERS	Minimal

PAR	YARDS	RATING	SLOPE
71	6047	66.7	102
71	5756	65.4	99
72	5374	68.1	100

1992 GREEN FEES $

HIGH	$24
LOW	$10
SPECIALS	May through Oct. special rates

THE COURSE COMMENTARY

This course was designed with the senior golfer in mind. It is always in good condition.

TOUGHEST HOLE	THE 398 YARD PAR-4 14TH HOLE. THE LENGTH MAKES THIS HOLE DIFFICULT TO MAKE PAR.
BIRDIE HOLE	THE 453 YARD PAR-5 16TH IS THE SHORTEST PAR-5 ON THE COURSE AND IS REACHABLE IN 2 WITH GOOD ACCURACY.
WATER IN PLAY ON...	0 HOLES
OVERALL STRATEGY	YOU NEED TO HIT IT STRAIGHT OUT HERE OR YOU WILL FIND TROUBLE VERY EASILY.
CART REQUIRED?	NO
PRACTICE FACILITIES?	DRIVING RANGE PUTTING GREEN CHIPPING GREEN
COURSE IS OPEN...	MAY 1 TO OCTOBER 31
OVERSEEDING	OCTOBER FOR 4 WEEKS. TEES, GREENS, AND FAIRWAYS.
RESTAURANT?	APACHE WELLS COUNTRY CLUB RESTAURANT
ACCOMMODATIONS?	N/A
DON'T FORGET YOUR..	DRINKING WATER
COURSE DESIGNER	N/A
# OF ROUNDS ANNUALLY	40,000
DIRECTIONS	3 BLOCKS NORTH OF MCKELLIPS BETWEEN HIGLEY RD. AND RECKER RD.

COURSE LAYOUT

HOLE	1	2	3	4	5	6	7	8	9	10	11	12	13	14	15	16	17	18
CHAMP	330	154	392	151	342	353	210	536	348	348	458	159	520	398	228	453	169	498
MENS	319	140	378	137	321	337	185	516	331	340	444	147	501	387	199	433	154	487
LADIES	308	135	392	105	283	330	176	462	316	319	416	136	475	310	172	430	148	461
PAR	4	3	4	3	4	4	3	5	4	4	5	3	5	4	3	5	3	5
M.HCP	14	18	2	16	8	10	12	4	6	9	11	17	3	1	7	15	13	5
L.HCP	8	16	6	18	14	4	12	2	10	11	9	17	1	7	13	5	15	3

ARIZONA BILTMORE C.C.- ADOBE COURSE

PUBLIC   18 HOLES

24th St. & Missouri Ave. Phoenix, AZ 85016   *602-955-9655*

DESERT ⃝   **TRADITIONAL** ⬤   **LINKS** ⃝

TERRAIN	TREES	WATER

GREENS	Bermuda	**COURSE FAVORS A...**	Fade
FAIRWAYS	Bermuda	**WIDTH OF FAIRWAYS**	Forgiving
BUNKERS	Regular	**AMT. OF BUNKERS**	Average

PAR	YARDS	RATING	SLOPE
72	6767	71.5	121
72	6455	70.0	116
73	6101	74.3	116

1992 GREEN FEES $

HIGH	$80
LOW	$35
SPECIALS	9 hole rate is 1/2 price + $1

THE COURSE COMMENTARY

Former site of the LPGA Samaritan Turquoise Classic and site of the 1992 U.S. Open Qualifier. This mature course has gentle rolling terrain with wider fairways than the Links course.

TOUGHEST HOLE	THE 422 YARD PAR-4 3RD HOLE. WATER AND A BUNKER TO THE RIGHT GUARD THE GREEN.
BIRDIE HOLE	THE 175 YARD PAR-3 12TH IS THE EASIEST HOLE ON THE COURSE.
WATER IN PLAY ON...	2 HOLES
OVERALL STRATEGY	HIT IT LONG AND STRAIGHT.
CART REQUIRED?	YES
PRACTICE FACILITIES?	DRIVING RANGE PUTTING GREEN CHIPPING GREEN
COURSE IS OPEN...	YES
OVERSEEDING	OCTOBER FOR 2 WEEKS. TEES, GREENS, AND FAIRWAYS.
RESTAURANT?	RESTAURANT IS OPEN FOR BREAKFAST AND LUNCH ONLY.
ACCOMMODATIONS?	THE 5-STAR ARIZONA BILTMORE HOTEL BUILT BY FRANK LLOYD WRIGHT.
DON'T FORGET YOUR..	BALL RETRIEVER OR GINTY
COURSE DESIGNER	WILLIAM BELL
# OF ROUNDS ANNUALLY	100,000
DIRECTIONS	1 BLOCK NORTH OF CAMELBACK RD. ON 24TH ST

HOLE	1	2	3	4	5	6	7	8	9	10	11	12	13	14	15	16	17	18
CHAMP	491	240	422	363	395	479	375	440	146	378	443	175	396	448	335	525	208	508
MENS	473	218	404	351	375	469	363	415	140	363	419	157	374	425	321	512	193	483
LADIES	446	177	365	348	366	442	354	406	124	363	389	154	362	354	314	507	149	481
PAR	5	3	4	4	4	5	4	4	3	4	4	3	4	4	4	5	3	5
M.HCP	5	15	1	13	7	11	9	3	17	10	4	18	12	2	14	6	16	8
L.HCP	3	15	1	13	7	5	11	9	17	8	6	16	10	12	14	2	18	4

ARIZONA BILTMORE C.C.- LINKS COURSE

PUBLIC   18 HOLES

24th Street and Missouri   Phoenix, AZ 85016

602-955-9655

DESERT ○   TRADITIONAL ○   LINKS ●

TERRAIN	TREES	WATER

GREENS	Bermuda	COURSE FAVORS A...	Fade
FAIRWAYS	Bermuda	WIDTH OF FAIRWAYS	Tight
BUNKERS	Regular	AMT. OF BUNKERS	Average

	PAR	YARDS	RATING	SLOPE
	71	6300	69.3	122
	71	5726	66.6	115
	71	4747	68.0	N/A

1992 GREEN FEES

HIGH	$80
LOW	$35
SPECIALS	9 hole rate is 1/2 price + $1

THE COURSE COMMENTARY

The front nine winds its way through many of the beautiful homes which circle The Arizona Biltmore. The back nine takes you on a tour of the rolling hills behind the Arizona Biltmore Hotel.

TOUGHEST HOLE THE 532 YARD PAR-5 2ND HOLE IS THE NUMBER 1 HANDICAP HOLE FOR BOTH MEN AND WOMEN.

BIRDIE HOLE THE 334 YARD PAR-4 7TH HOLE IS SHORT AND STRAIGHTAWAY WITH NO HAZARDS TO WORRY ABOUT.

WATER IN PLAY ON... 2 HOLES

OVERALL STRATEGY JUST RELAX AND PLAY IT SAFE ON THIS COURSE OR IT WILL EAT YOU ALIVE.

CART REQUIRED? YES

PRACTICE FACILITIES? DRIVING RANGE   PUTTING GREEN   CHIPPING GREEN

COURSE IS OPEN... YES

OVERSEEDING OCTOBER FOR 2 WEEKS. TEES, GREENS, AND FAIRWAYS.

RESTAURANT? RESTAURANT IS OPEN FOR BREAKFAST AND LUNCH.

ACCOMMODATIONS? THE 5-STAR ARIZONA BILTMORE HOTEL BUILT BY FRANK LLOYD WRIGHT.

DON'T FORGET YOUR.. BALL RETRIEVER

COURSE DESIGNER VERNON SWABACK AND BILL JOHNSON

 # OF ROUNDS ANNUALLY 100,000

DIRECTIONS 1 BLOCK NORTH OF CAMELBACK ON 24TH STREET

HOLE	1	2	3	4	5	6	7	8	9	10	11	12	13	14	15	16	17	18
CHAMP	351	532	151	365	130	402	334	129	529	549	176	336	343	340	183	387	451	521
MENS	333	500	132	351	125	360	319	117	488	502	159	282	384	311	162	353	367	481
LADIES	220	454	77	341	92	292	296	106	429	428	117	257	313	264	116	281	256	406
PAR	4	5	3	4	3	4	4	3	5	5	3	4	4	4	3	4	4	5
M.HCP	9	1	13	7	17	3	11	15	5	4	18	14	2	12	16	10	6	8
L.HCP	11	1	17	5	13	7	9	15	3	2	18	12	6	10	16	8	14	4

ARIZONA CITY G.C.

PUBLIC   18 HOLES

Box B   Arizona City, AZ 85223

602-466-5327

DESERT ○   **TRADITIONAL** ●   **LINKS** ○

TERRAIN	TREES	WATER

GREENS *Bermuda*   **COURSE FAVORS A...** *Fade*

FAIRWAYS *Bermuda*   **WIDTH OF FAIRWAYS** *Forgiving*

BUNKERS *Regular*   **AMT. OF BUNKERS** *Average*

PAR	YARDS	RATING	SLOPE	1992 GREEN FEES $
72	6775	71.6	117	**HIGH** $29
72	6440	70.3	114	**LOW** $17
72	5959	72.0	117	**SPECIALS** Afternoon 21.00 w/ cart

THE COURSE COMMENTARY

The signature hole is the 430 yard par-4 9th in which your tee shot must go between two palm trees with an approach over water to an island green.

TOUGHEST HOLE THE 430 YARD PAR-4 9TH IS THE SIGNATURE HOLE AND REQUIRES TWO GREAT SHOTS TO REACH THE GREEN.

BIRDIE HOLE THE 508 YARD PAR-5 6TH IS REACHABLE IN TWO. THE FAIRWAY BUNKER DOES NOT COME INTO PLAY.

WATER IN PLAY ON... 6 HOLES

OVERALL STRATEGY STAY ON THE FAIRWAY. MOST HOLES HAVE OUT-OF-BOUNDS ON BOTH SIDES OF THE FAIRWAY.

CART REQUIRED? NO

PRACTICE FACILITIES? DRIVING RANGE   PUTTING GREEN   CHIPPING GREEN

COURSE IS OPEN... YES

OVERSEEDING OCTOBER FOR 2 WEEKS. TEES, GREENS, AND FAIRWAYS.

RESTAURANT? RESTAURANT AND LOUNGE

ACCOMMODATIONS? SEVERAL MOTELS WITHIN 3 MILES. OVER 50 DISCOUNT OUTLET STORES WITHIN 10 MILES.

DON'T FORGET YOUR.. ROCK IRON

COURSE DESIGNER ARTHUR JACK SNYDER

 # OF ROUNDS ANNUALLY 40,000

DIRECTIONS TAKE I-10 SOUTH TO THE SUNLAND GIN RD. EXIT, GO 4 MILES SOUTH TO ARIZONA CITY

COURSE LAYOUT

HOLE	1	2	3	4	5	6	7	8	9	10	11	12	13	14	15	16	17	18
CHAMP	349	480	401	230	410	508	441	140	430	419	520	363	382	205	385	395	162	555
MENS	346	472	389	191	396	486	419	131	390	395	500	338	374	195	372	380	143	523
LADIES	325	462	310	162	341	462	350	107	383	380	486	324	355	173	358	366	128	487
PAR	4	5	4	3	4	5	4	3	4	4	5	4	4	3	4	4	3	5
M.HCP	15	11	7	13	1	9	5	17	3	2	10	16	6	14	12	4	18	8
L.HCP	13	7	11	15	3	5	9	17	1	2	6	18	12	14	10	8	16	4

ARROWHEAD C.C.

SEMI PRIVATE   18 HOLES

19888 N. 73rd Ave. Glendale, AZ 85308   *602-561-9625*

DESERT ●   TRADITIONAL ○   LINKS ○

TERRAIN	TREES	WATER

GREENS	*Bent*	**COURSE FAVORS A...**	*Fade*
FAIRWAYS	*Bermuda*	**WIDTH OF FAIRWAYS**	*Normal*
BUNKERS	*Silicon*	**AMT. OF BUNKERS**	*Many*

PAR	YARDS	RATING	SLOPE	1992 GREEN FEES $	
72	7001	73.3	128	**HIGH**	*$58*
72	6302	70.2	125	**LOW**	*$35*
72	5291	70.4	120	**SPECIALS**	*Call*

THE COURSE COMMENTARY

This is one of the valley's newer courses. It winds through an equally new home development set in the quiet setting of the northwestern valley. The course is in excellent condition with manicured tees and fairways.

TOUGHEST HOLE	THE 572 YARD PAR-5 6TH HOLE IS A DOGLEG LEFT WITH WATER OFF THE TEE MAKING A VERY DIFFICULT TEE SHOT!
BIRDIE HOLE	THE 180 YARD PAR-3 15TH HOLE PLAYS TO A LARGE GREEN.
WATER IN PLAY ON...	11 HOLES
OVERALL STRATEGY	YOUR TEE SHOT MUST BE IN THE FAIRWAY OR YOUR IN FOR A LONG DAY.
CART REQUIRED?	YES
PRACTICE FACILITIES?	DRIVING RANGE PUTTING GREEN CHIPPING GREEN
COURSE IS OPEN...	YES
OVERSEEDING	YES. INCLUDES EVERYTHING.
RESTAURANT?	YES
ACCOMMODATIONS?	NO
DON'T FORGET YOUR..	FAVORITE DRIVER
COURSE DESIGNER	ARNOLD PALMER
# OF ROUNDS ANNUALLY	N/A
DIRECTIONS	HALF MILE WEST OF 67TH AVE ON THE SOUTH SIDE OF BEARDSLY RD. (YOU CANNOT TURN INTO THE ENTRANCE GOING WEST ON BEARDSLY SO GO PAST THE COURSE AND MAKE A U-TURN HEADING EAST ON BEARDSLY)

COURSE LAYOUT

HOLE	1	2	3	4	5	6	7	8	9	10	11	12	13	14	15	16	17	18
CHAMP	396	533	202	387	433	572	205	396	381	446	206	550	397	424	180	393	423	477
MENS	347	485	184	343	390	523	181	354	350	414	163	507	353	381	160	363	354	450
LADIES	298	440	131	314	343	432	137	256	300	366	120	459	278	320	120	286	313	378
PAR	4	5	3	4	4	5	3	4	4	4	3	5	4	4	3	4	4	5
M.HCP	11	3	15	13	5	1	17	7	9	4	16	2	10	6	18	14	12	8
L.HCP	13	3	17	11	5	1	15	7	9	8	16	2	10	12	18	14	6	4

ARROYO DUNES MUNICIPAL G.C.

PUBLIC   18 HOLES

32nd St. and Avenue A   Yuma, AZ 85364   *602-726-8350*

DESERT ●   TRADITIONAL ○   LINKS ○

TERRAIN	TREES	WATER

GREENS	Bermuda		COURSE FAVORS A...	Mix
FAIRWAYS	Bermuda		WIDTH OF FAIRWAYS	Normal
BUNKERS	Other		AMT. OF BUNKERS	Average

PAR	YARDS	RATING	SLOPE	1992 GREEN FEES $	
N/A	N/A	N/A	N/A	HIGH	$10
54	1123	N/A	N/A	LOW	$6
N/	N/A	N/A	N/A	SPECIALS	None

THE COURSE COMMENTARY There are no bunkers and no water on this 18 hole executive course which sports all par-3's... a hackers dream. 9 holes are lighted. The front 9 is flat and the back nine is more rolling hills. A great course for senior's.

TOUGHEST HOLE THE 172 YARD PAR-3 17TH HOLE. THERE'S NOTHING FANCY ABOUT THIS ONE - JUST LONG AND STRAIGHT.

BIRDIE HOLE THE 67 YARD PAR-3 9TH HOLE. TAKE OUT YOUR FAVORITE WEDGE AND AIM FOR THE PIN.

WATER IN PLAY ON... 0 HOLES

OVERALL STRATEGY HIT IT STRAIGHT OFF THE TEE.

CART REQUIRED? No

PRACTICE FACILITIES? DRIVING RANGE   PUTTING GREEN

COURSE IS OPEN... YES

OVERSEEDING SEPT. FOR 4 WEEKS. INCLUDES EVERYTHING.

RESTAURANT? No

ACCOMMODATIONS? No

DON'T FORGET YOUR.. L-WEDGE

COURSE DESIGNER N/A

 # OF ROUNDS ANNUALLY 35,000

DIRECTIONS TAKE THE 32ND ST. EXIT FROM I-18 SOUTH TO AVENUE A.

HOLE	1	2	3	4	5	6	7	8	9	10	11	12	13	14	15	16	17	18
CHAMP																		
MENS	138	100	115	82	180	128	117	124	67	115	65	152	90	125	120	138	172	146
LADIES																		
PAR	3	3	3	3	3	3	3	3	3	3	3	3	3	3	3	3	3	3
M.HCP	4	14	10	16	2	8	12	6	18	11	17	3	15	7	13	5	1	9
L.HCP	4	14	10	16	2	8	12	6	18	11	17	3	15	7	13	5	1	9

ARTHUR PACK DESERT G.C.

PUBLIC   18 HOLES

9101 N. Thornydale Rd. Tucson, AZ 85741   602-744-3322

DESERT ●   TRADITIONAL ○   LINKS ○

TERRAIN   **TREES**   **WATER**

GREENS *Bermuda*	**COURSE FAVORS A...** *Draw*	
FAIRWAYS *Bermuda*	**WIDTH OF FAIRWAYS** *Forgiving*	
BUNKERS *Other*	**AMT. OF BUNKERS** *Many*	

PAR	YARDS	RATING	SLOPE	1992 GREEN FEES $	
72	6896	71.6	118	**HIGH**	*$19*
72	6384	69.2	113	**LOW**	*$12*
72	5068	67.6	108	**SPECIALS**	*Resident card rates*

THE COURSE COMMENTARY *This course hosts qualifying for the PGA Tour Northern Telecom Tucson Open. Red sand bunkers highlight a beautiful desert landscape.*

TOUGHEST HOLE THE 569 YARD PAR-5 8TH HOLE. YOU WANT TO BE LONG OFF THE TEE ON THIS HOLE.

BIRDIE HOLE THE 364 PAR-4 12TH HOLE HAS A WIDE OPEN LANDING AREA OFF THE TEE AND A LARGE GREEN.

WATER IN PLAY ON... 4 HOLES

OVERALL STRATEGY LENGTH OFF THE TEE IS A BIG PLUS.

CART REQUIRED? NO

PRACTICE FACILITIES? DRIVING RANGE   PUTTING GREEN   CHIPPING GREEN

COURSE IS OPEN... YES

OVERSEEDING OCT. AND APR. FOR 2 WEEKS. FAIRWAYS AND GREENS.

RESTAURANT? COFFEE SHOP

ACCOMMODATIONS? NO

DON'T FORGET YOUR.. 3 WEDGES

COURSE DESIGNER LEE TREVINO

 # OF ROUNDS ANNUALLY N/A

DIRECTIONS 2 MILES NORTH OF INA RD. ON THORNYDALE RD.

HOLE	1	2	3	4	5	6	7	8	9	10	11	12	13	14	15	16	17	18
CHAMP	402	189	374	578	381	413	140	569	406	391	538	364	180	438	553	215	374	391
MENS	382	157	353	488	362	375	137	522	359	383	496	353	158	419	520	193	357	370
LADIES	287	131	282	364	283	289	124	413	302	317	421	280	129	318	421	123	322	262
PAR	4	3	4	5	4	4	3	5	4	4	5	4	3	4	5	3	4	4
M.HCP	9	15	13	3	11	5	17	1	7	8	10	18	14	2	6	4	16	12
L.HCP	5	17	11	3	13	9	15	1	7	12	6	14	4	10	2	18	8	16

BELLAIR G.C.

PUBLIC   18 HOLES

17233 North 45th Ave. Phoenix, AZ 85308   *602-978-0330*

DESERT ○   TRADITIONAL ●   LINKS ○

TERRAIN	TREES	WATER

GREENS	*Bermuda*	**COURSE FAVORS A...**	*Mix*
FAIRWAYS	*Bermuda*	**WIDTH OF FAIRWAYS**	*Normal*
BUNKERS	*Regular*	**AMT. OF BUNKERS**	*Average*

PAR	YARDS	RATING	SLOPE	1992 GREEN FEES $	
59	3493	56.2	90	**HIGH**	*$15*
59	3412	55.8	89	**LOW**	*$10*
60	3340	55.3	81	**SPECIALS**	*None*

THE COURSE COMMENTARY

An 18 hole executive style layout with 5 par-4's, and 13 par-3's. The signature hole is the 281 yard par-4 10th. Your tee shot carries over a lake and it continues to affect play up the right side of the fairway.

TOUGHEST HOLE THE 184 YARD PAR-3 3RD HOLE IS AS GOOD A TEST AS ANY PAR-3 IN THE VALLEY.

BIRDIE HOLE THE 254 YARD PAR-4 1ST HOLE PLAYS TO A 15 HANDICAP. IF YOU PITCH WELL YOU'RE LOOKING AT A BIRDIE.

WATER IN PLAY ON... 3 HOLES

OVERALL STRATEGY GET IN A RHYTHM WITH SHORT TO MIDDLE IRONS.

CART REQUIRED? NO

PRACTICE FACILITIES? DRIVING RANGE   PUTTING GREEN   CHIPPING GREEN

COURSE IS OPEN... YES

OVERSEEDING OCTOBER FOR 2 WEEKS. TEES, GREENS, AND FAIRWAYS

RESTAURANT? RESTAURANT AND COFFEE SHOP

ACCOMMODATIONS? NO

DON'T FORGET YOUR.. FAVORITE WEDGE

COURSE DESIGNER N/A

 # OF ROUNDS ANNUALLY N/A

DIRECTIONS 1/2 MILE NORTH OF BELL RD. ON 45TH AVE.

COURSE LAYOUT

HOLE	1	2	3	4	5	6	7	8	9	10	11	12	13	14	15	16	17	18
CHAMP	254	104	184	135	188	121	146	286	275	281	140	150	217	123	164	168	203	354
MENS	248	102	178	130	188	121	144	284	272	263	137	140	217	118	158	163	200	349
LADIES	244	94	165	130	170	100	125	255	255	265	131	135	200	105	145	140	175	335
PAR	4	3	3	3	3	3	3	4	4	4	3	3	3	3	3	3	3	4
M.HCP	13	17	1	11	3	15	9	5	7	8	14	16	2	18	10	12	4	6
L.HCP	7	17	9	11	1	15	13	3	5	8	12	16	18	14	10	6	4	2

BOULDERS CLUB - NORTH

34631 N. Tom Darlington Rd. Carefree, AZ 85377   *602-488-9028*

DESERT ●   TRADITIONAL ○   LINKS ○

TERRAIN	TREES	WATER

GREENS	*Bent*
FAIRWAYS	*Other*
BUNKERS	*Regular*

COURSE FAVORS A...	*Mix*
WIDTH OF FAIRWAYS	*Forgiving*
AMT. OF BUNKERS	*Average*

PAR	YARDS	RATING	SLOPE	1992 GREEN FEES $	
72	6731	73.7	131	HIGH	*$135*
72	6291	70.6	128	LOW	
72	4893	70.5	117	SPECIALS	*Specials w/ dinner*

THE COURSE COMMENTARY

The Boulders sports 2 championship 18 hole layouts. This Jay Morrish designed layout is the longer and is cut through the desert with undulating greens and fantastic scenery. One of the top courses in all of Arizona. This is target golf at its best.

TOUGHEST HOLE	THE 548 YARD PAR-5 3RD HOLE PLAYS VERY LONG. YOU'LL NEED TO REALLY CARRY THE BALL OFF THE TEE.
BIRDIE HOLE	THE 175 YARD PAR-3 14TH HOLE. SHOOT FOR THE PIN.
WATER IN PLAY ON...	3 HOLES
OVERALL STRATEGY	YOU NEED TO BE ABLE TO CARRY THE BALL OFF THE TEE!!!
CART REQUIRED?	YES
PRACTICE FACILITIES?	DRIVING RANGE PUTTING GREEN CHIPPING GREEN
COURSE IS OPEN...	YES
OVERSEEDING	OCTOBER FOR 2 WEEKS. FAIRWAYS ONLY.
RESTAURANT?	1 RESTAURANT AT THE GOLF SHOP AND 2 IN THE RESORT.
ACCOMMODATIONS?	THE BOULDERS RESORT IS ONE OF THE TOP RESORTS IN ALL OF THE SOUTHWEST.
DON'T FORGET YOUR..	ROCK IRON
COURSE DESIGNER	JAY MORRISH
# OF ROUNDS ANNUALLY	N/A
DIRECTIONS	HALF MILE NORTH OF CAREFREE HWY. OFF SCOTTSDALE RD. TO THE RESORT ENTRANCE.

COURSE LAYOUT

HOLE	1	2	3	4	5	6	7	8	9	10	11	12	13	14	15	16	17	18
CHAMP	485	195	548	404	410	142	345	350	347	435	442	531	405	175	483	419	195	420
MENS	481	150	517	396	400	133	338	330	340	429	395	479	375	127	468	357	176	400
LADIES	331	120	415	325	317	93	290	252	258	400	310	378	272	80	340	250	110	352
PAR	5	3	5	4	4	3	4	4	4	4	4	5	4	3	5	4	3	4
M.HCP	3	15	1	7	5	17	11	9	13	6	12	2	4	18	8	10	16	14
L.HCP	3	17	1	13	5	15	11	9	7	8	14	6	10	18	2	12	16	4

BOULDERS CLUB - SOUTH

34631 N. Tom Darlington Rd. Carefree, AZ 85377   *602-488-9028*

DESERT ●   **TRADITIONAL** ○   **LINKS** ○

TERRAIN   **TREES**   **WATER**

GREENS *Bent*	**COURSE FAVORS A...** *Mix*	
FAIRWAYS *Other*	**WIDTH OF FAIRWAYS** *Forgiving*	
BUNKERS *Regular*	**AMT. OF BUNKERS** *Many*	

PAR	YARDS	RATING	SLOPE	1992 GREEN FEES $	
71	6543	70.7	125	**HIGH**	*$135*
71	6073	68.6	121	**LOW**	
71	4706	68.7	112	**SPECIALS**	*Specials w/ dinner*

THE COURSE COMMENTARY

The Boulders sports 2 championship 18 hole layouts. This Jay Morrish designed layout is the shorter and is cut through the desert with undulating greens and fantastic scenery. One of the top courses in all of Arizona. This is target golf at its best.

TOUGHEST HOLE	THE 455 YARD PAR-4 8TH HOLE HAS A LONG CARRY OFF THE TEE.
BIRDIE HOLE	THE 143 YARD PAR-3 15TH HOLE. KEEP IT HIGH OFF THE TEE.
WATER IN PLAY ON...	2 HOLES
OVERALL STRATEGY	YOU NEED TO BE ABLE TO CARRY THE BALL OFF THE TEE!!!
CART REQUIRED?	YES
PRACTICE FACILITIES?	DRIVING RANGE PUTTING GREEN CHIPPING GREEN
COURSE IS OPEN...	YES
OVERSEEDING	OCTOBER FOR 2 WEEKS. FAIRWAYS ONLY.
RESTAURANT?	1 RESTAURANT AT THE GOLF SHOP AND 2 IN THE RESORT.
ACCOMMODATIONS?	THE BOULDERS RESORT IS ONE OF THE TOP RESORTS IN ALL OF THE SOUTHWEST.
DON'T FORGET YOUR..	ROCK IRON
COURSE DESIGNER	JAY MORRISH
# OF ROUNDS ANNUALLY	N/A
DIRECTIONS	HALF MILE NORTH OF CAREFREE HWY. OFF SCOTTSDALE RD. TO THE RESORT ENTRANCE.

COURSE LAYOUT

HOLE	1	2	3	4	5	6	7	8	9	10	11	12	13	14	15	16	17	18
CHAMP	421	135	407	384	529	352	182	455	400	198	557	343	424	527	143	198	420	468
MENS	381	115	360	349	525	345	155	435	356	188	499	321	369	511	140	176	380	468
LADIES	305	9.5	280	270	375	285	95	329	252	125	393	250	261	418	95	141	324	413
PAR	4	3	4	4	5	4	3	4	4	3	5	4	4	5	3	3	4	5
M.HCP	3	17	9	7	1	13	15	5	11	16	4	17	8	6	18	10	2	12
L.HCP	5	15	9	11	3	13	17	1	7	16	2	12	10	4	18	14	6	8

CAMELOT G.C. - 18

PUBLIC   18 HOLES

6210 McKellips Rd. Mesa, AZ 85205   *602-832-0156*

DESERT ○   **TRADITIONAL** ●   **LINKS** ○

TERRAIN	**TREES**	**WATER**

GREENS *Bermuda*   **COURSE FAVORS A...** *Fade*

FAIRWAYS *Bermuda*   **WIDTH OF FAIRWAYS** *Forgiving*

BUNKERS *Regular*   **AMT. OF BUNKERS** *Minimal*

	PAR	**YARDS**	**RATING**	**SLOPE**
	N/A	N/A	N/A	N/A
	70	5600	64.6	92
	70	4687	69.2	105

1992 GREEN FEES $

HIGH	*$33*
LOW	*$24*
SPECIALS	*Coupons available*

THE COURSE COMMENTARY

This is the 18 hole championship layout that accompanies the 9 executive hole layout.

TOUGHEST HOLE	THE 520 YARD PAR-5 8TH HOLE IS LONG WITH O.B. OFF THE TEE.
BIRDIE HOLE	THE 270 YARD PAR-4 9TH HOLE PLAYS TO A LARGE GREEN AND IS REACHABLE FROM THE TEE.
WATER IN PLAY ON...	0 HOLES
OVERALL STRATEGY	N/A
CART REQUIRED?	NO
PRACTICE FACILITIES?	DRIVING RANGE PUTTING GREEN
COURSE IS OPEN...	YES
OVERSEEDING	OCTOBER FOR 2 WEEKS. INCLUDES EVERYTHING.
RESTAURANT?	YES
ACCOMMODATIONS?	NO
DON'T FORGET YOUR..	FAVORITE PUTTER
COURSE DESIGNER	N/A
# OF ROUNDS ANNUALLY	125,000
DIRECTIONS	1 BLOCK EAST OF RECKER RD. ON MCKELLIPS RD.

COURSE LAYOUT

HOLE	1	2	3	4	5	6	7	8	9	10	11	12	13	14	15	16	17	18
CHAMP	476	124	189	315	353	145	323	487	245	497	493	163	327	320	170	154	320	381
MENS	476	121	179	278	338	120	315	479	236	470	465	158	302	307	160	150	323	371
LADIES	451	106	159	266	323	107	227	420	227	400	386	125	253	270	155	140	312	360
PAR	5	3	3	4	4	3	4	5	4	5	5	3	4	4	3	3	4	4
M.HCP	3	17	13	9	5	15	7	1	11	4	2	14	12	8	16	18	10	6
L.HCP	3	17	13	9	5	15	7	1	11	4	2	14	12	8	16	18	10	6

CAMELOT G.C. - 9

PUBLIC   9 HOLES

6210 McKellips Rd. Mesa, AZ 85205   602-832-0156

DESERT ○   **TRADITIONAL** ●   **LINKS** ○

TERRAIN	TREES	WATER

GREENS	Bermuda	COURSE FAVORS A...	Fade
FAIRWAYS	Bermuda	WIDTH OF FAIRWAYS	Forgiving
BUNKERS	Regular	AMT. OF BUNKERS	Minimal

PAR	YARDS	RATING	SLOPE	1992 GREEN FEES $
30	1830	29.4	N/A	HIGH $10
30	1742	N/A	N/A	LOW $10
30	1686	29.0	N/A	SPECIALS Coupons available

THE COURSE COMMENTARY

This is the 9 hole layout that accompanies the championship 18 hole layout. It's very straightaway and short with large greens and wide fairway's on the 3 par-4's.

TOUGHEST HOLE	THE 303 YARD PAR-4 3RD HOLE IS STRAIGHTAWAY WITH A TRICKY GREEN. A LONG DRIVE LEAVES YOU A SHORT IRON.
BIRDIE HOLE	THE 140 YARD PAR-3 7TH HOLE TAKES A MEDIUM IRON TO THE GREEN. WATCH FOR PALM TREES ON THE LEFT.
WATER IN PLAY ON...	0 HOLES
OVERALL STRATEGY	SHOOT FOR THE PIN.
CART REQUIRED?	NO
PRACTICE FACILITIES?	DRIVING RANGE PUTTING GREEN
COURSE IS OPEN...	YES
OVERSEEDING	OCTOBER FOR 2 WEEKS. INCLUDES EVERYTHING.
RESTAURANT?	YES
ACCOMMODATIONS?	NO
DON'T FORGET YOUR..	3 WOOD
COURSE DESIGNER	N/A
# OF ROUNDS ANNUALLY	125,000
DIRECTIONS	1 BLOCK EAST OF RECKER RD. ON MCKELLIPS RD.

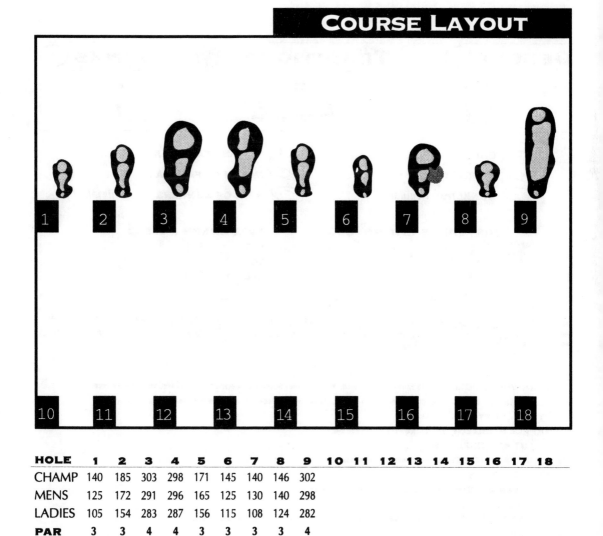

HOLE	1	2	3	4	5	6	7	8	9	10	11	12	13	14	15	16	17	18
CHAMP	140	185	303	298	171	145	140	146	302									
MENS	125	172	291	296	165	125	130	140	298									
LADIES	105	154	283	287	156	115	108	124	282									
PAR	3	3	4	4	3	3	3	3	4									
M.HCP	7	4	1	3	5	6	9	8	2									
L.HCP	7	4	1	3	5	6	9	8	2									

CANYON MESA C.C.

SEMI PRIVATE 9 HOLES

500 Jacks Canyon Rd. Sedona, AZ 86336   602-284-2176

DESERT ○   TRADITIONAL ●   LINKS ○

TERRAIN	TREES	WATER

GREENS *Bent*	**COURSE FAVORS A...** *Mix*	
FAIRWAYS *Other*	**WIDTH OF FAIRWAYS** *Tight*	
BUNKERS *Regular*	**AMT. OF BUNKERS** *Minimal*	

PAR	YARDS	RATING	SLOPE	1992 GREEN FEES	
28	1475	51.7	73	**HIGH**	*$15*
28	1300	51.7	73	**LOW**	*$10*
28	1010	51.7	73	**SPECIALS**	*Call*

THE COURSE COMMENTARY

This is a gorgeous course that backs up to the National Forest with great views of the Sedona red rocks. Greens are tiff grass. Hand carts are available. This Jack Snyder layout plays two sets of tees for 18 holes.

TOUGHEST HOLE	THE 185 YARD PAR-3 8TH HOLE. YOUR TEE SHOT PLAYS OVER A DITCH TO AN ELEVATED TWO-TIERED GREEN.
BIRDIE HOLE	THE 100 YARD PAR-3 7TH HOLE PLAYS TO A HUGE GREEN WITH BUNKERS THAT DON'T COME INTO PLAY.
WATER IN PLAY ON...	1 HOLE
OVERALL STRATEGY	HIT IT STRAIGHT AND AIM FOR THE PIN.
CART REQUIRED?	NO
PRACTICE FACILITIES?	PUTTING GREEN CHIPPING GREEN
COURSE IS OPEN...	YES
OVERSEEDING	OCTOBER FOR 2 WEEKS. FAIRWAYS ONLY.
RESTAURANT?	NO
ACCOMMODATIONS?	CASITAS AND RENTALS ARE ON PROPERTY. GOLF PACKAGES ARE AVAILABLE.
DON'T FORGET YOUR..	THIRD WEDGE
COURSE DESIGNER	JACK SNYDER
# OF ROUNDS ANNUALLY	N/A
DIRECTIONS	8 MILES WEST OFF I-17 ON STATE RD. 179.

COURSE LAYOUT

HOLE	1	2	3	4	5	6	7	8	9	10	11	12	13	14	15	16	17	18
CHAMP	135	170	145	295	180	105	100	185	160	135	170	145	295	180	105	100	185	160
MENS	115	160	100	280	150	95	70	175	120	125	140	130	265	170	80	85	160	145
LADIES	103	130	88	234	97	70	77	116	93	105	130	65	255	140	70	60	95	90
PAR	3	3	3	4	3	3	3	3	3	3	3	3	4	3	3	3	3	3
M.HCP	11	5	13	3	7	15	17	1	9	14	10	12	4	2	18	16	6	8
L.HCP	7	5	15	1	3	13	17	9	11	8	6	16	2	4	14	18	10	12

CAVE CREEK G.C

PUBLIC   18 HOLES

15202 N. 19th Ave. Phoenix, AZ 85023   602-866-8076

DESERT ○   TRADITIONAL ●   LINKS ○

| TERRAIN | TREES | WATER |

GREENS	Bermuda	COURSE FAVORS A...	Fade
FAIRWAYS	Bermuda	WIDTH OF FAIRWAYS	Forgiving
BUNKERS	Regular	AMT. OF BUNKERS	Average

PAR	YARDS	RATING	SLOPE	1992 GREEN FEES $
72	6876	71.9	122	HIGH $18
72	6290	68.3	117	LOW $12
72	5614	68.9	109	SPECIALS None

THE COURSE COMMENTARY

The Cave Creek wash runs right through the middle of the course making this a very undulated layout. Wide open fairways let you rip it off the tee.

TOUGHEST HOLE	THE 450 YARD PAR-4 8TH HOLE IS LONG AND NARROW WITH O.B. ON THE LEFT PLAYING TO A SMALL GREEN.
BIRDIE HOLE	THE 173 YARD PAR-3 13TH HOLE HAS BUNKERS SHORT OF THE GREEN THAT REALLY DON'T COME INTO PLAY.
WATER IN PLAY ON...	8 HOLES
OVERALL STRATEGY	HIT IT LONG AND STRAIGHT OFF THE TEE. SHOOT FOR THE PIN TO AVOID LONG PUTTS.
CART REQUIRED?	NO
PRACTICE FACILITIES?	DRIVING RANGE PUTTING GREEN
COURSE IS OPEN...	YES
OVERSEEDING	OCTOBER FOR 2 WEEKS. TEES AND GREENS.
RESTAURANT?	YES
ACCOMMODATIONS?	NO
DON'T FORGET YOUR..	ROCK IRON
COURSE DESIGNER	JACK SNYDER
# OF ROUNDS ANNUALLY	100,000
DIRECTIONS	ON 19TH AVE BETWEEN GREENWAY RD. AND THUNDERBIRD RD.

HOLE	1	2	3	4	5	6	7	8	9	10	11	12	13	14	15	16	17	18
CHAMP	363	520	198	391	385	559	199	450	415	353	550	378	173	399	389	536	212	406
MENS	334	483	153	361	355	529	170	400	388	323	515	341	150	370	358	508	176	376
LADIES	305	426	123	330	325	500	120	370	360	296	408	314	106	344	334	477	136	340
PAR	4	5	3	4	4	5	3	4	4	4	5	4	3	4	4	5	3	4
M.HCP	15	3	17	11	9	13	7	1	5	16	2	14	18	10	12	6	8	4
L.HCP	15	5	17	9	11	3	13	1	7	18	2	14	16	6	8	4	12	10

CLIFF VALLEY G.C.

PUBLIC 18 HOLES

5910 N. Oracle Rd. Tucson, AZ 85704

602-887-6161

DESERT ● **TRADITIONAL** ○ **LINKS** ○

TERRAIN	TREES	WATER

GREENS *Bermuda*	**COURSE FAVORS A...** *Mix*
FAIRWAYS *Bermuda*	**WIDTH OF FAIRWAYS** *Forgiving*
BUNKERS *Other*	**AMT. OF BUNKERS** *Average*

	PAR	YARDS	RATING	SLOPE
	N/A	N/A	N/A	N/A
	54	2261	N/A	N/A
	54	2155	N/A	N/A

1992 GREEN FEES $

HIGH	$9
LOW	$8
SPECIALS	$5.50 Apr.- Oct. Unlimited

THE COURSE COMMENTARY

This course is all par 3's but it doesn't mean that you'll only hit your pitching wedge. The back nine is predominantly more difficult than the front nine.

TOUGHEST HOLE THE 108 YARD PAR-3 7TH PLAYS TO A SMALL GREEN WITH OUT-OF-BOUNDS TO THE RIGHT.

BIRDIE HOLE THE 125 YARD PAR-3 18TH IS WIDE OPEN WITH A LARGE GREEN AND NO HAZARDS.

WATER IN PLAY ON... 3 HOLES

OVERALL STRATEGY STAY BELOW THE PIN ON EVERY TEE SHOT.

CART REQUIRED? NO

PRACTICE FACILITIES? PUTTING GREEN

COURSE IS OPEN... YES

OVERSEEDING SEPTEMBER FOR 4 WEEKS. TEES, GREENS, AND FAIRWAYS

RESTAURANT? BREAKFAST AND LUNCH SERVED DAILY.

ACCOMMODATIONS? CLIFF MANOR INN NEARBY

DON'T FORGET YOUR.. ALL YOUR SHORT YARDAGE CLUBS.

COURSE DESIGNER GIL KAMMERT

 # OF ROUNDS ANNUALLY 50,000 - 60,000

DIRECTIONS HALF MILE NORTH OF ORANGE GROVE RD. ON ORACLE RD. AT THE CORNER OF RUDASIL AND ORACLE RDS.

HOLE	1	2	3	4	5	6	7	8	9	10	11	12	13	14	15	16	17	18
CHAMP																		
MENS	125	110	130	141	120	123	108	100	108	133	125	125	160	150	125	150	103	125
LADIES	125	110	130	141	56	123	108	68	108	133	125	125	160	150	125	150	93	125
PAR	3	3	3	3	3	3	3	3	3	3	3	3	3	3	3	3	3	3
M.HCP	11	14	7	2	8	12	15	16	18	10	4	9	3	5	6	1	17	13
L.HCP	11	14	8	3	17	12	15	16	18	10	5	9	4	6	7	2	1	13

COCOPAH BEND R.V. & G.R.

6800 Strand Ave Yuma, AZ 85634   602-343-1663

DESERT ○   **TRADITIONAL** ●   **LINKS** ○

TERRAIN	TREES	WATER

	GREENS	Bermuda		COURSE FAVORS A...	Mix
	FAIRWAYS	Bermuda		WIDTH OF FAIRWAYS	Tight
	BUNKERS	Regular		AMT. OF BUNKERS	Average

	PAR	YARDS	RATING	SLOPE	1992 GREEN FEES $	
	N/A	N/A	N/A	N/A	HIGH	$16
	70	5264	64	97	LOW	$8
	70	4709	64.8	99	SPECIALS	Free to residents in Sept/Oct

THE COURSE COMMENTARY

This course is not very long but should be fun to play for all levels of golfing skills. It is a difficult course to par and is easy to walk around.

TOUGHEST HOLE	THE 220 YARD PAR-3 17TH IS LONG AND HAS OUT-OF-BOUNDS TO THE RIGHT OF THE GREEN.
BIRDIE HOLE	THE 266 YARD PAR-4 6TH IS VERY FORGIVING OFF THE TEE.
WATER IN PLAY ON...	3 HOLES
OVERALL STRATEGY	HIT EVERY CLUB IN YOUR BAG STRAIGHT.
CART REQUIRED?	NO
PRACTICE FACILITIES?	DRIVING RANGE PUTTING GREEN
COURSE IS OPEN...	YES
OVERSEEDING	OCTOBER FOR 4 WEEKS. TEES, GREENS, AND FAIRWAYS.
RESTAURANT?	SNACK BAR OCT. THRU MAY
ACCOMMODATIONS?	800 SPACE RV RESORT.
DON'T FORGET YOUR..	YOUR FAVORITE DRIVER.
COURSE DESIGNER	N/A
# OF ROUNDS ANNUALLY	40,000
DIRECTIONS	TAKE THE WINTERHAVEN 4TH AVE EXIT OFF I-8 TO FIRST ST. , GO WEST AND FOLLOW THE SIGNS.

COURSE LAYOUT

HOLE	1	2	3	4	5	6	7	8	9	10	11	12	13	14	15	16	17	18
CHAMP																		
MENS	153	308	330	200	439	266	358	442	213	220	354	507	300	175	267	269	220	243
LADIES	140	283	300	182	352	244	333	408	178	195	329	423	280	155	244	245	192	226
PAR	3	4	4	3	5	4	4	5	3	4	4	5	4	3	4	4	3	4
M.HCP	3	15	13	5	9	17	11	1	7	16	10	6	14	8	12	18	2	4
L.HCP	3	15	13	5	9	17	11	1	7	16	10	6	14	8	12	18	2	4

CONTINENTAL G.C.

PUBLIC   18 HOLES

7920 E. Osborn Rd. Scottsdale, AZ 85251   *602-941-1585*

DESERT ○   **TRADITIONAL** ●   **LINKS** ○

TERRAIN	TREES	WATER

	GREENS	Bermuda		COURSE FAVORS A...	Mix
	FAIRWAYS	Bermuda		WIDTH OF FAIRWAYS	Normal
	BUNKERS	Regular		AMT. OF BUNKERS	Average

	PAR	YARDS	RATING	SLOPE	1992 GREEN FEES	
	N/A	N/A	N/A	N/A	HIGH	$33
	60	3766	57.4	86	LOW	$15
	60	3381	57.1	78	SPECIALS	None

THE COURSE COMMENTARY   This challenging 18 hole executive style layout is located in a green riverbed in the heart of Scottsdale.

TOUGHEST HOLE	THE 340 YARD PAR-4 18TH HOLE HAS WATER ON BOTH SIDES OF THE FAIRWAY AND GREEN.
BIRDIE HOLE	THE 117 YARD PAR-3 3RD HOLE IS SHORT FOR ANY SKILL LEVEL.
WATER IN PLAY ON...	3 HOLES
OVERALL STRATEGY	A GOOD PUTTER WILL SCORE WELL.
CART REQUIRED?	No
PRACTICE FACILITIES?	DRIVING RANGE PUTTING GREEN CHIPPING GREEN
COURSE IS OPEN...	YES
OVERSEEDING	OCTOBER FOR 2 WEEKS. INCLUDES EVERYTHING.
RESTAURANT?	YES
ACCOMMODATIONS?	MANY HOTELS NEARBY IN SCOTTSDALE.
DON'T FORGET YOUR..	FAVORITE WEDGE
COURSE DESIGNER	CITY ENGINEERS OF SCOTTSDALE
# OF ROUNDS ANNUALLY	N/A
DIRECTIONS	1 BLOCK WEST OF HAYDEN ON OSBORN.

COURSE LAYOUT

HOLE	1	2	3	4	5	6	7	8	9	10	11	12	13	14	15	16	17	18
CHAMP																		
MENS	317	133	117	338	141	182	171	138	360	305	158	113	188	157	123	329	156	340
LADIES	301	117	105	318	107	166	147	108	330	280	139	103	170	134	95	309	133	319
PAR	4	3	3	4	3	3	3	3	4	4	3	3	3	3	3	4	3	4
M.HCP	6	14	18	4	12	8	10	16	2	5	11	17	7	9	15	3	13	1
L.HCP	6	14	18	4	12	8	10	16	2	5	11	17	7	9	15	3	13	1

CORONADO G.C.

PUBLIC   9 HOLES

2829 N. Miller Rd. Scottsdale, AZ 85257   602-947-8364

DESERT ⚪   **TRADITIONAL** ⚫   **LINKS** ⚪

TERRAIN	TREES	WATER

GREENS *Bermuda*	**COURSE FAVORS A...** *Fade*
FAIRWAYS *Bermuda*	**WIDTH OF FAIRWAYS** *Normal*
BUNKERS *Regular*	**AMT. OF BUNKERS** *Average*

	PAR	YARDS	RATING	SLOPE	1992 GREEN FEES $
	N/A	N/A	N/A	N/A	**HIGH** $10
	31	1850	56.7	92	**LOW** $5
	31	1850	59.5	91	**SPECIALS** N/A

THE COURSE COMMENTARY *This golf course is excellent for beginners and retirees. The driving range is all grass and lighted for night use.*

TOUGHEST HOLE	THE 362 YARD PAR-4 3RD HOLE IS A DOGLEG LEFT WITH WATER TO THE RIGHT. KEEP YOUR TEE SHOT TO THE RIGHT.
BIRDIE HOLE	THE 111 YARD PAR-3 2ND HOLE IS STRAIGHT AWAY WITH NO HAZARDS.
WATER IN PLAY ON...	5 HOLES
OVERALL STRATEGY	A CONSISTENT SHORT GAME WILL WORK WELL FOR YOU ON THIS COURSE.
CART REQUIRED?	NO
PRACTICE FACILITIES?	DRIVING RANGE PUTTING GREEN CHIPPING GREEN
COURSE IS OPEN...	YES
OVERSEEDING	OCTOBER FOR 2 WEEKS. TEES AND GREENS.
RESTAURANT?	NO
ACCOMMODATIONS?	CLOSE TO DOWNTOWN SCOTTSDALE
DON'T FORGET YOUR..	PITCHING WEDGE
COURSE DESIGNER	MILT COGGINS, SR.
# OF ROUNDS ANNUALLY	65,000
DIRECTIONS	1 BLOCK SOUTH OF THOMAS ON MILLER RD.

COURSE LAYOUT

HOLE	1	2	3	4	5	6	7	8	9	10	11	12	13	14	15	16	17	18
CHAMP																		
MENS	255	111	362	148	160	278	130	145	261	255	111	362	148	160	278	130	145	261
LADIES																		
PAR	4	3	4	3	3	4	3	3	4	4	3	4	3	3	4	3	3	4
M.HCP	5	17	1	11	9	3	15	13	7	6	18	2	12	10	4	16	14	8
L.HCP	5	17	1	11	9	3	15	13	7	6	18	2	12	10	4	16	14	8

CYPRESS G.C.

PUBLIC   18 HOLES

10801 E. McDowell Scottsdale, AZ 85256   602-946-5155

DESERT ○   TRADITIONAL ●   LINKS ○

TERRAIN	TREES	WATER

GREENS Bermuda	**COURSE FAVORS A...** Mix	
FAIRWAYS Bermuda	**WIDTH OF FAIRWAYS** Forgiving	
BUNKERS Regular	**AMT. OF BUNKERS** Average	

PAR	YARDS	RATING	SLOPE	1992 GREEN FEES $	
68	5164	N/A	N/A	HIGH	$16
68	4946	N/A	N/A	LOW	$11
68	4678	N/A	N/A	SPECIALS	N/A

THE COURSE COMMENTARY

This course has a short nine and a long nine. The front nine is the longest in the valley.

TOUGHEST HOLE THE 593 YARD PAR-5 3RD HOLE ON THE LONG NINE TAKES 3 LONG, STRAIGHT SHOTS IN A ROW TO HAVE A CHANCE AT PAR.

BIRDIE HOLE THE 95 YARD PAR-3 9TH HOLE ON THE SHORT NINE IS A CHIP AND A PUTT FOR A BIRDIE.

WATER IN PLAY ON... 7 HOLES

OVERALL STRATEGY THE COURSE IS STRAIGHT, STRAIGHT, STRAIGHT. HIT IT STRAIGHT AND YOU'LL DO FINE.

CART REQUIRED? No

PRACTICE FACILITIES? DRIVING RANGE   PUTTING GREEN   CHIPPING GREEN

COURSE IS OPEN... YES

OVERSEEDING OCTOBER FOR 2 WEEKS, TEES AND GREENS.

RESTAURANT? SNACK BAR WITH DRINKS, SANDWICHES AND HOT DOGS.

ACCOMMODATIONS? N/A

DON'T FORGET YOUR.. YOUR FAVORITE DRIVER.

COURSE DESIGNER N/A

 # OF ROUNDS ANNUALLY 50,000

DIRECTIONS HALF MILE WEST OF COUNTRY CLUB DR. ON MCDOWELL RD.

COURSE LAYOUT

HOLE	1	2	3	4	5	6	7	8	9	10	11	12	13	14	15	16	17	18
CHAMP										510	195	593	268	485	349	475	425	166
MENS	165	175	140	165	305	223	135	295	95	495	180	580	253	470	330	435	355	150
LADIES										480	170	500	235	410	310	415	330	130
PAR	3	3	3	3	4	4	3	4	3	5	3	5	4	5	4	5	4	3
M.HCP	11	5	15	9	1	7	13	3	17	6	16	2	14	8	12	4	10	18
L.HCP	11	5	15	9	1	7	13	3	17	6	16	2	14	8	12	4	10	18

DESERT SANDS G.C.

SEMI PRIVATE 18 HOLES

7400 E. Baseline Rd. Mesa, AZ 85208   *602-832-0210*

DESERT ○   **TRADITIONAL** ●   **LINKS** ○

TERRAIN	TREES	WATER

GREENS *Bermuda*   **COURSE FAVORS A...** *Mix*
FAIRWAYS *Bermuda*   **WIDTH OF FAIRWAYS** *Forgiving*
BUNKERS *Other*   **AMT. OF BUNKERS** *Average*

PAR	YARDS	RATING	SLOPE	1992 GREEN FEES $	
N/A	N/A	N/A	N/A	HIGH	$14
65	3914	56.5	N/A	LOW	$7
N/	N/A	N/A	N/A	SPECIALS	Call

THE COURSE COMMENTARY   This 18 hole executive course is very mature with undulating greens that are in excellent condition. No bunkers on this course.

TOUGHEST HOLE   THE 437 YARD PAR-4 13TH HOLE PLAYS STRAIGHTAWAY TO A LARGE GREEN.

BIRDIE HOLE   THE 100 YARD PAR-3 5TH HOLE IS SHORT TO A WIDE GREEN WITH NO TROUBLE.

WATER IN PLAY ON...   2 HOLES

OVERALL STRATEGY   YOU NEED TO PUTT WELL!

CART REQUIRED?   No

PRACTICE FACILITIES?   DRIVING RANGE   PUTTING GREEN   CHIPPING GREEN

COURSE IS OPEN...   YES

OVERSEEDING   OCTOBER FOR 2 WEEKS. INCLUDES EVERYTHING.

RESTAURANT?   No

ACCOMMODATIONS?   No

DON'T FORGET YOUR..   FAVORITE PUTTER

COURSE DESIGNER   N/A

 # OF ROUNDS ANNUALLY   60,000

DIRECTIONS   HALF MILE EAST OF POWER RD. ON BASELINE.

COURSE LAYOUT

HOLE	1	2	3	4	5	6	7	8	9	10	11	12	13	14	15	16	17	18
CHAMP																		
MENS	305	125	140	263	100	218	283	147	128	130	283	322	437	115	138	253	294	233
LADIES																		
PAR	4	3	3	4	3	4	4	3	3	3	4	4	4	3	3	4	4	4
M.HCP	2	14	16	4	18	8	6	12	10	13	9	3	1	17	15	5	7	11
L.HCP	2	14	16	4	18	8	6	12	10	13	9	3	1	17	15	5	7	11

DESRT HILLS MUNI. G.C.

PUBLIC   18 HOLES

1245 Desert Hills Dr. Yuma, AZ 85364   602-341-0644

DESERT ○   **TRADITIONAL** ●   **LINKS** ○

TERRAIN	**TREES**	**WATER**

GREENS	Bermuda	**COURSE FAVORS A...**	Draw
FAIRWAYS	Bermuda	**WIDTH OF FAIRWAYS**	Normal
BUNKERS	Regular	**AMT. OF BUNKERS**	Many

PAR	YARDS	RATING	SLOPE	1992 GREEN FEES
72	6853	71.2	115	**HIGH** $16
72	6372	69.2	111	**LOW** $8
73	5726	72.4	122	**SPECIALS** N/A

THE COURSE COMMENTARY

Home of The Ben Hogen Tour "Yuma Open" and the future Nike Tour "Yuma Open."

TOUGHEST HOLE	THE 430 YARD PAR 4 5TH HOLE IS UPHILL AND PLAYS INTO A NORTH WIND.
BIRDIE HOLE	THE 471 YARD PAR-5 11TH HOLE IS REACHABLE IN TWO WITH A STRONG DRAW OFF THE TEE.
WATER IN PLAY ON...	4 HOLES
OVERALL STRATEGY	PAY ATTENTION TO THE SLOPING GREENS.
CART REQUIRED?	NO
PRACTICE FACILITIES?	DRIVING RANGE PUTTING GREEN CHIPPING GREEN
COURSE IS OPEN...	YES
OVERSEEDING	OCTOBER FOR 4 WEEKS. TEES, GREENS, AND FAIRWAYS.
RESTAURANT?	BREAKFAST & LUNCH, AND BAR.
ACCOMMODATIONS?	PLENTY OF HOTELS NEARBY.
DON'T FORGET YOUR..	N/A
COURSE DESIGNER	N/A
# OF ROUNDS ANNUALLY	80,000
DIRECTIONS	TAKE 32ND ST. TO AVENUE A, THEN GO SOUTH.

HOLE	1	2	3	4	5	6	7	8	9	10	11	12	13	14	15	16	17	18
CHAMP	415	510	373	167	430	545	381	166	420	381	471	394	339	420	260	594	185	402
MENS	400	480	350	140	415	515	360	140	390	348	464	374	311	353	235	566	147	384
LADIES	340	451	314	113	367	493	337	118	357	314	438	344	250	324	203	463	124	346
PAR	4	5	4	3	4	5	4	3	4	4	5	4	4	4	3	5	3	4
M.HCP	5	9	11	15	1	3	13	17	7	14	10	8	18	12	4	2	16	6
L.HCP	13	11	5	17	1	3	7	15	9	12	2	4	18	14	16	6	10	8

DOBSON RANCH G.C.

PUBLIC   18 HOLES

2155 S. Dobson Rd   Mesa, AZ 85202   *602-644-2291*

DESERT ○   TRADITIONAL ●   LINKS ○

TERRAIN	TREES	WATER

GREENS	*Bermuda*		**COURSE FAVORS A...**	*Mix*
FAIRWAYS	*Bermuda*		**WIDTH OF FAIRWAYS**	*Forgiving*
BUNKERS	*Regular*		**AMT. OF BUNKERS**	*Many*

PAR	YARDS	RATING	SLOPE	1992 GREEN FEES $
72	6593	71.0	117	**HIGH** *$18+*
72	6176	69.1	113	**LOW**
72	5598	71.3	116	**SPECIALS** *Twilight specials*

THE COURSE COMMENTARY

This course is wide open and fairly easy for any skill level. The terrain is fairly flat making it great for walking. Large fairways and greens let you enjoy the game of golf.

TOUGHEST HOLE	THE 417 YARD PAR-4 8TH HOLE. WATER ALL THE WAY DOWN THE RIGHT SIDE LEADS TO A WELL PROTECTED GREEN.
BIRDIE HOLE	THE 357 YARD PAR-4 15TH HOLE IS A WIDE OPEN DOGLEG LEFT. FAIRWAY TRAPS GUARD THE LEFT SIDE.
WATER IN PLAY ON...	7 HOLES
OVERALL STRATEGY	YOU CAN REACH BACK FOR EVERYTHING YOU'VE GOT OFF THE TEE... THE FAIRWAYS ARE FORGIVING.
CART REQUIRED?	No
PRACTICE FACILITIES?	DRIVING RANGE PUTTING GREEN CHIPPING GREEN
COURSE IS OPEN...	YES
OVERSEEDING	OCTOBER FOR 2 WEEKS. TEES, GREENS, AND FAIRWAYS.
RESTAURANT?	YES
ACCOMMODATIONS?	No
DON'T FORGET YOUR..	FAVORITE DRIVER
COURSE DESIGNER	N/A
# OF ROUNDS ANNUALLY	N/A
DIRECTIONS	HALF MILE SOUTH OF BASELINE RD. ON DOBSON RD.

COURSE LAYOUT

HOLE	1	2	3	4	5	6	7	8	9	10	11	12	13	14	15	16	17	18
CHAMP	547	430	380	154	513	393	149	417	568	357	406	183	488	195	357	378	188	490
MENS	516	400	352	153	489	373	140	402	546	331	340	163	465	175	341	357	168	465
LADIES	503	364	330	125	470	360	118	358	387	301	315	147	444	156	314	337	151	418
PAR	5	4	4	3	5	4	3	4	5	4	4	3	5	3	4	4	3	5
M.HCP	5	3	13	11	15	9	17	1	7	8	2	10	12	14	18	4	6	16
L.HCP	3	7	13	15	1	11	17	5	9	8	6	14	2	16	12	10	18	4

DORADO G.C.

6601 E. Speedway Blvd. Tucson, AZ 85710   602-855-6751

DESERT ○   **TRADITIONAL** ●   **LINKS** ○

TERRAIN	TREES	WATER

GREENS	Bent	COURSE FAVORS A...	Draw
FAIRWAYS	Bermuda	WIDTH OF FAIRWAYS	Tight
BUNKERS	Regular	AMT. OF BUNKERS	Minimal

	PAR	YARDS	RATING	SLOPE
★	N/A	N/A	N/A	N/A
	62	3751	57.3	85
	62	3187	57.3	90

1992 GREEN FEES $

HIGH	$15
LOW	$15
SPECIALS	None

THE COURSE COMMENTARY

This 18 hole executive course is challenging even though it's short. Houses down the both sides of the fairway come into play.

TOUGHEST HOLE THE 278 YARD PAR-4 6TH HOLE. FAIRWAY BUNKERS MAKE YOU HIT A STRAIGHT TEE SHOT. WATER RIGHT OF THE GREEN.

BIRDIE HOLE THE 128 YARD PAR-3 13TH HOLE PLAYS TO A LARGE GREEN WITH BUNKERS ONLY ON THE BACK SIDE.

WATER IN PLAY ON... 6 HOLES

OVERALL STRATEGY KEEP IT STRAIGHT AND HIT IT LONG.

CART REQUIRED? No

PRACTICE FACILITIES? N/A

COURSE IS OPEN... YES

OVERSEEDING OCTOBER FOR 1 WEEK. TEES ONLY.

RESTAURANT? No

ACCOMMODATIONS? No

DON'T FORGET YOUR.. N/A

COURSE DESIGNER N/A

 # OF ROUNDS ANNUALLY 50,000

DIRECTIONS 2 BLOCKS EAST OF WILMOT ON SPEEDWAY BLVD.

COURSE LAYOUT

HOLE	1	2	3	4	5	6	7	8	9	10	11	12	13	14	15	16	17	18
CHAMP																		
MENS	287	140	259	180	162	278	148	162	243	242	165	325	128	254	146	264	168	200
LADIES	268	125	227	151	138	248	88	138	181	222	133	298	112	182	128	246	138	164
PAR	4	3	4	3	3	4	3	3	4	4	3	4	3	4	3	4	3	3
M.HCP	5	13	9	15	11	1	3	17	7	8	10	2	18	4	16	6	14	12
L.HCP	5	13	9	15	11	1	3	17	7	8	10	2	18	4	16	6	14	12

DREAMLAND VILLA G.C.

PUBLIC   9 HOLES

5641 E. Albany   Mesa, AZ 85205   *602-985-6591*

DESERT ○   **TRADITIONAL** ●   **LINKS** ○

TERRAIN   **TREES**   **WATER**

GREENS	Bermuda		COURSE FAVORS A...	Mix
FAIRWAYS	Bermuda		WIDTH OF FAIRWAYS	Tight
BUNKERS	Other		AMT. OF BUNKERS	Average

	PAR	YARDS	RATING	SLOPE	1992 GREEN FEES $	
★	N/A	N/A	N/A	N/A	HIGH	$9
	31	1950	57.6	N/A	LOW	$4
	31	1882	N/A	N/A	SPECIALS	Call

THE COURSE COMMENTARY   This is a great course for seniors. This is a very open layout with water coming into play on every par-3. There are no bunkers. The same tees apply for an 18 hole round.

TOUGHEST HOLE	THE 338 PAR-4 7TH HOLE IS LONG AND STRAIGHTAWAY.
BIRDIE HOLE	THE 130 YARD PAR-3 4TH HOLE PLAYS TO A SMALLER GREEN WITH WATER IN FRONT AND TO THE RIGHT.
WATER IN PLAY ON...	5 HOLES
OVERALL STRATEGY	HIT IT STRAIGHT.
CART REQUIRED?	NO
PRACTICE FACILITIES?	N/A
COURSE IS OPEN...	YES
OVERSEEDING	OCTOBER FOR 2 WEEKS. INCLUDES EVERYTHING.
RESTAURANT?	COFFEE SHOP
ACCOMMODATIONS?	NO
DON'T FORGET YOUR..	3 WOOD
COURSE DESIGNER	N/A
# OF ROUNDS ANNUALLY	125,000
DIRECTIONS	1 BLOCK NORTH OF MAIN ON 56TH ST.

HOLE	1	2	3	4	5	6	7	8	9	10	11	12	13	14	15	16	17	18
CHAMP																		
MENS	328	263	150	130	271	181	338	118	171									
LADIES	328	245	150	130	261	171	328	108	161									
PAR	4	4	3	3	4	3	4	3	3									
M.HCP	4	5	11	17	7	13	1	15	9									
L.HCP	4	5	11	17	7	13	1	15	9									

EL CARO G.C.

PUBLIC   18 HOLES

2222 W. Royal Palm Rd.   Phoenix, AZ 85021   602-995-3664

DESERT ○   TRADITIONAL ●   LINKS ○

TERRAIN	TREES	WATER

GREENS	Bermuda	**COURSE FAVORS A...**	Mix
FAIRWAYS	Bermuda	**WIDTH OF FAIRWAYS**	Forgiving
BUNKERS	Other	**AMT. OF BUNKERS**	Average

PAR	YARDS	RATING	SLOPE	1992 GREEN FEES $	
N/A	N/A	N/A	N/A	**HIGH**	$18
60	3330	54.7	73	**LOW**	$7
60	3021	55.1	74	**SPECIALS**	Call

THE COURSE COMMENTARY

This is one of the top executive courses in the valley.

TOUGHEST HOLE	THE 273 YARD PAR-4 6TH HOLE IS A SHARP DOGLEG LEFT WITH WATER WAITING IF YOU DRIVE THE BALL TO THE RIGHT.
BIRDIE HOLE	THE 115 YARD PAR-3 16TH HOLE PLAYS TO A LARGE GREEN. A LAKE IN FRONT DOES NOT AFFECT YOUR SHOT.
WATER IN PLAY ON...	6 HOLES
OVERALL STRATEGY	ACCURACY OFF THE TEE IS MORE IMPORTANT THAN DISTANCE.
CART REQUIRED?	NO
PRACTICE FACILITIES?	DRIVING RANGE PUTTING GREEN
COURSE IS OPEN...	YES
OVERSEEDING	OCTOBER FOR 4 WEEKS. INCLUDES EVERYTHING.
RESTAURANT?	YES
ACCOMMODATIONS?	NO
DON'T FORGET YOUR..	3 WOOD
COURSE DESIGNER	N/A
# OF ROUNDS ANNUALLY	80,000
DIRECTIONS	1 BLOCK NORTH OF NORTHERN ON 23RD AVE.

COURSE LAYOUT

HOLE	1	2	3	4	5	6	7	8	9	10	11	12	13	14	15	16	17	18
CHAMP																		
MENS	136	157	134	297	254	273	133	167	152	242	146	110	161	111	257	115	155	330
LADIES	126	137	114	293	238	254	116	153	130	227	99	102	139	91	243	99	140	320
PAR	3	3	3	4	4	4	3	3	3	4	3	3	3	3	4	3	3	4
M.HCP	15	9	17	3	5	1	13	7	11	4	8	14	12	16	6	18	10	2
L.HCP	15	9	17	3	5	1	13	7	11	4	8	14	12	16	6	18	10	2

EL CONQUISTADOR C.C.-SUNRISE COURSE

HOTEL GUEST PRIORITY 18 HOLES

10555 N. La Canada Tucson, AZ 85704   602-544-1800

DESERT ●   **TRADITIONAL** ○   **LINKS** ○

TERRAIN	TREES	WATER

GREENS	Bermuda	**COURSE FAVORS A...**	Fade
FAIRWAYS	Bermuda	**WIDTH OF FAIRWAYS**	Tight
BUNKERS	Regular	**AMT. OF BUNKERS**	Average

PAR	YARDS	RATING	SLOPE	1992 GREEN FEES $	
72	6819	71.7	123	**HIGH**	$95
72	6288	69.0	113	**LOW**	$40
72	5255	69.4	116	**SPECIALS**	None

THE COURSE COMMENTARY

This course uses a unique mowing technique. The visual impact of the grass strips set El Conquistador apart from all others in the region. Voted Most Improved Course in 1990-91 in the Southwest Region.

TOUGHEST HOLE	THE 460 YARD PAR-4 12TH HOLE IS STRAIGHT AWAY AND VERY LONG. O.B. ON BOTH SIDES.
BIRDIE HOLE	THE 354 YARD PAR-4 1ST HOLE IS SHORT AND CAN START YOUR DAY OFF WITH A SMILE.
WATER IN PLAY ON...	1 HOLE
OVERALL STRATEGY	KEEP THE BALL IN THE MIDDLE OF THE FAIRWAY.
CART REQUIRED?	YES
PRACTICE FACILITIES?	DRIVING RANGE PUTTING GREEN CHIPPING GREEN
COURSE IS OPEN...	YES
OVERSEEDING	AUGUST FOR 3-4 WEEKS. TEES, GREENS, AND FAIRWAYS.
RESTAURANT?	RESTAURANT, LOUNGE, AND FULL SNACK BAR.
ACCOMMODATIONS?	THE SHERATON EL CONQUISTADOR IS 4 1/2 MILES AWAY WITH 440 DELUXE GUEST ROOMS AND 100 SUITES..
DON'T FORGET YOUR..	ROCK IRON
COURSE DESIGNER	JEFF HARDEN & GREG NASH
# OF ROUNDS ANNUALLY	N/A
DIRECTIONS	GO EAST ON INA RD. TO LA CANADA, THEN GO NORTH 4. 5 MILES

COURSE LAYOUT

HOLE	1	2	3	4	5	6	7	8	9	10	11	12	13	14	15	16	17	18
CHAMP	354	167	402	315	362	573	437	188	568	426	374	460	195	338	335	558	379	388
MENS	341	153	382	286	272	540	406	167	534	398	365	390	165	316	291	543	367	372
LADIES	295	114	310	241	265	505	365	141	453	363	276	291	111	194	216	477	289	349
PAR	4	3	4	4	4	5	4	3	5	4	4	4	3	4	4	5	4	4
M.HCP	11	16	3	17	12	1	7	9	6	4	18	8	5	14	15	2	10	13
L.HCP	11	17	3	05	13	1	7	5	9	6	10	12	18	16	14	2	8	4

EL RIO G.C.

PUBLIC   18 HOLES

1400 W. Speedway Blvd. Tucson, AZ 85745   *602-791-4336*

DESERT ○   **TRADITIONAL** ○   **LINKS** ●

TERRAIN	TREES	WATER

GREENS	Bermuda	COURSE FAVORS A...	Draw
FAIRWAYS	Bermuda	WIDTH OF FAIRWAYS	Tight
BUNKERS	Regular	AMT. OF BUNKERS	Many

PAR	YARDS	RATING	SLOPE	1992 GREEN FEES $	
70	6418	69.6	110	HIGH	$18
70	6013	68.6	108	LOW	$16
73	5824	72.2	115	SPECIALS	$6 after 4pm

THE COURSE COMMENTARY *Easy to walk. It's not long but the small greens make it interesting. This course was the home of the PGA Tour's Tucson Open in the 1950's and '60's.*

TOUGHEST HOLE	THE 216 YARD PAR-3 8TH HOLE PLAYS TO A SMALL GREEN AND IS WELL BUNKERED IN FRONT.
BIRDIE HOLE	THE 510 YARD PAR-5 18TH. HIT A LONG FADE OFF THE TEE AND YOU CAN REACH THE GREEN IN TWO.
WATER IN PLAY ON...	4 HOLES
OVERALL STRATEGY	STAY IN THE FAIRWAY BECAUSE IT'S NOT TOO FORGIVING. MUST HAVE A GOOD SHORT GAME.
CART REQUIRED?	No
PRACTICE FACILITIES?	DRIVING RANGE PUTTING GREEN
COURSE IS OPEN...	YES
OVERSEEDING	OCTOBER FOR 2 WEEKS. TEES, GREENS, AND FAIRWAYS.
RESTAURANT?	YES
ACCOMMODATIONS?	LA QUINTA IS NEARBY
DON'T FORGET YOUR..	SHORT GAME!
COURSE DESIGNER	N/A
# OF ROUNDS ANNUALLY	80,000
DIRECTIONS	TAKE THE SPEEDWAY EXIT OFF I-10, THEN GO WEST FOR A HALF MILE.

COURSE LAYOUT

HOLE	1	2	3	4	5	6	7	8	9	10	11	12	13	14	15	16	17	18
CHAMP	368	450	343	186	330	360	424	216	522	389	420	425	119	450	165	392	349	510
MENS	340	412	297	181	307	344	402	201	508	368	390	415	103	428	143	364	331	479
LADIES	339	379	288	175	314	346	398	190	505	368	367	410	85	359	138	360	326	477
PAR	4	4	4	3	4	4	4	3	5	4	4	4	3	4	3	4	4	5
M.HCP	13	1	7	17	11	15	5	3	9	12	4	6	18	2	16	8	14	10
L.HCP	11	17	13	7	9	3	15	5	1	10	8	12	18	6	16	4	14	2

ENCANTO G.C.

PUBLIC   18 HOLES

2705 N. 15th Ave. Phoenix, AZ 85007

602-253-3963

DESERT ○   **TRADITIONAL** ●   **LINKS** ○

TERRAIN	TREES	WATER

GREENS	Bermuda	
FAIRWAYS	Bermuda	
BUNKERS	Regular	

COURSE FAVORS A...	Mix
WIDTH OF FAIRWAYS	Forgiving
AMT. OF BUNKERS	Many

	PAR	YARDS	RATING	SLOPE	1992 GREEN FEES $	
	N/A	N/A	N/A	N/A	**HIGH**	$18
	70	6195	69	N/A	**LOW**	$12
	72	5896	71	N/A	**SPECIALS**	None

THE COURSE COMMENTARY

Located in the heart of downtown Phoenix this course looks directly down on the Phoenix skyline. It's an easy course to shoot in the 80's but difficult to shoot to par.

TOUGHEST HOLE	THE 427 YARD PAR-4 9TH HOLE IS LONG AND STRAIGHTAWAY TO A LARGE GREEN.
BIRDIE HOLE	THE 159 YARD PAR-3 11TH HOLE IS FORGIVING ON AND OFF THE GREEN.
WATER IN PLAY ON...	4 HOLES
OVERALL STRATEGY	BOOM IT OFF THE TEE BECAUSE THE FAIRWAYS ARE QUITE FORGIVING.
CART REQUIRED?	No
PRACTICE FACILITIES?	DRIVING RANGE PUTTING GREEN CHIPPING GREEN
COURSE IS OPEN...	YES
OVERSEEDING	OCTOBER FOR 4 WEEKS. TEES AND GREENS.
RESTAURANT?	YES
ACCOMMODATIONS?	NEARBY IN DOWNTOWN PHOENIX.
DON'T FORGET YOUR..	EVERYTHING
COURSE DESIGNER	CITY PLANNERS
# OF ROUNDS ANNUALLY	80,000
DIRECTIONS	2 BLOCKS SOUTH OF THOMAS ON 15TH AVE.

COURSE LAYOUT

HOLE	1	2	3	4	5	6	7	8	9	10	11	12	13	14	15	16	17	18
CHAMP																		
MENS	485	318	195	377	188	352	115	562	427	300	159	508	388	217	426	403	393	388
LADIES	469	303	185	353	177	342	103	487	415	295	146	502	367	212	413	380	381	343
PAR	5	4	3	4	3	4	3	5	4	4	3	5	4	3	4	4	4	4
M.HCP	3	15	13	7	11	9	17	5	1	16	18	12	6	8	4	2	10	14
L.HCP	3	9	15	7	13	11	17	1	5	14	18	2	8	16	4	6	10	12

ENCANTO NINE G.C.

PUBLIC 9 HOLES

2300 N. 17th Ave. Phoenix, AZ 85007　　　　*602-261-8979*

DESERT ○　　**TRADITIONAL** ●　　**LINKS** ○

TERRAIN	TREES	WATER

GREENS	Bermuda	COURSE FAVORS A...	Mix
FAIRWAYS	Bermuda	WIDTH OF FAIRWAYS	Forgiving
BUNKERS	Regular	AMT. OF BUNKERS	Minimal

	PAR	YARDS	RATING	SLOPE	1992 GREEN FEES $	
	N/A	N/A	N/A	N/A	HIGH	$5
	30	1730	57.7	79	LOW	$5
	N/	N/A	N/A	N/A	SPECIALS	None

THE COURSE COMMENTARY

This 9 hole executive course plays the same tees for 18 holes. Located in the heart of downtown Phoenix, anyone can get a round in before heading to a meeting or the airport.

TOUGHEST HOLE	THE 312 YARD PAR-4 9TH HOLE IS THE #1 HANDICAP HOLE ON THE COURSE.
BIRDIE HOLE	THE 95 YARD PAR-3 2ND HOLE IS A SURE LOOK AT A BIRDIE.
WATER IN PLAY ON...	2 HOLES
OVERALL STRATEGY	YOUR MIDDLE IRONS NEED TO BE ON TARGET.
CART REQUIRED?	NO
PRACTICE FACILITIES?	DRIVING RANGE PUTTING GREEN CHIPPING GREEN
COURSE IS OPEN...	YES
OVERSEEDING	OCTOBER FOR 2 WEEKS. TEES AND GREENS.
RESTAURANT?	COFFEE SHOP
ACCOMMODATIONS?	DOWNTOWN HOTELS NEARBY
DON'T FORGET YOUR..	FAVORITE WEDGE
COURSE DESIGNER	CITY PLANNERS
# OF ROUNDS ANNUALLY	N/A
DIRECTIONS	17TH AVE. AND ENCANTO BLVD

COURSE LAYOUT

HOLE	1	2	3	4	5	6	7	8	9	10	11	12	13	14	15	16	17	18
CHAMP																		
MENS	267	95	150	140	245	156	180	165	312	267	95	150	140	245	156	180	165	312
LADIES																		
PAR	4	3	3	3	4	3	3	3	4	4	3	3	3	4	3	3	3	4
M.HCP	3	17	15	13	9	11	5	7	1	4	18	16	14	10	12	6	8	2
L.HCP																		

ESTRELLA MOUNTAIN G.C.

PUBLIC   18 HOLES

South Bullard Road   Goodyear, AZ 85338   *602-932-3714*

DESERT ●   **TRADITIONAL** ○   **LINKS** ○

| TERRAIN | TREES | WATER |

GREENS *Bermuda*   **COURSE FAVORS A...** *Mix*
FAIRWAYS *Bermuda*   **WIDTH OF FAIRWAYS** *Normal*
BUNKERS *Silicon*   **AMT. OF BUNKERS** *Average*

PAR	YARDS	RATING	SLOPE	1992 GREEN FEES $	
N/A	N/A	N/A	N/A	HIGH	$20
71	6415	69.3	112	LOW	$14
73	5374	69.8	113	SPECIALS	$10

THE COURSE COMMENTARY

Beautiful desert setting in the foothills of the Sierra Estrella Mountains.

TOUGHEST HOLE THE 392 YARD PAR-4 3RD HOLE. THERE IS O.B. LEFT AND WATER RIGHT WITH A NARROW OPENING TO THE GREEN.

BIRDIE HOLE THE 323 YARD PAR-4 2ND HOLE IS SHORT AND PLAYS TO A LARGE GREEN.

WATER IN PLAY ON... 3 HOLES

OVERALL STRATEGY EXCEPT FOR THE FIRST HOLE, STAY LEFT OFF THE TEE.

CART REQUIRED? NO

PRACTICE FACILITIES? DRIVING RANGE   PUTTING GREEN   CHIPPING GREEN

COURSE IS OPEN... YES

OVERSEEDING SEPTEMBER FOR 4 WEEKS. TEES, GREENS, AND FAIRWAYS

RESTAURANT? SNACK BAR

ACCOMMODATIONS? N/A

DON'T FORGET YOUR.. ROCK IRON

COURSE DESIGNER ROBERT (RED) LAWRENCE

 # OF ROUNDS ANNUALLY 51,000

DIRECTIONS HEAD WEST ON I-10 TO ESTRELLA PKWY, THEN EXIT AND GO SOUTH FOR 5 MILES

COURSE LAYOUT

HOLE	1	2	3	4	5	6	7	8	9	10	11	12	13	14	15	16	17	18
CHAMP																		
MENS	501	323	392	150	409	350	374	166	368	521	410	200	435	368	186	369	421	472
LADIES	446	281	263	115	356	329	330	121	281	475	325	136	392	301	93	321	408	401
PAR	5	4	4	3	4	4	4	3	4	5	4	3	4	4	3	4	4	5
M.HCP	3	13	7	17	1	11	5	15	9	4	10	16	2	14	18	12	6	8
L.HCP	3	13	7	17	1	11	5	15	9	4	10	16	2	14	18	12	6	8

FAIRFIELD FLAGSTAFF - ELDEN HILLS G.C.

PUBLIC   18 HOLES

2380 N. Oakmont Dr. Flagstaff, AZ 86004   602-527-7999

DESERT ○   **TRADITIONAL** ●   **LINKS** ○

TERRAIN	TREES	WATER

GREENS	Bermuda	
FAIRWAYS	Bermuda	
BUNKERS	Regular	

COURSE FAVORS A...	Mix
WIDTH OF FAIRWAYS	Forgiving
AMT. OF BUNKERS	Many

	PAR	YARDS	RATING	SLOPE	1992 GREEN FEES $
★	N/A	N/A	N/A	N/A	**HIGH** $38
	73	6104	67.8	122	**LOW**
	73	5280	67.7	106	**SPECIALS** Call

THE COURSE COMMENTARY

One of two courses at the Fairfield Flagstaff Resort. This course is shorter and forgiving. Your ball should carry a little longer because of the altitude.

TOUGHEST HOLE	THE 513 YARD PAR-5 18TH HOLE. YOUR TEE SHOT PLAYS TO A NARROW LANDING AREA WITH WATER TO THE LEFT.
BIRDIE HOLE	THE 310 YARD PAR-4 1ST HOLE IS STRAIGHTAWAY AND REACHABLE IN 1 BECAUSE OF THE ALTITUDE.
WATER IN PLAY ON...	5 HOLES
OVERALL STRATEGY	BE LONG AND STRAIGHT OFF THE TEE.
CART REQUIRED?	NO
PRACTICE FACILITIES?	DRIVING RANGE PUTTING GREEN CHIPPING GREEN
COURSE IS OPEN...	CLOSED WHEN SNOW COVERED.
OVERSEEDING	N/A
RESTAURANT?	YES
ACCOMMODATIONS?	NO
DON'T FORGET YOUR..	1 IRON
COURSE DESIGNER	N/A
# OF ROUNDS ANNUALLY	N/A
DIRECTIONS	TAKE THE COUNTRY CLUB DR. EXIT OFF I-40 AND GO SOUTH FOR A HALF MILE TO OAKMONT DR.

COURSE LAYOUT NOT AVAILABLE

HOLE	1	2	3	4	5	6	7	8	9	10	11	12	13	14	15	16	17	18
CHAMP																		
MENS	310	302	440	170	460	400	335	183	515	332	344	390	140	470	150	318	332	513
LADIES	282	268	408	140	438	300	295	156	440	312	322	330	115	410	142	304	245	473
PAR	4	4	5	3	5	4	4	3	5	4	4	4	3	5	3	4	4	5
M.HCP	16	14	8	18	6	4	10	12	2	9	7	3	17	5	15	13	11	1
L.HCP	16	14	8	18	4	12	10	6	2	9	7	3	17	5	15	11	13	1

Fiesta Lakes G.C.

PUBLIC   9 HOLES

1415 S. Westwood Cir. Mesa, AZ 85210   602-969-0377

DESERT ○   **TRADITIONAL** ●   **LINKS** ○

TERRAIN	TREES	WATER

GREENS	Bermuda	**COURSE FAVORS A...**	Mix
FAIRWAYS	Bermuda	**WIDTH OF FAIRWAYS**	Normal
BUNKERS	Regular	**AMT. OF BUNKERS**	Minimal

	PAR	YARDS	RATING	SLOPE
	N/A	N/A	N/A	N/A
	29	1503	N/A	N/A
	N/	N/A	N/A	N/A

1992 GREEN FEES $

HIGH	$8
LOW	$6
SPECIALS	Call

THE COURSE COMMENTARY

This course is great for juniors and small company tournaments. The course plays fairly straight-away with all 9 holes built around a large central lake.

TOUGHEST HOLE	THE 274 YARD PAR-4 4TH HOLE IS A DOGLEG RIGHT WITH WATER ON THE LEFT.
BIRDIE HOLE	THE 117 YARD PAR-3 6TH HOLE PLAYS TO A LARGE GREEN WITH NO TROUBLE.
WATER IN PLAY ON...	4 HOLES
OVERALL STRATEGY	RELAX AND ENJOY YOUR ROUND.
CART REQUIRED?	NO
PRACTICE FACILITIES?	DRIVING RANGE
COURSE IS OPEN...	YES
OVERSEEDING	OCTOBER FOR 2 WEEKS. TEES AND GREENS.
RESTAURANT?	NO
ACCOMMODATIONS?	NO
DON'T FORGET YOUR..	3 WOOD
COURSE DESIGNER	N/A
# OF ROUNDS ANNUALLY	N/A
DIRECTIONS	TAKE THE ALMA SCHOOL EXIT OFF STATE 360, THEN GO NORTH TO HOLME AND THEN EAST FOR A HALF MILE.

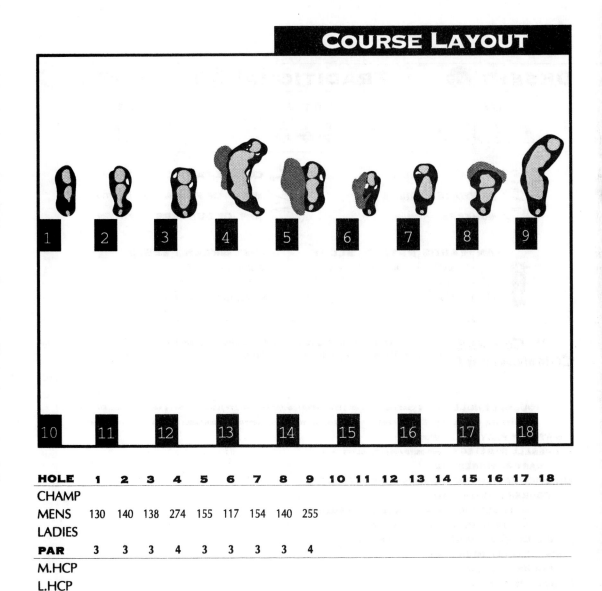

HOLE	1	2	3	4	5	6	7	8	9	10	11	12	13	14	15	16	17	18
CHAMP																		
MENS	130	140	138	274	155	117	154	140	255									
LADIES																		
PAR	3	3	3	4	3	3	3	3	4									
M.HCP																		
L.HCP																		

FOUNTAIN HILLS G.C.

SEMI PRIVATE 18 HOLES

10440 Indian Wells Dr. Fountain Hills, AZ 85268   602-837-1173

DESERT ●   **TRADITIONAL** ○   **LINKS** ○

TERRAIN	TREES	WATER

	GREENS	Bermuda		COURSE FAVORS A...	Draw
	FAIRWAYS	Bermuda		WIDTH OF FAIRWAYS	Normal
	BUNKERS	Regular		AMT. OF BUNKERS	Average

PAR	YARDS	RATING	SLOPE	1992 GREEN FEES $	
71	6087	68.9	119	HIGH	$65
71	5743	67.3	111	LOW	$22
71	5035	68.9	112	SPECIALS	40% less after 2pm

THE COURSE COMMENTARY

This course is hilly, narrow and very competitive. The signature hole is the 153 yard par-3 16th that sports a great view and a great chance at a birdie.

TOUGHEST HOLE	THE 386 YARD PAR-4 9TH HOLE IS A NARROW DOGLEG LEFT WITH TROUBLE AND TREES AROUND THE GREEN.
BIRDIE HOLE	THE 153 YARD PAR-3 16TH. IT'S A RELIEF TO HIT A TEE SHOT TO A GREEN LARGER THAN MOST OF THE FAIRWAYS.
WATER IN PLAY ON...	2 HOLES
OVERALL STRATEGY	DON'T DRIVE FOR DISTANCE OFF THE TEE.
CART REQUIRED?	YES
PRACTICE FACILITIES?	DRIVING RANGE PUTTING GREEN
COURSE IS OPEN...	YES
OVERSEEDING	OCTOBER FOR 4 WEEKS. TEES, GREENS, AND FAIRWAYS.
RESTAURANT?	RESTAURANT AND LOUNGE
ACCOMMODATIONS?	MARRIOT HOTEL 4 MILES AWAY.
DON'T FORGET YOUR..	ROCK IRON AND PATIENCE.
COURSE DESIGNER	N/A
# OF ROUNDS ANNUALLY	N/A
DIRECTIONS	1 MILE NORTH OF SHEA BLVD. ON SAGUARO BLVD. TO INDIAN WELLS DR. GO WEST UP THE HILL.

HOLE	1	2	3	4	5	6	7	8	9	10	11	12	13	14	15	16	17	18
CHAMP	346	186	372	497	358	360	318	158	386	322	380	484	184	493	392	153	340	358
MENS	336	172	367	463	332	338	303	146	370	291	372	464	155	475	384	141	309	325
LADIES	261	140	313	414	294	284	274	131	338	217	328	432	147	445	336	99	280	302
PAR	4	3	4	5	4	4	4	3	4	4	4	5	3	5	4	3	4	4
M.HCP	5	7	3	15	9	11	13	17	1	16	6	14	10	4	2	18	12	8
L.HCP	11	15	1	3	13	7	9	17	5	14	10	8	16	2	4	18	12	6

FRED ENKE G.C.

PUBLIC   18 HOLES

8251 E. Irvington Tucson, AZ 85730   *602-296-8607*

DESERT ●   TRADITIONAL ○   LINKS ○

| TERRAIN | TREES | WATER |

GREENS Bermuda	**COURSE FAVORS A...** Mix	
FAIRWAYS Bermuda	**WIDTH OF FAIRWAYS** Tight	
BUNKERS Regular	**AMT. OF BUNKERS** Many	

PAR	YARDS	RATING	SLOPE	1992 GREEN FEES $	
72	6809	73.3	137	HIGH	$18
72	6363	70.4	129	LOW	$7
72	5026	68.8	111	SPECIALS	$7 after 2pm

THE COURSE COMMENTARY

This is a resort-style course without the resort price. This is the only course in Tucson that is a target style layout. Watch for the wildlife. Excellent practice facilities.

TOUGHEST HOLE THE 455 YARD PAR-4 9TH HOLE. TROUBLE ON BOTH SIDES OFF THE TEE. THE GREEN IS SURROUNDED BY BUNKERS.

BIRDIE HOLE THE 152 YARD PAR-3 13TH HOLE PLAYS TO A HUGE GREEN. UNFORTUNATELY, BUNKERS SURROUND THE HOLE.

WATER IN PLAY ON... 2 HOLES

OVERALL STRATEGY ACCURACY OFF THE TEE IS AT A PREMIUM.

CART REQUIRED? NO

PRACTICE FACILITIES? DRIVING RANGE   PUTTING GREEN   CHIPPING GREEN

COURSE IS OPEN... YES

OVERSEEDING OCTOBER FOR 2 WEEKS. INCLUDES EVERYTHING.

RESTAURANT? YES

ACCOMMODATIONS? NO

DON'T FORGET YOUR.. ROCK IRON

COURSE DESIGNER BECK AND CAVANAUGH

 # OF ROUNDS ANNUALLY 60,000

DIRECTIONS TAKE THE VALENCIA EXIT OFF I-10 EAST TO KOLB RD., GO NORTH 2 MILES TO IRVINGTON, EAST 2 MILES.

HOLE	1	2	3	4	5	6	7	8	9	10	11	12	13	14	15	16	17	18
CHAMP	378	229	528	347	566	164	396	392	455	404	573	213	327	416	152	367	393	507
MENS	356	167	504	326	539	135	378	364	423	379	547	183	303	400	119	353	376	476
LADIES	295	109	412	278	446	87	305	287	333	308	474	118	251	230	90	260	311	432
PAR	4	3	5	4	5	3	4	4	4	4	5	3	4	4	3	4	4	5
M.HCP	13	5	7	15	3	17	11	9	1	12	8	6	16	4	18	10	2	14
L.HCP	13	15	11	9	1	17	5	7	3	6	4	10	12	14	18	16	2	8

G.C. Of Rancho Manana

SEMI PRIVATE 18 HOLES

5734 E. Rancho Manana Blvd. Cave Creek, AZ 85331   602-252-3245

DESERT ●   **TRADITIONAL ○**   **LINKS ○**

| TERRAIN | TREES | WATER |

| | | |

GREENS *Bent*	COURSE FAVORS A... *Mix*
FAIRWAYS *Bermuda*	WIDTH OF FAIRWAYS *Tight*
BUNKERS *Regular*	AMT. OF BUNKERS *Many*

PAR	YARDS	RATING	SLOPE	1992 GREEN FEES $
72	6378	69.7	N/A	**HIGH** *$65*
72	5910	69.1	N/A	**LOW** *$35*
73	5011	68.8	N/A	**SPECIALS** *None*

THE COURSE COMMENTARY

This course is nestled between the base of Black Mountain and Skull Mesa in the heart of the Sonoran Desert. The hillsides plunge into lush fairways with water or sand at every turn.

TOUGHEST HOLE	THE 317 YARD PAR-4 4TH HOLE IS SHAPED LIKE AN "L" AGAINST THE HILL AND IS DANGEROUS TO REACH IN ONE STROKE.
BIRDIE HOLE	THE 158 YARD PAR-3 17TH HOLE PLAYS SHORT TO A WELL GUARDED GREEN.
WATER IN PLAY ON...	3 HOLES
OVERALL STRATEGY	KEEP IT IN THE FAIRWAY OFF THE TEE.
CART REQUIRED?	YES
PRACTICE FACILITIES?	DRIVING RANGE PUTTING GREEN CHIPPING GREEN
COURSE IS OPEN...	YES
OVERSEEDING	OCTOBER FOR 2 WEEKS. INCLUDES EVERYTHING.
RESTAURANT?	YES
ACCOMMODATIONS?	NO
DON'T FORGET YOUR..	ROCK IRON!!!
COURSE DESIGNER	BILL JOHNSTON
# OF ROUNDS ANNUALLY	N/A
DIRECTIONS	GO NORTH ON SCOTTSDALE RD. TO CAVE CREEK RD., GO WEST 4 MILES UNTIL YOU SEE THE SIGN.

COURSE LAYOUT

HOLE	1	2	3	4	5	6	7	8	9	10	11	12	13	14	15	16	17	18
CHAMP	404	381	364	317	165	466	331	199	488	376	397	408	381	157	366	479	158	541
MENS	365	340	334	311	137	444	326	182	481	350	375	370	340	135	330	444	136	510
LADIES	302	274	264	269	112	292	308	149	411	313	312	366	284	114	243	404	114	412
PAR	4	4	4	4	3	5	4	3	5	4	4	4	4	3	4	5	3	5
M.HCP	7	5	9	1	15	11	17	13	3	14	8	6	10	16	12	2	18	4
L.HCP	7	5	9	1	15	11	17	13	3	14	8	6	10	16	12	2	18	49

GAINEY RANCH G.C. - ARROYO/LAKES

HOTEL GUESTS ONLY   18 HOLES

7600 E. Gainey Club Dr. Scottsdale, AZ 85258   602-951-0896

DESERT ◯   **TRADITIONAL** ●   **LINKS** ◯

TERRAIN	TREES	WATER

GREENS	Bermuda	
FAIRWAYS	Bermuda	
BUNKERS	Silicon	

COURSE FAVORS A...	Mix
WIDTH OF FAIRWAYS	Normal
AMT. OF BUNKERS	Many

PAR	YARDS	RATING	SLOPE	1992 GREEN FEES $	
72	6800	72.9	125	HIGH	$99
72	6252	70.0	120	LOW	$60
72	5312	70.4	116	SPECIALS	None

THE COURSE COMMENTARY Gainey Ranch is a 27 hole layout with three 9-hole courses. The Arroyo course is the longest of the three courses. A lake provides great views of the Hyatt and lots of boats. A dry river bed runs thru the course.

TOUGHEST HOLE THE 555 YARD PAR-5 9TH HOLE ON THE ARROYO 9 IS LONG AND NARROW.

BIRDIE HOLE THE 196 YARD PAR-3 8TH HOLE ON THE LAKES 9 PLAYS TO A LARGE GREEN AND MINIMAL TROUBLE.

WATER IN PLAY ON... 3 HOLES

OVERALL STRATEGY HIT IT STRAIGHT OFF THE TEE.

CART REQUIRED? YES

PRACTICE FACILITIES? DRIVING RANGE   PUTTING GREEN   CHIPPING GREEN

COURSE IS OPEN... YES

OVERSEEDING OCTOBER FOR 2 WEEKS. TEES AND FAIRWAYS.

RESTAURANT? ON PROPERTY.

ACCOMMODATIONS? HYATT RESORT ON PROPERTY.

DON'T FORGET YOUR.. BALL RETRIEVER

COURSE DESIGNER BENZ AND POELETTE

 # OF ROUNDS ANNUALLY N/A

DIRECTIONS HALF MILE EAST OF SCOTTSDALE RD. ON DOUBLETREE RANCH RD.

COURSE LAYOUT

HOLE	1	2	3	4	5	6	7	8	9	10	11	12	13	14	15	16	17	18
CHAMP	386	207	374	404	533	173	384	408	555	394	365	395	190	521	411	410	198	492
MENS	356	182	345	374	495	165	349	390	527	363	333	352	170	493	386	379	156	437
LADIES	310	142	311	306	449	125	294	345	453	280	264	304	114	447	346	326	109	387
PAR	4	3	4	4	5	3	4	4	5	4	4	4	3	5	4	4	3	5
M.HCP	9	17	13	7	3	15	11	5	1	12	14	8	16	4	10	2	18	6
L.HCP	7	17	9	11	3	15	13	5	1	12	14	6	16	2	10	8	18	4

GAINEY RANCH G.C. - DUNES/ARROYO

7600 E. Gainey Club Dr. Scottsdale, AZ 85258   602-951-0896

DESERT ○   **TRADITIONAL** ○   **LINKS** ●

TERRAIN	TREES	WATER

GREENS *Bermuda*   **COURSE FAVORS A...** *Mix*

FAIRWAYS *Bermuda*   **WIDTH OF FAIRWAYS** *Normal*

BUNKERS *Silicon*   **AMT. OF BUNKERS** *Many*

PAR	YARDS	RATING	SLOPE	1992 GREEN FEES $	
72	6662	71.4	119	HIGH	$99
72	6133	68.9	116	LOW	$60
72	5151	68.5	113	SPECIALS	None

THE COURSE COMMENTARY

Gainey Ranch is a 27 hole layout with three 9-hole courses. The signature hole on the Lakes course is the beautiful 9th hole which plays to a green with a waterfall in back and sprinkling springs along the fairway.

TOUGHEST HOLE THE 555 YARD PAR-5 9TH HOLE ON THE ARROYO 9 PLAYS VERY LONG AND NARROW.

BIRDIE HOLE THE 305 YARD PAR-4 2ND HOLE ON THE DUNES 9 IS REACHABLE IN ONE FOR THE LONG HITTER.

WATER IN PLAY ON... 3 HOLES

OVERALL STRATEGY THIS COMBINATION PLAYS THE LONGEST 9 AND THE SHORTEST 9 TOGETHER. YOU WILL USE ALL YOUR CLUBS.

CART REQUIRED? YES

PRACTICE FACILITIES? DRIVING RANGE   PUTTING GREEN   CHIPPING GREEN

COURSE IS OPEN... YES

OVERSEEDING OCTOBER FOR 2 WEEKS. TEES AND FAIRWAYS.

RESTAURANT? ON PROPERTY.

ACCOMMODATIONS? HYATT RESORT ON PROPERTY.

DON'T FORGET YOUR.. BALL RETRIEVER

COURSE DESIGNER BENZ AND POELETTE

 # OF ROUNDS ANNUALLY N/A

DIRECTIONS HALF MILE EAST OF SCOTTSDALE RD. ON DOUBLETREE RANCH RD.

Course Layout

HOLE	1	2	3	4	5	6	7	8	9	10	11	12	13	14	15	16	17	18
CHAMP	388	305	345	187	381	506	390	186	550	386	207	374	404	533	173	384	408	555
MENS	357	284	315	150	336	481	365	156	506	356	182	345	374	495	165	349	390	527
LADIES	312	229	265	92	279	406	260	119	454	310	142	311	306	449	125	294	345	453
PAR	4	4	4	3	4	5	4	3	5	4	3	4	4	5	3	4	4	5
M.HCP	6	14	12	16	8	4	10	18	2	9	17	13	7	3	15	11	5	1
L.HCP	6	14	8	18	10	4	12	16	2	7	17	9	11	3	15	13	5	1

GAINEY RANCH G.C. - LAKES/DUNES

7600 E. Gainey Club Dr. Scottsdale, AZ 85258   602-951-0896

DESERT ○   TRADITIONAL ●   LINKS ○

TERRAIN	TREES	WATER

GREENS *Bermuda*   **COURSE FAVORS A...** *Mix*

FAIRWAYS *Bermuda*   **WIDTH OF FAIRWAYS** *Normal*

BUNKERS *Silicon*   **AMT. OF BUNKERS** *Many*

PAR	YARDS	RATING	SLOPE	1992 GREEN FEES $	
72	6614	N/A	N/A	HIGH	$99
72	6019	N/A	N/A	LOW	$60
72	4933	N/A	N/A	SPECIALS	None

THE COURSE COMMENTARY Gainey Ranch is a 27 hole layout with three great 9-hole courses. The signature hole on the Lakes course is the beautiful 9th hole which plays to a green with a waterfall in back and sprinkling springs along the fairway.

TOUGHEST HOLE	THE 550 YARD PAR-5 18TH HOLE ON THE DUNES 9 IS VERY LONG WITH TROUBLE ON BOTH SIDES.
BIRDIE HOLE	THE 492 YARD PAR-5 9TH HOLE ON THE LAKES 9. REACHABLE IN TWO BUT WATCH OUT FOR THE WATER.
WATER IN PLAY ON...	6 HOLES
OVERALL STRATEGY	HIT THE BALL STRAIGHT AND TAKE IN THE BEAUTY.
CART REQUIRED?	YES
PRACTICE FACILITIES?	DRIVING RANGE PUTTING GREEN CHIPPING GREEN
COURSE IS OPEN...	YES
OVERSEEDING	OCTOBER FOR 2 WEEKS. TEES AND FAIRWAYS.
RESTAURANT?	ON PROPERTY.
ACCOMMODATIONS?	HYATT RESORT ON PROPERTY.
DON'T FORGET YOUR..	BALL RETRIEVER
COURSE DESIGNER	BENZ AND POELETTE
# OF ROUNDS ANNUALLY	N/A
DIRECTIONS	HALF MILE EAST OF SCOTTSDALE RD. ON DOUBLETREE RANCH RD.

COURSE LAYOUT

HOLE	1	2	3	4	5	6	7	8	9	10	11	12	13	14	15	16	17	18
CHAMP	394	365	395	190	521	411	410	198	492	388	305	345	187	381	506	390	186	550
MENS	363	333	352	170	493	386	379	156	437	357	284	315	150	336	481	365	156	506
LADIES	280	264	304	114	447	346	326	109	387	312	229	265	92	279	406	260	119	454
PAR	4	4	4	3	5	4	4	3	5	4	4	4	3	4	5	4	3	5
M.HCP	11	13	7	15	3	9	1	17	5	6	14	12	16	8	4	10	18	2
L.HCP	11	13	5	15	1	9	7	17	3	6	14	8	18	12	4	12	16	2

GENERAL WILLIAM BLANCHARD G.C.

SEMI PRIVATE 18 HOLES

Box 15034 Tucson, AZ 85707   602-750-3734

DESERT ○   **TRADITIONAL** ●   **LINKS** ○

| TERRAIN | TREES | WATER |

GREENS Bermuda	**COURSE FAVORS A...** Mix
FAIRWAYS Bermuda	**WIDTH OF FAIRWAYS** Normal
BUNKERS Silicon	**AMT. OF BUNKERS** Many

PAR	YARDS	RATING	SLOPE	1992 GREEN FEES $
72	6611	70.5	113	**HIGH** $15
72	6155	68.4	108	**LOW** $12
73	5792	71.5	113	**SPECIALS** $9 unlimited in June-Sept.

THE COURSE COMMENTARY

Fees are based on rank. The signature hole is the 316 yard par-4 16th hole that has a fairway bunker in the shape of an F-10 jet.

TOUGHEST HOLE	THE 413 YARD PAR-4 7TH HOLE PLAYS EVEN LONGER DUE TO THE PREVAILING WIND IN YOUR FACE.
BIRDIE HOLE	THE 282 YARD PAR-4 10TH HOLE IS SHORT, SIMPLE, AND STRAIGHT AWAY.
WATER IN PLAY ON...	0 HOLES
OVERALL STRATEGY	STAY OUT OF THE ROUGH IN THE SUMMER... IT'S TOUGH TO GET OUT OF.
CART REQUIRED?	NO
PRACTICE FACILITIES?	DRIVING RANGE PUTTING GREEN
COURSE IS OPEN...	YES
OVERSEEDING	OCT/MAR FOR 3 WEEKS. TEES AND GREENS.
RESTAURANT?	RESTAURANT AND FULL-SERVICE SNACK BAR.
ACCOMMODATIONS?	N/A
DON'T FORGET YOUR..	CAMERA FOR THE BUNKER THAT LOOKS LIKE AN F-10 JET.
COURSE DESIGNER	N/A
# OF ROUNDS ANNUALLY	7,000
DIRECTIONS	AT CRAYCROFT & GOLF LINKS RD. AT DAVIS-MONTHAN AIR FORCE BASE.

HOLE	1	2	3	4	5	6	7	8	9	10	11	12	13	14	15	16	17	18
CHAMP	397	159	524	380	385	504	438	363	165	358	405	150	528	390	208	342	515	400
MENS	386	145	489	362	327	488	426	292	132	313	386	135	508	376	191	325	497	377
LADIES	375	144	458	344	255	474	413	265	116	282	371	120	487	361	173	316	478	360
PAR	4	3	5	4	4	5	4	4	3	4	4	3	5	4	3	4	5	43
M.HCP	3	15	7	13	5	9	1	17	11	18	2	16	6	8	4	14	12	10
L.HCP	2	12	4	10	6	8	14	16	18	15	1	17	3	9	13	5	11	7

GLEN LAKES G.C.

PUBLIC   9 HOLES

5450 W. Northern Ave.   Glendale, AZ 85301   602-939-7541

DESERT ○   **TRADITIONAL** ●   **LINKS** ○

TERRAIN	TREES	WATER

GREENS *Bermuda*   **COURSE FAVORS A...** *Mix*

FAIRWAYS *Bermuda*   **WIDTH OF FAIRWAYS** *Forgiving*

BUNKERS *Regular*   **AMT. OF BUNKERS** *Many*

PAR	YARDS	RATING	SLOPE	1992 GREEN FEES $	
N/A	N/A	N/A	N/A	HIGH	$7
33	2396	60.4	N/A	LOW	$7
33	2215	61.7	N/A	SPECIALS	$5 after 3pm

THE COURSE COMMENTARY   Mature trees and fairways make this a challenging 9 hole executive course. Practice facilities include a lighted driving range. One of the busiest courses in town.

TOUGHEST HOLE THE 200 YARD PAR-3 4TH HOLE PLAYS TO A SMALL GREEN WITH WATER LEFT AND RIGHT.

BIRDIE HOLE THE 126 YARD PAR-3 3RD HOLE PLAYS TO A LARGE GREEN WITH NOTHING BETWEEN YOU AND THE GREEN.

WATER IN PLAY ON... 6 HOLES

OVERALL STRATEGY HIT YOUR MIDDLE IRONS WELL.

CART REQUIRED? NO

PRACTICE FACILITIES? DRIVING RANGE   PUTTING GREEN   CHIPPING GREEN

COURSE IS OPEN... YES

OVERSEEDING NO

RESTAURANT? SNACK BAR

ACCOMMODATIONS? NO

DON'T FORGET YOUR.. 3 WOOD

COURSE DESIGNER N/A

 # OF ROUNDS ANNUALLY N/A

DIRECTIONS ON THE CORNER OF 55TH AVE. AND NORTHERN AVE.

COURSE LAYOUT

HOLE	1	2	3	4	5	6	7	8	9	10	11	12	13	14	15	16	17	18
CHAMP																		
MENS	393	350	126	200	180	285	294	294	274									
LADIES	373	330	106	180	143	265	270	274	254									
PAR	4	4	3	3	3	4	4	4	4									
M.HCP	3	5	17	1	7	15	9	11	13									
L.HCP	3	5	17	1	7	15	9	11	13									

GOLD CANYON G.C.

PUBLIC   18 HOLES

6100 S. Kings Ranch Rd   Apache Junction, AZ 85219   602-982-9449

DESERT ●   **TRADITIONAL** ○   **LINKS** ○

TERRAIN	TREES	WATER

GREENS	Bermuda	**COURSE FAVORS A...**	Draw
FAIRWAYS	Bermuda	**WIDTH OF FAIRWAYS**	Tight
BUNKERS	Regular	**AMT. OF BUNKERS**	Average

PAR	YARDS	RATING	SLOPE	1992 GREEN FEES $
71	6398	N/A	N/A	**HIGH** $65
71	6004	70.7	124	**LOW** $32
72	4876	67.5	112	**SPECIALS** Twilight rates are $34 to $18

THE COURSE COMMENTARY   Gold Canyon has hosted regional qualifying for The Oldsmobile Scramble and The 1992 March of Dimes Lou Boudreau Classic. The Superstition Mountains provide an excellent backdrop for the course, especially on the back nine.

TOUGHEST HOLE	THE 400 YARD PAR-4 7TH HAS WATER DOWN THE RIGHT SIDE. USE A LONG IRON TO REACH THE WELL PROTECTED GREEN.
BIRDIE HOLE	THE 385 YARD 15TH IS A SHORT PAR-4 AND IS REACHABLE IF YOU CUT THE CORNER.
WATER IN PLAY ON...	1 HOLE
OVERALL STRATEGY	LENGTH IS NOT IMPORTANT. KEEP IT IN THE FAIRWAY.
CART REQUIRED?	YES
PRACTICE FACILITIES?	DRIVING RANGE PUTTING GREEN CHIPPING GREEN
COURSE IS OPEN...	YES
OVERSEEDING	SEPTEMBER FOR 2 1/2 WEEKS. EVERYTHING.
RESTAURANT?	RESTAURANT AND LOUNGE.
ACCOMMODATIONS?	CASITAS ON PROPERTY.
DON'T FORGET YOUR..	ROCK IRON
COURSE DESIGNER	NASH AND KAVANAUGH
# OF ROUNDS ANNUALLY	30-35,000
DIRECTIONS	GO 7 MILES EAST OF APACHE JUNCTION ON US 60/89 TO KINGS RANCH RD., THEN GO EAST FOR 1 MILE.

COURSE LAYOUT

HOLE	1	2	3	4	5	6	7	8	9	10	11	12	13	14	15	16	17	18
CHAMP	398	170	522	375	325	215	428	400	494	295	194	495	479	169	385	511	148	395
MENS	375	148	485	355	310	193	418	385	471	285	180	481	445	130	375	481	129	358
LADIES	301	132	438	320	295	141	332	332	325	195	152	410	325	89	265	415	98	311
PAR	4	3	5	4	4	3	4	4	5	4	3	5	4	3	4	5	3	4
M.HCP	11	17	3	5	15	13	1	9	7	12	14	4	2	16	8	6	18	10
L.HCP	11	17	3	5	15	13	1	9	7	12	14	4	2	16	8	6	18	10

Happy Trails G.R.

PUBLIC   18 HOLES

17200 W. Bell Rd. Suprise, AZ 85374   *602-975-5500*

DESERT ○   TRADITIONAL ○   LINKS ●

TERRAIN	TREES	WATER

GREENS *Bent*	**COURSE FAVORS A...** *Mix*	
FAIRWAYS *Bermuda*	**WIDTH OF FAIRWAYS** *Forgiving*	
BUNKERS *Silicon*	**AMT. OF BUNKERS** *Many*	

PAR	YARDS	RATING	SLOPE	1992 GREEN FEES $	
72	6646	72.1	124	HIGH	*$39*
72	5939	69.7	119	LOW	*$20*
72	5146	69.7	117	SPECIALS	*Call*

THE COURSE COMMENTARY *A hidden gem on the west side of town. This course boast's some of the best green's in the entire valley. Moguls make for some interesting lies. Don't hit your driver until the 5th hole.*

TOUGHEST HOLE	THE 545 YARD PAR-5 1ST HOLE IS LONG AND NARROW WITH WATER ON THE LEFT. HIT AN IRON OF THE TEE!
BIRDIE HOLE	THE 170 YARD PAR-3 11TH HOLE IS SURROUNDED BY WATER THAT REALLY DOESN'T COME INTO PLAY.
WATER IN PLAY ON...	4 HOLES
OVERALL STRATEGY	GET READY TO HIT YOUR 1 OR 2 IRON OFF THE TEE ON POSSIBLY 6 TO 8 HOLES.
CART REQUIRED?	YES
PRACTICE FACILITIES?	DRIVING RANGE PUTTING GREEN CHIPPING GREEN
COURSE IS OPEN...	YES
OVERSEEDING	OCTOBER FOR 2 WEEKS. ONLY FAIRWAYS.
RESTAURANT?	YES
ACCOMMODATIONS?	LODGING NEARBY
DON'T FORGET YOUR..	1 IRON
COURSE DESIGNER	MCCORMICK & NASH
# OF ROUNDS ANNUALLY	50,000
DIRECTIONS	WEST ON BELL RD. TO COTTON LN. (5 MILES WEST OF GRAND AVE.)

COURSE LAYOUT

HOLE	1	2	3	4	5	6	7	8	9	10	11	12	13	14	15	16	17	18
CHAMP	545	320	324	142	481	388	323	217	420	398	170	582	385	225	441	320	512	453
MENS	520	307	294	118	440	348	293	172	379	362	142	534	343	172	390	262	474	389
LADIES	474	272	259	100	399	303	247	118	338	312	121	479	285	120	344	224	410	341
PAR	5	4	4	3	5	4	4	3	4	4	3	5	4	3	4	4	5	4
M.HCP	1	9	15	17	5	7	13	11	3	10	18	2	14	12	8	16	6	4
L.HCP	1	9	11	17	5	7	13	15	3	10	16	2	14	18	8	12	4	6

HILLCREST G.C.

PUBLIC   18 HOLES

20002 Star Ridge Dr. Sun City West, AZ 85375   *602-975-1000*

DESERT ○   TRADITIONAL ●   LINKS ○

TERRAIN	TREES	WATER

GREENS	Bermuda		COURSE FAVORS A...	Fade
FAIRWAYS	Bermuda		WIDTH OF FAIRWAYS	Forgiving
BUNKERS	Regular		AMT. OF BUNKERS	Many

PAR	YARDS	RATING	SLOPE	1992 GREEN FEES	
72	6900	73.5	126	HIGH	$49
72	6600	70.6	122	LOW	$16
74	5800	72.5	119	SPECIALS	Twilight - $17 w/ cart

THE COURSE COMMENTARY

This is one of the nicest courses in the valley... and the one of the toughest! The signature hole is the 546 yard par-5 13th hole nicknamed "Jaws". A long dogleg left with water down the right side and in front of the green.

TOUGHEST HOLE	THE 422 YARD PAR-4 16TH HOLE IS STRAIGHT AWAY WITH WATER DOWN THE RIGHT AND BUNKERS DOWN THE LEFT.
BIRDIE HOLE	THE 496 YARD PAR-5 10TH HOLE. HIT YOUR DRIVE LONG AND ON THE LEFT SIDE OF THE FAIRWAY TO BIRDIE.
WATER IN PLAY ON...	12 HOLES
OVERALL STRATEGY	STAY AWAY FROM THE WATER!!!
CART REQUIRED?	YES
PRACTICE FACILITIES?	DRIVING RANGE PUTTING GREEN CHIPPING GREEN
COURSE IS OPEN...	YES
OVERSEEDING	OCTOBER FOR 2 WEEKS. TEES, GREENS, AND FAIRWAYS.
RESTAURANT?	YES.
ACCOMMODATIONS?	WINDMILL INN NEARBY.
DON'T FORGET YOUR..	BRING EVERYTHING YOU CAN CARRY.
COURSE DESIGNER	GREG NASH
# OF ROUNDS ANNUALLY	55,000
DIRECTIONS	TAKE BELL RD. TO R.H. JOHNSON BLVD., THEN GO EAST ON CAMINO DEL SOL FOR 1 BLOCK TO STAR RIDGE.

COURSE LAYOUT

HOLE	1	2	3	4	5	6	7	8	9	10	11	12	13	14	15	16	17	18
CHAMP	376	352	215	573	430	373	555	161	454	496	364	339	546	207	399	422	237	461
MENS	341	332	181	533	390	353	528	141	403	476	344	319	526	168	359	402	197	428
LADIES	292	287	146	486	365	333	488	110	404	436	330	299	477	137	328	382	180	400
PAR	4	4	3	5	4	4	5	3	4	5	4	4	5	3	4	4	3	4
M.HCP	17	15	11	3	7	9	1	13	5	8	12	18	2	14	10	6	16	4
L.HCP	11	13	15	1	7	9	3	17	5	4	12	14	2	18	10	8	16	6

IRONWOOD G.C.

PUBLIC   9 HOLES

2945 W. 8th St. Yuma, AZ 85364   602-343-1466

DESERT ○   **TRADITIONAL** ●   **LINKS** ○

TERRAIN	TREES	WATER

GREENS	Bermuda	COURSE FAVORS A... Mix
FAIRWAYS	Bermuda	WIDTH OF FAIRWAYS Normal
BUNKERS	Other	AMT. OF BUNKERS Average

PAR	YARDS	RATING	SLOPE	1992 GREEN FEES $
N/A	N/A	N/A	N/A	HIGH $10
29	1460	N/A	N/A	LOW $5
N/	N/A	N/A	N/A	SPECIALS None

THE COURSE COMMENTARY The sloping greens are where you'll find the challenge here. This is the home of the Annual Easter Seals Night Golf Championship.

TOUGHEST HOLE THE 260 YARD PAR-4 5TH HOLE. IT IS SHORT BUT ONCE YOUR ON THE GREEN IT'S NOT EASY TO SINK YOUR PUTT.

BIRDIE HOLE THE 250 YARD PAR-4 3RD HOLE IS AN EAGLE POSSIBILITY. THERE IS A WIDE OPEN FAIRWAY TO THE GREEN.

WATER IN PLAY ON... 2 HOLES

OVERALL STRATEGY TAKE TIME TO READ THE GREENS.

CART REQUIRED? NO

PRACTICE FACILITIES? PUTTING GREEN

COURSE IS OPEN... YES

OVERSEEDING OCTOBER FOR 2 WEEKS. TEES, GREENS, AND FAIRWAYS.

RESTAURANT? N/A

ACCOMMODATIONS? N/A

DON'T FORGET YOUR.. YOUR FAVORITE PUTTER

COURSE DESIGNER N/A

 # OF ROUNDS ANNUALLY 20,000

DIRECTIONS 1/2 MILE WEST OF AVE. B ON 8TH STREET.

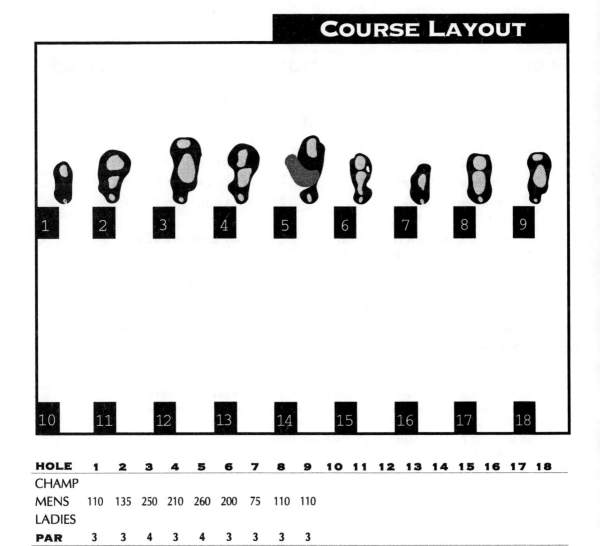

Course Layout

HOLE	1	2	3	4	5	6	7	8	9	10	11	12	13	14	15	16	17	18
CHAMP																		
MENS	110	135	250	210	260	200	75	110	110									
LADIES																		
PAR	3	3	4	3	4	3	3	3	3									
M.HCP	6	5	2	3	1	4	9	7	8									
L.HCP																		

KARSTEN G.C. AT ASU

PUBLIC   18 HOLES

1125 E. Rio Salado Pkwy. Tempe, AZ 85281   *602-921-8070*

DESERT ○   **TRADITIONAL** ○   **LINKS** ●

TERRAIN	TREES	WATER

GREENS	*Bent*	**COURSE FAVORS A...**	*Draw*
FAIRWAYS	*Bermuda*	**WIDTH OF FAIRWAYS**	*Tight*
BUNKERS	*Regular*	**AMT. OF BUNKERS**	*Many*

PAR	YARDS	RATING	SLOPE	1992 GREEN FEES
72	7057	74.3	133	**HIGH** *$70+*
71	6272	70.3	125	**LOW**
71	4760	63.4	110	**SPECIALS** *Student and alumni*

THE COURSE COMMENTARY   *This is a classic Pete Dye "Scottish Links" layout in stadium tradition. Hosted NCAA Championship, Pac-10 Championship, U.S. Open Qualifying and more. You'll be in danger quickly if you step up the tee and blast your tee shots.*

TOUGHEST HOLE	THE 446 YARD PAR-4 9TH HOLE. WATER DOWN THE RIGHT AND TROUBLE ALL AROUND THE GREEN.
BIRDIE HOLE	THE 402 YARD PAR-4 1ST HOLE IS THE MOST FORGIVING HOLE ON THE COURSE. DON'T GET USED TO IT.
WATER IN PLAY ON...	5 HOLES
OVERALL STRATEGY	HIT YOUR TEE SHOTS TO SET UP YOUR FAVORITE APPROACH CLUB.
CART REQUIRED?	YES
PRACTICE FACILITIES?	DRIVING RANGE PUTTING GREEN CHIPPING GREEN
COURSE IS OPEN...	YES
OVERSEEDING	OCTOBER FOR 2 WEEKS. TEES AND FAIRWAYS.
RESTAURANT?	YES
ACCOMMODATIONS?	NO
DON'T FORGET YOUR..	L-WEDGE
COURSE DESIGNER	PETE DYE
# OF ROUNDS ANNUALLY	55,000
DIRECTIONS	1/2 MILE NORTH OF UNIVERSITY DR. ON SCOTTSDALE RD. AT RIO SALADO PKWY.

COURSE LAYOUT

HOLE	1	2	3	4	5	6	7	8	9	10	11	12	13	14	15	16	17	18
CHAMP	402	323	423	420	500	209	155	380	446	546	410	209	350	527	457	248	581	471
MENS	341	296	373	389	462	176	134	323	399	504	363	161	308	488	419	175	537	424
LADIES	255	208	266	288	363	131	89	268	284	409	300	106	199	402	308	132	417	340
PAR	4	4	4	4	5	3	3	4	4	5	4	3	4	5	4	3	5	4
M.HCP	13	17	9	1	11	5	15	7	3	6	16	12	18	10	2	8	14	4
L.HCP	11	13	9	3	1	15	17	7	5	2	8	18	16	12	4	14	10	6

KEN McDONALD G.C.

PUBLIC   18 HOLES

800 Divot Dr. Tempe, AZ 85283

602-350-5250

DESERT ○   **TRADITIONAL** ●   **LINKS** ○

TERRAIN	TREES	WATER

GREENS Bermuda	**COURSE FAVORS A...** Mix
FAIRWAYS Bermuda	**WIDTH OF FAIRWAYS** Forgiving
BUNKERS Regular	**AMT. OF BUNKERS** Average

PAR	YARDS	RATING	SLOPE	1992 GREEN FEES	
72	6743	70.8	115	**HIGH**	$25
72	6316	68.7	111	**LOW**	$10
73	5872	70.4	112	**SPECIALS**	None

THE COURSE COMMENTARY

One of the more popular Tempe city golf courses. This course is not really easy or hard. You will hit every club in your bag.

TOUGHEST HOLE	THE 436 YARD PAR-4 2ND HOLE IS LONG WITH A NARROW LANDING AREA OFF THE TEE.
BIRDIE HOLE	THE 364 YARD PAR-4 15TH HOLE PLAYS TO A FORGIVING FAIRWAY WITH A LARGE GREEN.
WATER IN PLAY ON...	7 HOLES
OVERALL STRATEGY	RELAX. YOU'LL HAVE FUN AND GET A SOLID CHALLENGE
CART REQUIRED?	NO
PRACTICE FACILITIES?	DRIVING RANGE PUTTING GREEN CHIPPING GREEN
COURSE IS OPEN...	YES
OVERSEEDING	OCTOBER FOR 2 WEEKS. EVERYTHING.
RESTAURANT?	COFFEE SHOP AND " PETE'S 19TH HOLE RESTAURANT."
ACCOMMODATIONS?	NO
DON'T FORGET YOUR..	FAVORITE DRIVER
COURSE DESIGNER	ARTHUR JACK SNYDER
# OF ROUNDS ANNUALLY	N/A
DIRECTIONS	HALF MILE SOUTH OF GUADALUPE RD. ON RURAL RD.

COURSE LAYOUT

HOLE	1	2	3	4	5	6	7	8	9	10	11	12	13	14	15	16	17	18
CHAMP	341	436	515	170	402	216	359	529	443	364	570	397	513	184	364	356	195	389
MENS	324	414	489	145	387	183	341	507	424	346	514	374	490	161	351	332	171	363
LADIES	308	395	461	127	321	157	320	476	415	325	447	355	473	142	337	312	153	348
PAR	4	4	5	3	4	3	4	5	4	4	5	4	5	3	4	4	3	4
M.HCP	17	1	7	15	11	5	13	9	3	14	2	12	4	16	18	10	8	6
L.HCP	13	1	3	17	11	15	9	5	7	12	4	6	2	18	10	14	16	8

LA PALOMA C.C. - CANYON/HILL

3660 E. Sunrise Dr. Tucson, AZ 85718   1-880-222-1249/602-299-1500

DESERT ●   TRADITIONAL ○   LINKS ○

TERRAIN	TREES	WATER

GREENS	Bent	COURSE FAVORS A...	Fade
FAIRWAYS	Bermuda	WIDTH OF FAIRWAYS	Tight
BUNKERS	Regular	AMT. OF BUNKERS	Many

	PAR	YARDS	RATING	SLOPE	1992 GREEN FEES $	
	72	6997	N/A	N/A	HIGH	$95
	72	6997	73.9	139	LOW	$60
	72	5057	69.0	118	SPECIALS	None

THE COURSE COMMENTARY

A classic Jack Nicklaus designed course that blends in beautifully with the surrounding desert. Home of The Rolex Junior Golf Tournament. This 27 hole layout combines 3 difficult 9 hole combinations. One of Golf Digest 75 Best Resort Courses.

TOUGHEST HOLE	THE 542 YARD PAR-5 5TH HOLE ON THE CANYON COURSE. YOUR APPROACH PLAYS OVER A WASH TO A SMALL GREEN.
BIRDIE HOLE	THE 157 YARD PAR-3 8TH HOLE ON THE HILL COURSE IS THE EASIEST OF THE PAR THREES.
WATER IN PLAY ON...	0 HOLES
OVERALL STRATEGY	BRING EVERYTHING
CART REQUIRED?	YES
PRACTICE FACILITIES?	DRIVING RANGE PUTTING GREEN CHIPPING GREEN
COURSE IS OPEN...	YES
OVERSEEDING	OCTOBER FOR 6 WEEKS. TEES AND FAIRWAYS.
RESTAURANT?	YES
ACCOMMODATIONS?	WESTIN LA PALOMA RESORT HOTEL ON PROPERTY.
DON'T FORGET YOUR..	EVERYTHING
COURSE DESIGNER	JACK NICKLAUS
# OF ROUNDS ANNUALLY	60,000
DIRECTIONS	BETWEEN CAMPBELL & SWAN ON E. SUNRISE.

COURSE LAYOUT

HOLE	1	2	3	4	5	6	7	8	9	10	11	12	13	14	15	16	17	18
CHAMP	454	514	178	417	542	355	445	211	418	340	381	561	185	467	419	538	157	415
MENS	417	497	166	383	517	337	426	190	379	320	321	484	171	421	385	516	132	391
LADIES	356	363	113	289	445	228	368	134	331	225	271	383	94	348	302	421	84	302
PAR	4	5	3	4	5	4	4	3	4	4	4	5	3	4	4	5	3	4
M.HCP	7	5	4	9	1	6	2	8	3	7	4	3	8	6	5	1	9	2
L.HCP	1	3	8	5	2	9	4	7	6	7	5	6	9	3	4	2	8	1

LA PALOMA C.C. - HILL/RIDGE

3660 E. Sunrise Dr. Tucson, AZ 85718   1-880-222-1249/602-299-1500

DESERT ●   **TRADITIONAL** ○   **LINKS** ○

TERRAIN	TREES	WATER

GREENS	Bent	**COURSE FAVORS A...**	Fade
FAIRWAYS	Bermuda	**WIDTH OF FAIRWAYS**	Tight
BUNKERS	Regular	**AMT. OF BUNKERS**	Many

	PAR	YARDS	RATING	SLOPE	1992 GREEN FEES $	
	72	7017	N/A	N/A	**HIGH**	$95
	72	7017	73.7	135	**LOW**	$60
	72	4878	67.8	115	**SPECIALS**	None

THE COURSE COMMENTARY

A classic Jack Nicklaus designed course that blends in beautifully with the surrounding desert. Home of The Rolex Junior Golf Tournament. This 27 hole layout combines 3 difficult 9 hole combinations. One of Golf Digest 75 Best Resort Courses.

TOUGHEST HOLE	THE 436 YARD PAR-4 8TH HOLE ON THE RIDGE COURSE IS A SHARP DOGLEG LEFT GUARDED BY A BUNKER AND DESERT.
BIRDIE HOLE	THE 157 YARD PAR-3 8TH HOLE ON THE HILL COURSE IS THE EASIEST OF THE PAR THREES.
WATER IN PLAY ON...	0 HOLES
OVERALL STRATEGY	HIT YOUR LONG IRONS LONG AND HIGH.
CART REQUIRED?	YES
PRACTICE FACILITIES?	DRIVING RANGE PUTTING GREEN
COURSE IS OPEN...	YES
OVERSEEDING	OCTOBER FOR 6 WEEKS. TEES AND FAIRWAYS.
RESTAURANT?	YES
ACCOMMODATIONS?	WESTIN LA PALOMA RESORT HOTEL ON PROPERTY.
DON'T FORGET YOUR..	ANYTHING
COURSE DESIGNER	JACK NICKLAUS
# OF ROUNDS ANNUALLY	60,000
DIRECTIONS	BETWEEN CAMPBELL & SWAN ON E. SUNRISE.

COURSE LAYOUT

HOLE	1	2	3	4	5	6	7	8	9	10	11	12	13	14	15	16	17	18
CHAMP	340	381	561	185	467	419	538	157	415	381	411	517	199	420	459	171	436	560
MENS	320	321	484	171	421	385	516	132	391	364	374	482	176	381	449	153	395	549
LADIES	225	271	383	94	348	302	421	84	302	264	309	372	112	306	262	105	285	433
PAR	4	4	5	3	4	4	5	3	4	4	4	5	3	4	4	3	4	5
M.HCP	7	4	3	8	6	5	1	9	2	5	7	2	8	4	6	9	1	3
L.HCP	7	5	6	9	3	4	2	8	1	7	3	4	8	2	6	9	5	1

LA PALOMA C.C. - RIDGE/CANYON

3660 E. Sunrise Dr. Tucson, AZ 85718   1-880-222-1249/602-299-1500

DESERT ●   TRADITIONAL ○   LINKS ○

TERRAIN	TREES	WATER

GREENS *Bent*	**COURSE FAVORS A...** *Fade*	
FAIRWAYS *Bermuda*	**WIDTH OF FAIRWAYS** *Tight*	
BUNKERS *Regular*	**AMT. OF BUNKERS** *Many*	

	PAR	YARDS	RATING	SLOPE	1992 GREEN FEES $	
	N/A	7088	N/A	N/A	HIGH	$95
	72	7088	75.8	147	LOW	$60
	72	5075	68.9	116	SPECIALS	None

THE COURSE COMMENTARY

A classic Jack Nicklaus designed course that blends in beautifully with the surrounding desert. Home of The Rolex Junior Golf Tournament. This 27 hole layout combines 3 difficult 9 hole combinations. One of Golf Digest 75 Best Resort Courses.

TOUGHEST HOLE THE 436 YARD PAR-4 8TH HOLE ON THE RIDGE COURSE IS A SHARP DOGLEG LEFT GUARDED BY A BUNKER AND DESERT.

BIRDIE HOLE THE 381 YARD PAR-4 1ST HOLE ON THE RIDGE COURSE. A LONG DRIVE LEAVES YOU WITH A SHORT PITCH.

WATER IN PLAY ON... 0 HOLES

OVERALL STRATEGY HIT YOUR LONG IRONS LONG AND HIGH.

CART REQUIRED? YES

PRACTICE FACILITIES? DRIVING RANGE   PUTTING GREEN

COURSE IS OPEN... YES

OVERSEEDING OCTOBER FOR 6 WEEKS. TEES AND FAIRWAYS.

RESTAURANT? YES

ACCOMMODATIONS? WESTIN LA PALOMA RESORT HOTEL ON PROPERTY.

DON'T FORGET YOUR.. ANYTHING

COURSE DESIGNER JACK NICKLAUS

 # OF ROUNDS ANNUALLY "60,000

DIRECTIONS BETWEEN CAMPBELL & SWAN ON E. SUNRISE.

COURSE LAYOUT

HOLE	1	2	3	4	5	6	7	8	9	10	11	12	13	14	15	16	17	18
CHAMP	381	411	517	199	420	459	171	436	560	454	514	178	417	542	355	455	211	418
MENS	364	374	482	176	381	449	153	395	549	417	497	166	383	517	337	426	190	379
LADIES	264	309	372	112	306	262	105	285	433	356	363	113	289	445	228	368	134	331
PAR	4	4	5	3	4	4	3	4	5	4	5	3	4	5	4	4	3	4
M.HCP	5	7	2	8	4	6	9	1	3	7	5	4	9	1	6	2	8	3
L.HCP	7	3	4	8	2	6	9	5	1	1	3	8	5	2	9	4	7	6

LEGEND G.C.

PUBLIC   18 HOLES

21027 N. 67th Ave. Glendale, AZ 85308   602-249-1007 or 602-561-0953

DESERT ○   **TRADITIONAL** ●   **LINKS** ○

TERRAIN	TREES	WATER

GREENS *Bermuda*   **COURSE FAVORS A...** *Draw*

FAIRWAYS *Bermuda*   **WIDTH OF FAIRWAYS** *Normal*

BUNKERS *Regular*   **AMT. OF BUNKERS** *Many*

	PAR	YARDS	RATING	SLOPE	1992 GREEN FEES $
★	72	7005	73.0	129	**HIGH** $66
	72	6013	68.8	118	**LOW** $22
	72	5233	71.2	119	**SPECIALS** N/A

THE COURSE COMMENTARY

The Legend was designed by Arnold Palmer and features a traditional layout with fairway bunkers and mounds placed throughout the course to make you think about every shot and use every club.

TOUGHEST HOLE THE 529 YARD PAR-5 6TH HOLE. HIT YOUR TEE SHOT BETWEEN 2 FAIRWAY BUNKERS AND STAY LEFT OF A LAKE.

BIRDIE HOLE THE 396 YARD PAR-4 1ST HOLE IS WIDE OPEN FROM THE TEE. A FLAT GREEN MAKES FOR BIRDIE PUTTS.

WATER IN PLAY ON... 6 HOLES

OVERALL STRATEGY HIT IT LONG.

CART REQUIRED? YES

PRACTICE FACILITIES? DRIVING RANGE   PUTTING GREEN

COURSE IS OPEN... YES

OVERSEEDING OCTOBER FOR 2 WEEKS. TEES, GREENS, AND FAIRWAYS.

RESTAURANT? N/A

ACCOMMODATIONS? WYNDHAM HOTEL NEARBY

DON'T FORGET YOUR.. BALL RETRIEVER

COURSE DESIGNER ARNOLD PALMER

 # OF ROUNDS ANNUALLY 45,000

DIRECTIONS 1 MILE NORTH OF BEARDSLY ON 67TH AVE.

HOLE	1	2	3	4	5	6	7	8	9	10	11	12	13	14	15	16	17	18
CHAMP	396	511	429	161	426	529	392	206	413	552	388	414	441	185	456	169	407	530
MENS	371	476	393	143	401	507	361	197	390	517	352	399	418	162	405	153	370	494
LADIES	298	415	337	109	312	387	286	138	317	414	280	323	340	126	338	112	297	404
PAR	4	5	4	3	4	5	4	3	4	5	4	4	4	3	4	3	4	5
M.HCP	13	3	5	15	7	1	11	17	9	4	14	10	6	16	8	18	12	2
L.HCP	13	1	5	17	9	3	11	15	7	4	14	8	12	16	6	18	10	2

MARRIOT'S CAMELBACK G.C. - INDIAN BEND

7847 N. Mockingbird Ln. Scottsdale, AZ 85253   602-948-6770

DESERT ○   TRADITIONAL ○   LINKS ●

TERRAIN	TREES	WATER

GREENS	Bermuda	COURSE FAVORS A... Draw
FAIRWAYS	Bermuda	WIDTH OF FAIRWAYS Forgiving
BUNKERS	Regular	AMT. OF BUNKERS Average

PAR	YARDS	RATING	SLOPE	1992 GREEN FEES $
72	7014	72.6	126	HIGH $80
72	6486	72.3	122	LOW $30
72	5917	72.2	115	SPECIALS None

THE COURSE COMMENTARY

Marriott's Camelback Golf Club sports two championship 18 hole layouts, with the added plus of a premiere 5-star, 5-diamond resort in the heart of Scottsdale. The Indian Bend course is a links style layout with forgiving fairways and scenic views.

TOUGHEST HOLE	THE 432 YARD PAR-4 1ST HOLE WILL GET YOU OFF TO A TOUGH START WITH TWO LONG AND ACCURATE SHOTS.
BIRDIE HOLE	THE 185 YARD PAR-3 11TH HOLE IS LONG BUT IS GUARANTEED TO GIVE YOU A LOOK AT A BIRDIE.
WATER IN PLAY ON...	3 HOLES
OVERALL STRATEGY	HIT EVERYTHING LONG.
CART REQUIRED?	YES
PRACTICE FACILITIES?	DRIVING RANGE PUTTING GREEN CHIPPING GREEN
COURSE IS OPEN...	YES
OVERSEEDING	SEPTEMBER FOR 7 WEEKS. TEES, GREENS, AND FAIRWAYS
RESTAURANT?	YES
ACCOMMODATIONS?	THE 5-STAR, 5-DIAMOND MARRIOTT CAMELBACK.
DON'T FORGET YOUR..	EVERYTHING
COURSE DESIGNER	JACK SNYDER
# OF ROUNDS ANNUALLY	82,000
DIRECTIONS	3 MILES NORTH OF LINCOLN OFF SCOTTSDALE RD. TO CHENEY. GO WEST TO MOCKINGBIRD AND NORTH TO THE COURSE.432

COURSE LAYOUT NOT AVAILABLE

HOLE	1	2	3	4	5	6	7	8	9	10	11	12	13	14	15	16	17	18
CHAMP	432	550	180	400	440	540	410	200	430	400	185	412	570	370	185	380	400	530
MENS	400	535	150	380	414	510	372	170	400	370	140	385	540	360	145	345	360	510
LADIES	390	511	120	345	395	480	355	145	374	345	120	360	510	267	105	270	340	485
PAR	4	5	3	4	4	5	4	3	4	4	3	4	5	4	3	4	4	5
M.HCP	1	7	17	11	5	9	13	15	3	8	18	6	2	16	12	14	10	4
L.HCP	7	1	17	13	5	3	11	15	9	10	16	6	2	12	18	14	8	4

MARRIOTT'S CAMELBACK G.C. - PADRE

HOTEL GUEST PRIORITY 18 HOLES

7847 N. Mockingbird Ln. Scottsdale, AZ 85253   *602-948-6770*

DESERT ○   TRADITIONAL ○   LINKS ●

TERRAIN	TREES	WATER

 GREENS *Bermuda*   **COURSE FAVORS A...** *Draw*

FAIRWAYS *Bermuda*   **WIDTH OF FAIRWAYS** *Forgiving*

BUNKERS *Regular*   **AMT. OF BUNKERS** *Average*

PAR	YARDS	RATING	SLOPE	1992 GREEN FEES $	
71	6559	69.8	117	**HIGH**	*$80*
71	6019	67.7	117	**LOW**	*$30*
73	5626	70.9	116	**SPECIALS**	*None*

THE COURSE COMMENTARY *Marriott's Camelback Golf Club sports two championship 18 hole layouts, with the added plus of a premiere 5-star, 5-diamond resort in the heart of Scottsdale. The Padre course has tree lined fairways with elevated greens.*

TOUGHEST HOLE THE 447 YARD PAR-4 6TH HOLE TAKES TWO LONG SHOTS TO A GUARDED GREEN.

BIRDIE HOLE THE 145 YARD PAR-3 12TH HOLE PLAYS TO A LARGE GREEN WITH LITTLE TROUBLE.

WATER IN PLAY ON... 0 HOLES

OVERALL STRATEGY PLACEMENT OFF THE TEE IS CRITICAL.

CART REQUIRED? YES

PRACTICE FACILITIES? DRIVING RANGE   PUTTING GREEN   CHIPPING GREEN

COURSE IS OPEN... YES

OVERSEEDING SEPTEMBER FOR 7 WEEKS. TEES, GREENS, AND FAIRWAYS

RESTAURANT? YES

ACCOMMODATIONS? THE 5-STAR, 5-DIAMOND MARRIOTT CAMELBACK.

DON'T FORGET YOUR.. EVERYTHING

COURSE DESIGNER RED LAWERENCE

 # OF ROUNDS ANNUALLY 82,000

DIRECTIONS 3 MILES NORTH OF LINCOLN OFF SCOTTSDALE RD. TO CHENEY. GO WEST TO MOCKINGBIRD AND NORTH TO THE COURSE.

COURSE LAYOUT NOT AVAILABLE

HOLE	1	2	3	4	5	6	7	8	9	10	11	12	13	14	15	16	17	18
CHAMP	463	351	180	498	351	447	408	215	512	538	447	145	383	200	421	332	163	505
MENS	415	315	162	452	331	420	390	148	467	505	431	130	354	166	397	316	146	474
LADIES	400	291	141	439	308	398	361	131	450	480	412	110	320	151	372	300	108	454
PAR	4	4	3	5	4	4	4	3	5	5	4	3	4	3	4	4	3	5
M.HCP	3	17	13	7	11	1	5	15	9	4	2	18	8	10	6	12	16	14
L.HCP	17	11	13	5	9	1	3	15	7	4	14	18	10	12	2	8	16	6

MARRIOTT'S MOUNTAIN SHADOWS G.C.

PUBLIC   18 HOLES

5641 E. Lincoln Dr. Scottsdale, AZ 85253   *602-951-5427*

DESERT ○   TRADITIONAL ●   LINKS ○

TERRAIN	TREES	WATER

GREENS *Bermuda*   **COURSE FAVORS A...** *Draw*

FAIRWAYS *Bermuda*   **WIDTH OF FAIRWAYS** *Tight*

BUNKERS *Regular*   **AMT. OF BUNKERS** *Many*

PAR	YARDS	RATING	SLOPE
56	3081	57.6	89
56	2606	54.7	86
56	2606	54.7	86

1992 GREEN FEES $

HIGH	$44
LOW	$31
SPECIALS	Afternoon specials

THE COURSE COMMENTARY

This 18 hole executive layout sits at the base of Camelback mountain and is the most scenic executive layout in the valley. There are many elevated greens and tees.

TOUGHEST HOLE	THE 353 YARD PAR-4 6TH HOLE IS THE LONGEST HOLE ON THE COURSE. YOUR APPROACH IS KEY TO THIS TOUGH GREEN.
BIRDIE HOLE	THE 100 YARD PAR-3 10TH HOLE. SHOOT FOR THE PIN.
WATER IN PLAY ON...	6 HOLES
OVERALL STRATEGY	GET YOUR SHORT GAME READY FOR A TEST.
CART REQUIRED?	YES
PRACTICE FACILITIES?	DRIVING RANGE PUTTING GREEN
COURSE IS OPEN...	YES
OVERSEEDING	SEPT. FOR 2 WEEKS. INCLUDES EVERYTHING
RESTAURANT?	YES
ACCOMMODATIONS?	A FULL SERVICE MARRIOTT RESORT
DON'T FORGET YOUR..	FAVORITE WEDGE
COURSE DESIGNER	ARTHUR JACK SNYDER
# OF ROUNDS ANNUALLY	18,000
DIRECTIONS	A MILE AND A HALF EAST OF TATUM BLVD. ON LINCOLN DR.

COURSE LAYOUT

HOLE	1	2	3	4	5	6	7	8	9	10	11	12	13	14	15	16	17	18
CHAMP	160	187	162	176	165	353	180	126	175	100	104	175	83	165	295	130	240	105
MENS	130	150	137	140	150	322	120	90	160	100	104	140	80	120	278	115	190	80
LADIES	130	150	137	140	150	322	120	90	160	100	104	140	80	120	278	115	190	80
PAR	3	3	3	3	3	4	3	3	3	3	3	3	3	3	4	3	3	3
M.HCP	11	7	17	3	13	1	5	15	9	18	14	4	16	8	6	10	2	12
L.HCP	13	5	15	11	3	1	17	9	7	18	16	2	12	8	6	10	4	14

MARYVALE G.C.

PUBLIC   18 HOLES

5902 W. Indian School Rd. Phoenix, AZ 85033   602-846-4022

DESERT ○   TRADITIONAL ●   LINKS ○

TERRAIN	TREES	WATER

GREENS	Other	COURSE FAVORS A...	Draw
FAIRWAYS	Bermuda	WIDTH OF FAIRWAYS	Normal
BUNKERS	Regular	AMT. OF BUNKERS	Minimal

PAR	YARDS	RATING	SLOPE	1992 GREEN FEES $	
72	6539	70.0	116	HIGH	$18
72	6191	68.1	111	LOW	$12
72	5656	70.0	N/A	SPECIALS	$9 Twilight - Winter

THE COURSE COMMENTARY

This course is in a park-like setting with mature trees and several ponds.

TOUGHEST HOLE	THE 421 YARD PAR-4 3RD HOLE AND THE 438 YARD PAR-4 16TH HOLE WILL BOTH TEST YOUR LONG IRON SKILL.
BIRDIE HOLE	THE 484 YARD PAR-5 9TH HOLE IS REACHABLE IN TWO WITH A GOOD TEE SHOT.
WATER IN PLAY ON...	7 HOLES
OVERALL STRATEGY	KEEP THE BALL IN PLAY. THIS MAY SOUND ONLY NATURAL BUT IT'S DIFFICULT WHEN YOUR ON THE TEE.
CART REQUIRED?	NO
PRACTICE FACILITIES?	DRIVING RANGE PUTTING GREEN CHIPPING GREEN
COURSE IS OPEN...	YES
OVERSEEDING	OCTOBER FOR 2 WEEKS. TEES AND GREENS.
RESTAURANT?	YES
ACCOMMODATIONS?	N/A
DON'T FORGET YOUR..	N/A
COURSE DESIGNER	WILLIAM BELL
# OF ROUNDS ANNUALLY	84,000
DIRECTIONS	ON THE NORTHWEST CORNER OF 59TH AVE. AND INDIAN SCHOOL RD.

HOLE	1	2	3	4	5	6	7	8	9	10	11	12	13	14	15	16	17	18
CHAMP	492	213	421	162	331	329	368	389	484	501	159	562	359	372	368	438	206	385
MENS	475	195	349	145	308	315	354	375	455	477	142	539	343	357	348	420	169	375
LADIES	459	177	382	130	288	283	342	337	407	450	116	495	296	344	325	371	114	340
PAR	5	3	4	3	4	4	4	4	5	5	3	5	4	4	4	4	3	4
M.HCP	9	3	1	17	15	13	11	5	7	6	18	4	14	12	16	2	8	10
L.HCP	1	15	5	17	11	13	7	9	3	4	18	2	14	8	12	6	16	10

McCormick Ranch G.C. - Palm Course

PUBLIC   18 HOLES

7505 E. McCormick Pkwy. Scottsdale, AZ 85258   602-948-0260

DESERT ○   **TRADITIONAL** ●   **LINKS** ○

TERRAIN	TREES	WATER

GREENS *Bent*
FAIRWAYS *Bermuda*
BUNKERS *Regular*

COURSE FAVORS A... *Mix*
WIDTH OF FAIRWAYS *Normal*
AMT. OF BUNKERS *Many*

	PAR	YARDS	RATING	SLOPE	1992 GREEN FEES $	
	72	7032	73.7	133	HIGH	$75
	72	6279	69.9	127	LOW	$32
	72	5210	70.2	120	SPECIALS	N/A

THE COURSE COMMENTARY

Past tournaments include: The Arizona Open, The ASU Sun Devil Tournament, The State Amateur, and U.S. Open qualifying.

TOUGHEST HOLE	AGAIN, THE 408 YARD PAR-4 9TH HOLE HAS A LAKE TO LEFT ALL THE WAY TO THE GREEN AND A LAGOON IN THE MIDDLE.
BIRDIE HOLE	THE 187 YARD PAR-3 17TH HAS WATER TO THE LEFT BUT DOES NOT COME INTO PLAY. IT'S STILL NOT THAT EASY.
WATER IN PLAY ON...	15 HOLES
OVERALL STRATEGY	YOU HAVE GOT TO PLAN EVERY SHOT. IF YOUR A POWER HITTER, HUMBLE YOURSELF AND HIT YOUR IRONS OFF MOST TEES.
CART REQUIRED?	YES
PRACTICE FACILITIES?	DRIVING RANGE PUTTING GREEN CHIPPING GREEN
COURSE IS OPEN...	YES
OVERSEEDING	NOVEMBER FOR 2 WEEKS. TEES AND FAIRWAYS.
RESTAURANT?	BREAKFAST AND LUNCH.
ACCOMMODATIONS?	SEVERAL RESORTS WITHIN 5 MINUTES IN THE HEART OF SCOTTSDALE.
DON'T FORGET YOUR..	BALL RETRIEVER
COURSE DESIGNER	DESMOND MUIRHEAD
# OF ROUNDS ANNUALLY	100,000
DIRECTIONS	GO SOUTH OFF SHEA BLVD. ON SCOTTSDALE RD. TO MCCORMICK PKWY. GO LEFT UNTIL YOU SEE THE SIGN.

COURSE LAYOUT

HOLE	1	2	3	4	5	6	7	8	9	10	11	12	13	14	15	16	17	18
CHAMP	375	384	531	446	214	389	523	195	408	394	420	510	203	413	448	564	187	428
MENS	337	351	497	373	179	361	477	157	370	351	376	489	169	325	418	511	148	390
LADIES	284	301	418	277	122	298	398	101	330	295	332	427	136	276	349	461	76	335
PAR	4	4	5	4	3	4	5	3	4	4	4	5	3	4	4	5	3	4
M.HCP	13	9	5	7	15	11	1	17	3	14	10	6	16	12	4	2	18	8
L.HCP	13	9	5	7	15	11	1	17	3	14	10	6	16	12	4	2	18	8

McCormick Ranch G.C. - Pine Course

PUBLIC   18 HOLES

7505 E. McCormick Pkwy. Scottsdale, AZ 85258   602-948-0260

DESERT ○   **TRADITIONAL** ●   **LINKS** ○

| TERRAIN | TREES | WATER |

	GREENS	Bent		COURSE FAVORS A...	Mix
	FAIRWAYS	Bermuda		WIDTH OF FAIRWAYS	Normal
	BUNKERS	Regular		AMT. OF BUNKERS	Many

PAR	YARDS	RATING	SLOPE	1992 GREEN FEES
72	7013	73.2	133	**HIGH** $75
72	6346	69.9	125	**LOW** $32
72	5367	71.0	120	**SPECIALS** N/A

THE COURSE COMMENTARY

Past tournaments include: The Arizona Open, The ASU Sun Devil Tournament, The State Amateur, and U.S. Open qualifying.

TOUGHEST HOLE	THE 452 YARD PAR-4 13TH HOLE. BOTH YOUR TEE SHOT AND APPROACH ARE OVER LARGE LAKES WITH SMALL TARGETS.
BIRDIE HOLE	THE 174 YARD PAR-3 5TH HOLE IS SHORT WITH ONLY 2 TRAPS TO THE SIDE OF THE GREEN.
WATER IN PLAY ON...	5 HOLES
OVERALL STRATEGY	HIT YOUR TEE SHOTS TO THE MIDDLE OF THE FAIRWAY.
CART REQUIRED?	YES
PRACTICE FACILITIES?	DRIVING RANGE PUTTING GREEN CHIPPING GREEN
COURSE IS OPEN...	YES
OVERSEEDING	NOVEMBER FOR 2 WEEKS. TEES AND FAIRWAYS.
RESTAURANT?	BREAKFAST AND LUNCH.
ACCOMMODATIONS?	THE REGAL MCCORMICK RANCH HOTEL IS ON PROPERTY AND THERE ARE ALSO SEVERAL RESORTS WITHIN 5 MINUTES.
DON'T FORGET YOUR..	BALL RETRIEVER
COURSE DESIGNER	DESMOND MUIRHEAD
# OF ROUNDS ANNUALLY	100,000
DIRECTIONS	GO SOUTH OFF SHEA BLVD. ON SCOTTSDALE RD. TO MCCORMICK PKWY. GO LEFT UNTIL YOU SEE THE SIGN.

COURSE LAYOUT

HOLE	1	2	3	4	5	6	7	8	9	10	11	12	13	14	15	16	17	18
CHAMP	371	387	390	537	174	419	599	208	401	410	397	577	218	370	452	401	185	517
MENS	341	354	355	511	141	383	556	175	365	363	370	519	178	342	376	372	166	479
LADIES	289	308	310	469	96	336	468	125	326	276	320	476	115	271	311	328	100	443
PAR	4	4	4	5	3	4	5	3	4	4	4	5	3	4	4	4	3	5
M.HCP	14	12	8	6	18	4	2	16	10	13	7	3	15	11	1	9	17	5
L.HCP	14	12	8	6	18	4	2	16	10	13	7	3	15	11	1	9	17	5

MESA DEL SOL G.C.

PUBLIC   18 HOLES

10583 Camino Del Sol   Yuma, AZ 85365   602-342-1283

DESERT ○   **TRADITIONAL** ●   **LINKS** ○

TERRAIN	TREES	WATER

GREENS *Bermuda*	**COURSE FAVORS A...** *Fade*	
FAIRWAYS *Bermuda*	**WIDTH OF FAIRWAYS** *Normal*	
BUNKERS *Regular*	**AMT. OF BUNKERS** *Average*	

PAR	YARDS	RATING	SLOPE	1992 GREEN FEES
72	6767	72.6	124	**HIGH** *$25*
72	6299	69.7	116	**LOW** *$5*
73	5388	69.5	112	**SPECIALS** *Please call*

THE COURSE COMMENTARY

This is a challenging course even though it's not long. This course will test your short game.

TOUGHEST HOLE	THE 432 YARD PAR-4 4TH HOLE PLAYS INTO A PREVAILING NORTH WIND IN THE WINTER MONTHS.
BIRDIE HOLE	THE 460 YARD PAR-4 2ND HOLE GETS EVEN SHORTER IF YOU CAN CUT THE CORNER OF THE DOGLEG.
WATER IN PLAY ON...	9 HOLES
OVERALL STRATEGY	HIT IT STRAIGHT.
CART REQUIRED?	NO
PRACTICE FACILITIES?	DRIVING RANGE PUTTING GREEN
COURSE IS OPEN...	YES
OVERSEEDING	OCTOBER FOR 4 WEEKS. TEES, GREENS AND FAIRWAYS.
RESTAURANT?	DINNER DURING NOV.- APR. ON THURSDAY & FRIDAY NIGHTS.
ACCOMMODATIONS?	HOTELS NEARBY
DON'T FORGET YOUR..	BALL RETRIEVER
COURSE DESIGNER	ARNOLD PALMER
# OF ROUNDS ANNUALLY	50,000
DIRECTIONS	GO EAST FOR 10 MILES ON I-8 TO FORTUNA RD., EXIT, THEN GO NORTH ON THE FRONTAGE ROAD.

COURSE LAYOUT

HOLE	1	2	3	4	5	6	7	8	9	10	11	12	13	14	15	16	17	18
CHAMP	445	468	341	160	414	541	365	152	382	400	411	521	421	167	420	408	206	545
MENS	432	460	333	142	391	514	326	135	366	382	361	495	391	137	380	380	169	505
LADIES	401	442	285	126	356	443	271	119	305	318	319	401	298	95	358	319	131	401
PAR	4	5	4	3	4	5	4	3	4	4	4	5	4	3	4	4	3	5
M.HCP	1	11	13	15	7	5	9	17	3	12	8	2	10	18	14	6	16	4
L.HCP	7	1	11	17	13	3	9	15	5	12	10	8	14	16	6	4	18	2

OAK CREEK C.C.

SEMI PRIVATE 18 HOLES

690 Bell Rock Ave. Sedona, AZ 86336

602-284-1660

DESERT ○ TRADITIONAL ● LINKS ○

TERRAIN	TREES	WATER

GREENS	Bent		**COURSE FAVORS A...**	Mix
FAIRWAYS	Bent		**WIDTH OF FAIRWAYS**	Normal
BUNKERS	Regular		**AMT. OF BUNKERS**	Many

	PAR	YARDS	RATING	SLOPE	1992 GREEN FEES $	
	72	6854	71.9	129	**HIGH**	$45
	72	6286	69.4	121	**LOW**	$45
	72	5555	71.6	124	**SPECIALS**	$25 - Call for availability

THE COURSE COMMENTARY Designed by the famous golf course architect Robert Trent Jones. Spectacular views... especially on the back nine around the Bell Rock.

TOUGHEST HOLE THE 460 YARD PAR-4 9TH HOLE IS A DOGLEG LEFT WITH WATER ON THE RIGHT. THIS IS A GOOD TEST OF PLANNING.

BIRDIE HOLE 490 YARD PAR-5 15TH HOLE IS A SLIGHT DOGLEG RIGHT AND IS REACHABLE IN TWO WITH A LONG DRIVE.

WATER IN PLAY ON... 5 HOLES

OVERALL STRATEGY HIT YOUR DRIVES TO THE MIDDLE OF THE FAIRWAY.

CART REQUIRED? YES

PRACTICE FACILITIES? DRIVING RANGE   PUTTING GREEN   CHIPPING GREEN

COURSE IS OPEN... YES

OVERSEEDING N/A

RESTAURANT? BREAKFAST & LUNCH

ACCOMMODATIONS? THE BELL ROCK INN IS NEARBY.

DON'T FORGET YOUR.. CAMERA

COURSE DESIGNER ROBERT TRENT JONES

 # OF ROUNDS ANNUALLY 50,000

DIRECTIONS TAKE THE SEDONA EXIT FROM I-17, THEN GO 7 MILES NORTH ON STATE RD. 179, THEN GO .5 MILE WEST ON BELL ROCK BLVD.567

COURSE LAYOUT

HOLE	1	2	3	4	5	6	7	8	9	10	11	12	13	14	15	16	17	18
CHAMP	567	340	530	187	375	375	210	385	460	545	365	440	160	400	490	190	390	445
MENS	487	304	495	142	345	350	178	325	420	530	340	425	145	370	475	170	365	420
LADIES	440	270	450	105	310	320	155	290	380	490	290	355	115	295	450	130	330	380
PAR	5	4	5	3	4	4	3	4	4	5	4	4	3	4	5	3	4	4
M.HCP	7	13	15	17	5	3	11	9	1	8	14	2	18	6	16	12	10	4
L.HCP	3	13	1	17	11	7	15	9	5	6	12	10	18	14	2	16	8	4

OAKWOOD G.C.

SEMI PRIVATE 18 HOLES

25612 E. J. Robson Blvd. Sun Lakes, AZ 85248   602-895-7660

DESERT ○   **TRADITIONAL** ●   **LINKS** ○

TERRAIN	TREES	WATER

GREENS	Bermuda	COURSE FAVORS A...	Mix
FAIRWAYS	Bermuda	WIDTH OF FAIRWAYS	Normal
BUNKERS	Regular	AMT. OF BUNKERS	Average

PAR	YARDS	RATING	SLOPE	1992 GREEN FEES
72	6508	71.1	121	**HIGH** $42
72	6177	69.1	115	**LOW** $29
72	5343	68.8	113	**SPECIALS** Samaritan Tour Pass-

THE COURSE COMMENTARY

This course sports a lot of water and it will worry you from the third hole until you finish. Luckily, Kavanaugh, the architect, shows a little mercy in letting you get warmed up on the first two holes without being affected by the lakes.

TOUGHEST HOLE PAR-5 494 YARD 2ND HOLE IS A DOGLEG LEFT WITH WATER OFF THE TEE. YOUR TEE SHOT IS CRUCIAL

BIRDIE HOLE THE PAR-4 319 YARD 17TH HOLE IS A SURE BIRDIE IF YOUR HITTING YOUR PITCHING WEDGE WELL.

WATER IN PLAY ON... 14 HOLES

OVERALL STRATEGY LET IT FLY OFF THE TEE BUT BE CAUTIOUS ON YOUR APPROACH TO THE GREEN; THIS IS WHERE WATER WILL COME INTO PLAY.

CART REQUIRED? No

PRACTICE FACILITIES? DRIVING RANGE   PUTTING GREEN

COURSE IS OPEN... YES

OVERSEEDING OCTOBER FOR 4 WEEKS. TEES, GREENS, AND FAIRWAYS

RESTAURANT? THE BASHAI COFFEE SHOP IS A 1/2 MILE AWAY

ACCOMMODATIONS? N\A

DON'T FORGET YOUR.. BALL RETRIEVER

COURSE DESIGNER K. KAVANAUGH

 # OF ROUNDS ANNUALLY 60,000

DIRECTIONS EXIT I-10 AT RIGGS RD., AND THEN GO THREE MILES EAST.

132

COURSE LAYOUT

HOLE	1	2	3	4	5	6	7	8	9	10	11	12	13	14	15	16	17	18
CHAMP	372	494	354	179	388	358	188	394	522	510	133	412	385	375	186	544	319	395
MENS	359	482	338	170	374	345	156	377	502	490	126	367	352	358	190	517	291	383
LADIES	336	399	315	139	346	319	115	338	458	429	99	320	309	294	128	443	226	330
PAR	4	5	4	3	4	4	3	4	5	5	3	4	4	4	3	5	4	4
M.HCP	13	1	5	17	9	15	11	3	7	2	10	8	16	14	12	6	18	4
L.HCP	7	1	9	17	13	11	15	5	3	2	10	8	12	14	16	4	18	6

OCOTILLO G.C. - BLUE/GOLD

PUBLIC   18 HOLES

3751 S. Clubhouse Dr. Chandler, AZ 85248   602-275-4355

DESERT ○   **TRADITIONAL** ●   **LINKS** ○

TERRAIN	TREES	WATER

GREENS	Bermuda	COURSE FAVORS A...	Mix
FAIRWAYS	Bermuda	WIDTH OF FAIRWAYS	Normal
BUNKERS	Silicon	AMT. OF BUNKERS	Many

PAR	YARDS	RATING	SLOPE
72	6729	72.2	132
72	6379	70.6	129
72	5128	68.6	121

1992 GREEN FEES

HIGH	$65
LOW	$29
SPECIALS	$15 after 3:30pm/ walking

THE COURSE COMMENTARY

There is water on 24 of the Blue, White, and Gold courses 27 beautiful holes. It's really not as oceanic as it seems because the layout is quite forgiving. Multi-level greens and club selection make this course difficult.

TOUGHEST HOLE   THE 550 YARD PAR-5 6TH HOLE ON THE BLUE COURSE HAS BUNKERS ON THE RIGHT AND WATER ON THE LEFT.

BIRDIE HOLE   THE 382 YARD PAR-4 3RD HOLE ON THE GOLD COURSE PLAYS TO A LARGE GREEN. HIT AN IRON OFF THE TEE.

WATER IN PLAY ON...   24 OF 27 TOTAL HOLES HOLES

OVERALL STRATEGY   PLAY SAFELY AWAY FROM THE WATER.

CART REQUIRED?   YES

PRACTICE FACILITIES?   DRIVING RANGE   PUTTING GREEN

COURSE IS OPEN...   YES

OVERSEEDING   OCTOBER FOR 2 WEEKS. TEES, GREENS, AND FAIRWAYS.

RESTAURANT?   BEVERAGE CART, GRILL, AND PATIO RESTAURANT.

ACCOMMODATIONS?   NO

DON'T FORGET YOUR..   BALL RETRIEVER AND 1 IRON.

COURSE DESIGNER   TED ROBINSON

 # OF ROUNDS ANNUALLY   70,000

DIRECTIONS   3 AND A HALF MILES SOUTH OF CHANDLER BLVD. ON PRICE.

COURSE LAYOUT

HOLE	1	2	3	4	5	6	7	8	9	10	11	12	13	14	15	16	17	18
CHAMP	520	398	373	192	355	550	163	404	370	409	526	382	377	203	526	390	172	419
MENS	502	378	353	159	342	533	142	372	350	385	509	365	358	187	510	375	159	400
LADIES	404	331	289	108	304	454	107	311	261	298	415	310	269	142	402	298	116	309
PAR	5	4	4	3	4	5	3	4	4	4	5	4	4	3	5	4	3	4
M.HCP	5	13	9	11	17	1	15	3	7	8	4	16	10	12	2	14	18	6
L.HCP	5	13	9	15	7	1	17	3	11	6	2	10	8	16	4	12	18	14

OCOTILLO G.C. - BLUE/WHITE

PUBLIC   18 HOLES

3751 S. Clubhouse Dr. Chandler, AZ 85248

602-275-4355

DESERT ○   **TRADITIONAL** ●   **LINKS** ○

TERRAIN	TREES	WATER

GREENS	Bermuda	**COURSE FAVORS A...**	Mix
FAIRWAYS	Bermuda	**WIDTH OF FAIRWAYS**	Normal
BUNKERS	Silicon	**AMT. OF BUNKERS**	Many

PAR	YARDS	RATING	SLOPE	1992 GREEN FEES	
71	6533	71.4	128	**HIGH**	$65
71	6180	69.7	124	**LOW**	$29
71	5138	69.2	121	**SPECIALS**	$15 after 3:30; walking

THE COURSE COMMENTARY *There is water on 24 of the Blue, White, and Gold courses 27 beautiful holes. It's really not as oceanic as it seems because the layout is quite forgiving. Multi-level greens and club selection make this course so difficult.*

TOUGHEST HOLE	THE 550 YARD PAR-5 6TH HOLE ON THE BLUE COURSE HAS BUNKERS ON THE RIGHT AND WATER ON THE LEFT.
BIRDIE HOLE	THE 174 YARD PAR-3 7TH HOLE PLAYS TO A LARGE GREEN WITH NO TROUBLE.
WATER IN PLAY ON...	24 OF 27 TOTAL HOLES Holes
OVERALL STRATEGY	PLAY SAFELY AWAY FROM THE WATER.
CART REQUIRED?	YES
PRACTICE FACILITIES?	DRIVING RANGE PUTTING GREEN
COURSE IS OPEN...	YES
OVERSEEDING	OCTOBER FOR 2 WEEKS. TEES, GREENS, AND FAIRWAYS.
RESTAURANT?	BEVERAGE CART, GRILL, AND PATIO RESTAURANT.
ACCOMMODATIONS?	NO
DON'T FORGET YOUR..	BALL RETRIEVER AND 1 IRON.
COURSE DESIGNER	TED ROBINSON
# OF ROUNDS ANNUALLY	70,000
DIRECTIONS	3 AND A HALF MILES SOUTH OF CHANDLER BLVD. ON PRICE.

COURSE LAYOUT

HOLE	1	2	3	4	5	6	7	8	9	10	11	12	13	14	15	16	17	18
CHAMP	520	398	373	192	355	550	163	404	370	376	519	162	332	412	416	174	346	471
MENS	502	378	353	159	342	533	142	372	350	356	495	158	318	388	395	157	331	451
LADIES	404	331	289	108	304	454	107	311	261	314	426	112	259	323	341	117	294	379
PAR	5	4	4	3	4	5	3	4	4	4	5	3	4	4	4	3	4	4
M.HCP	5	13	9	11	17	1	15	3	7	12	2	14	10	8	6	18	16	4
L.HCP	5	13	9	15	7	1	17	3	11	10	2	14	16	6	8	18	12	4

OCOTILLO G.C. - GOLD/WHITE

PUBLIC   18 HOLES

3751 S. Clubhouse Dr.   Chandler, AZ 85428   *602-275-4355*

DESERT ○   TRADITIONAL ●   LINKS ○

TERRAIN	TREES	WATER

GREENS *Bermuda*   **COURSE FAVORS A...** *Mix*

FAIRWAYS *Bermuda*   **WIDTH OF FAIRWAYS** *Normal*

BUNKERS *Silicon*   **AMT. OF BUNKERS** *Many*

PAR	YARDS	RATING	SLOPE		1992 GREEN FEES $
71	6612	71.7	126	**HIGH**	$65
71	6297	70.2	123	**LOW**	$29
71	5124	69.0	120	**SPECIALS**	$15 after 3:30; walking

THE COURSE COMMENTARY

There is water on 24 of the Blue, White, and Gold courses 27 beautiful holes. It's really not as oceanic as it seems because the layout is quite forgiving. Multi-level greens and club selection make this course so difficult.

TOUGHEST HOLE THE 519 YARD PAR-5 2ND HOLE ON THE WHITE COURSE. WATER SPLITS THE FAIRWAY TOWARD A PROTECTED GREEN.

BIRDIE HOLE THE 174 YARD PAR-3 7TH HOLE ON THE WHITE COURSE PLAYS TO A LARGE GREEN WITH NO TROUBLE.

WATER IN PLAY ON... 24 OF 27 TOTAL HOLES Holes

OVERALL STRATEGY PLAY SAFELY AWAY FROM THE WATER.

CART REQUIRED? YES

PRACTICE FACILITIES? DRIVING RANGE   PUTTING GREEN

COURSE IS OPEN... YES

OVERSEEDING OCTOBER FOR 2 WEEKS. TEES, GREENS, AND FAIRWAYS.

RESTAURANT? BEVERAGE CART, GRILL, AND PATIO RESTAURANT.

ACCOMMODATIONS? NO

DON'T FORGET YOUR.. BALL RETRIEVER AND 1 IRON.

COURSE DESIGNER TED ROBINSON

 # OF ROUNDS ANNUALLY 70,000

DIRECTIONS 3 AND A HALF MILES SOUTH OF CHANDLER BLVD. ON PRICE.

COURSE LAYOUT

HOLE	1	2	3	4	5	6	7	8	9	10	11	12	13	14	15	16	17	18
CHAMP	409	526	382	377	203	526	390	172	419	376	519	162	332	412	416	174	346	471
MENS	385	509	365	358	187	510	375	159	400	356	495	158	318	388	395	157	331	451
LADIES	298	415	310	269	142	402	298	116	309	314	426	112	259	323	341	117	294	379
PAR	4	5	4	4	3	5	4	3	4	4	5	3	4	4	4	3	4	4
M.HCP	8	4	16	10	12	2	14	18	6	11	1	13	9	7	5	17	15	3
L.HCP	6	2	10	8	16	4	12	18	14	9	1	13	15	5	7	17	11	3

ORANGE TREE G.R.

PUBLIC 18 HOLES

10601 N. 56th St. Scottsdale, AZ 85254   602-948-6100

DESERT ⭕   **TRADITIONAL** ⚫   **LINKS** ⭕

TERRAIN   **TREES**   **WATER**

🚩 **GREENS** *Bermuda*	↳ **COURSE FAVORS A...** *Mix*
FAIRWAYS *Bermuda*	**WIDTH OF FAIRWAYS** *Forgiving*
BUNKERS *Other*	**AMT. OF BUNKERS** *Many*

	PAR	YARDS	RATING	SLOPE	1992 GREEN FEES
⭐	72	6762	71.3	122	**HIGH** *$75*
🧍	72	6398	69.5	118	**LOW** *$25*
🧍	72	5632	71.8	116	**SPECIALS** *Call*

THE COURSE COMMENTARY

This course is in great condition and is tucked away in the heart of the Scottsdale suburbs. Mature trees line the fairways. The newly added resort on property is great for a "golf getaway."

TOUGHEST HOLE	THE 494 YARD PAR-5 2ND HOLE IS A SHORT BUT CHALLENGING. BUNKERS MAKE IT TOUGH TO GET CLOSE IN TWO.
BIRDIE HOLE	THE 367 YARD PAR-4 1ST HOLE IS STAIGHTAWAY WITH A WIDE FAIRWAY AND NO TROUBLE.
WATER IN PLAY ON...	6 HOLES
OVERALL STRATEGY	THE FAIRWAYS ARE FORGIVING ENOUGH TO HIT FOR LENGTH OFF THE TEE. BUNKERS ARE STRATEGICALLY PLACED THROUGHOUT.
CART REQUIRED?	YES
PRACTICE FACILITIES?	DRIVING RANGE PUTTING GREEN CHIPPING GREEN
COURSE IS OPEN...	YES
OVERSEEDING	OCTOBER FOR 2 WEEKS. TEES, GREENS, AND FAIRWAYS.
RESTAURANT?	YES
ACCOMMODATIONS?	NEWLY CONSTRUCTED 160 LUXURY ROOM RESORT WITH APPOINTED GUEST AND CONFERENCE ROOMS.
DON'T FORGET YOUR..	EVERYTHING
COURSE DESIGNER	JOHNNY BULLA
# OF ROUNDS ANNUALLY	50,000
DIRECTIONS	ON THE NORTH-EAST CORNER OF 56TH ST. AND SHEA.

COURSE LAYOUT

HOLE	1	2	3	4	5	6	7	8	9	10	11	12	13	14	15	16	17	18
CHAMP	367	494	383	161	386	476	211	411	379	402	413	188	580	399	194	406	509	403
MENS	355	475	375	147	379	468	162	403	366	379	360	182	542	376	162	388	494	388
LADIES	324	449	332	119	350	432	138	331	317	335	328	150	459	350	105	345	428	340
PAR	4	5	4	3	4	5	3	4	4	4	4	3	5	4	3	4	5	4
M.HCP	13	1	11	15	9	5	17	3	7	12	10	16	2	14	18	4	8	6
L.HCP	13	1	11	15	7	3	17	5	9	14	12	16	2	10	18	8	4	6

PAPAGO G.C.

PUBLIC   18 HOLES

5595 E. Moreland   Phoenix, AZ 85008   602-275-8428

DESERT ○   **TRADITIONAL** ●   **LINKS** ○

TERRAIN	TREES	WATER
	🌲 🌲 🌲	〜〜〜

🚩 **GREENS**	Bermuda	**COURSE FAVORS A...**	Mix
FAIRWAYS	Bermuda	**WIDTH OF FAIRWAYS**	Normal
BUNKERS	Regular	**AMT. OF BUNKERS**	Many

	PAR	YARDS	RATING	SLOPE
★	72	7068	73.3	132
	72	6590	70.7	123
	72	5937	72.4	119

1992 GREEN FEES $

HIGH	$18
LOW	$9
SPECIALS	$5.50 - call for availabiltiy

THE COURSE COMMENTARY   Long considered one of the best public courses in America. It is the home of Phoenix Open qualifying and the 1972 National PubLinks Championship. Arrive EARLY on the weekends to get a tee time. For the money, one of the best courses to play in Arizona.

TOUGHEST HOLE	THE 458 YARD PAR-4 3RD HOLE. KEEP YOUR DRIVE TO THE LEFT/MIDDLE SIDE FOR A LONG IRON TO A SMALL GUARDED GREEN.
BIRDIE HOLE	THE 520 YARD PAR-5 10TH HOLE WILL TAKE AN ACCURATE WEDGE TO THE GREEN FOR A BIRDIE PUTT.
WATER IN PLAY ON...	5 HOLES
OVERALL STRATEGY	DONT GET GREEDY OFF THE TEE... YOU DON'T WANT TO END UP IN THE DESERT.
CART REQUIRED?	No
PRACTICE FACILITIES?	DRIVING RANGE PUTTING GREEN CHIPPING GREEN
COURSE IS OPEN...	YES
OVERSEEDING	OCTOBER FOR 2 WEEKS.
RESTAURANT?	COFFEE SHOP. BREAKFAST AND LUNCH.
ACCOMMODATIONS?	No
DON'T FORGET YOUR..	ROCK IRON
COURSE DESIGNER	WILLIAM BEIL (ALSO DESIGNED TOREY PINES IN SAN DIEGO)
# OF ROUNDS ANNUALLY	98,000
DIRECTIONS	1 MILE SOUTH OF MCDOWELL ON 52ND ST. AND MORELAND. TURN LEFT AT MORELAND.

COURSE LAYOUT

HOLE	1	2	3	4	5	6	7	8	9	10	11	12	13	14	15	16	17	18
CHAMP	552	368	458	215	390	420	417	198	517	520	187	353	408	396	555	444	227	443
MENS	500	350	430	167	365	405	386	166	480	510	152	338	387	373	530	418	213	420
LADIES	480	335	363	146	331	345	367	151	470	491	121	315	351	317	484	338	186	346
PAR	5	4	4	3	4	4	4	3	5	5	3	4	4	4	5	4	3	4
M.HCP	15	13	1	9	7	5	3	11	17	18	14	16	6	10	12	2	8	4
L.HCP	7	13	3	17	11	9	1	15	5	2	18	14	6	12	4	10	16	8

PARADISE VALLEY PARK G.C.

PUBLIC   18 HOLES

3505 E. Union Hills Dr.   Phoenix, AZ 85032   *602-992-7190*

DESERT ○   TRADITIONAL ●   LINKS ○

TERRAIN	TREES	WATER

GREENS *Bermuda*   **COURSE FAVORS A...** *Mix*

FAIRWAYS *Bermuda*   **WIDTH OF FAIRWAYS** *Forgiving*

BUNKERS *Regular*   **AMT. OF BUNKERS** *Average*

PAR	YARDS	RATING	SLOPE	1992 GREEN FEES $	
61	3994	N/A	N/A	HIGH	$15
61	3794	57.0	79	LOW	$10
61	3499	57.9	85	SPECIALS	Call

THE COURSE COMMENTARY

This 18 hole executive course has a new back 9. Leave your driver at home. Lighted driving range.

TOUGHEST HOLE	THE 339 PAR-4 10TH HOLE IS STRAIGHTAWAY WITH A POND TO THE RIGHT OF THE GREEN.
BIRDIE HOLE	THE 99 YARD PAR-3 8TH HOLE. GRAB YOUR WEDGE AND SHOOT FOR THE PIN.
WATER IN PLAY ON...	2 HOLES
OVERALL STRATEGY	HIT LONG IRONS OFF THE TEE FOR SHORT PITCHES TO THE GREEN.
CART REQUIRED?	NO
PRACTICE FACILITIES?	DRIVING RANGE PUTTING GREEN CHIPPING GREEN
COURSE IS OPEN...	YES
OVERSEEDING	OCTOBER. TEES AND GREENS.
RESTAURANT?	COFFEE SHOP
ACCOMMODATIONS?	NO
DON'T FORGET YOUR..	ROCK IRON AND 1 IRON
COURSE DESIGNER	N/A
# OF ROUNDS ANNUALLY	N/A
DIRECTIONS	SOUTHEAST CORNER OF 32ND ST. AND UNION HILLS. ENTRANCE IS HALF MILE EAST ON UNION HILLS OFF 32ND ST.

COURSE LAYOUT

HOLE	1	2	3	4	5	6	7	8	9	10	11	12	13	14	15	16	17	18
CHAMP	336	187	155	132	157	313	159	99	477	339	175	170	188	298	158	215	151	327
MENS	330	157	149	126	131	260	146	99	445	333	169	164	182	292	110	209	145	321
LADIES	315	147	135	117	117	245	121	90	421	318	154	151	160	275	105	192	118	294
PAR	4	3	3	3	3	4	3	3	5	4	3	3	3	4	3	3	3	4
M.HCP	4	8	10	14	16	6	12	18	2	1	11	13	9	5	17	7	15	3
L.HCP	4	8	10	14	16	6	12	18	2	1	11	13	9	5	17	7	15	3

PAVILLION LAKES G.C.

PUBLIC   18 HOLES

7331 N. Pima Rd. Scottsdale, AZ 85258   602-948-3370

DESERT ○   TRADITIONAL ●   LINKS ○

TERRAIN	TREES	WATER

GREENS *Bermuda*   **COURSE FAVORS A...** *Draw*

FAIRWAYS *Bermuda*   **WIDTH OF FAIRWAYS** *Forgiving*

BUNKERS *Regular*   **AMT. OF BUNKERS** *Average*

PAR	YARDS	RATING	SLOPE	1992 GREEN FEES $
70	6477	70.3	115	**HIGH** $47
70	6192	67.1	106	**LOW** $42
70	5128	67.7	107	**SPECIALS** Afternoon rates

THE COURSE COMMENTARY

This is the newly re-designed "Pima Country Club" with a new name, new ownership, and a much nicer facility than in the past. 800 trees, 3 lakes and a creek are new. It is the site of the 1993 Phoenix Open Qualifier. It opened November 1992.

TOUGHEST HOLE THE 463 YARD PAR-4 5TH HOLE IS A LONG NARROW DOGLEG RIGHT. HIT YOUR TEE SHOT TO THE MIDDLE-RIGHT SIDE.

BIRDIE HOLE THE 476 YARD PAR-5 9TH HOLE IS STRAIGHT AND WIDE. A PERFECT LONG IRON TO THE GREEN SPELLS EAGLE.

WATER IN PLAY ON... 8 HOLES

OVERALL STRATEGY 11 OUT 12 HOLES (EXCLUDING THE PAR-3'S) FAVOR A DRAW.

CART REQUIRED? YES

PRACTICE FACILITIES? DRIVING RANGE   PUTTING GREEN

COURSE IS OPEN... YES

OVERSEEDING OCTOBER FOR 3 WEEKS. INCLUDES EVERYTHING.

RESTAURANT? A FOOD SERVICE WITH SOFT DRINKS, HOT DOGS, CHIPS ECT...

ACCOMMODATIONS? RAMADA INN ACROSS THE STREET.

DON'T FORGET YOUR.. 3-WOOD, SPOON, AND 1 IRON.

COURSE DESIGNER N/A

 # OF ROUNDS ANNUALLY OPENED NOV. 1992

DIRECTIONS ON PIMA RD. JUST NORTH OF INDIAN BEND RD. LOCATED NORTH OF THE SCOTTSDALE PAVILIONS SHOPPING COMPLEX.

COURSE LAYOUT

HOLE	1	2	3	4	5	6	7	8	9	10	11	12	13	14	15	16	17	18
CHAMP	401	155	368	184	463	479	195	424	476	426	170	378	187	545	444	493	254	435
MENS	391	135	335	145	451	474	167	399	467	398	155	351	177	535	425	465	224	421
LADIES	323	76	296	96	388	379	157	299	408	325	69	327	149	502	342	419	133	349
PAR	4	3	4	3	4	5	3	4	5	4	3	4	3	5	4	5	3	4
M.HCP	11	17	15	5	1	7	13	3	9	12	14	16	10	6	2	4	18	8
L.HCP	11	17	15	5	1	7	13	3	9	12	14	16	10	6	2	4	18	8

PEPPERWOOD G.C.

PUBLIC   9 HOLES

647 W. Baseline Rd. Tempe, AZ 85283   *602-831-9457*

DESERT ◯   TRADITIONAL ●   LINKS ◯

TERRAIN	TREES	WATER

GREENS *Bermuda*   **COURSE FAVORS A...** *Draw*

FAIRWAYS *Bermuda*   **WIDTH OF FAIRWAYS** *Normal*

BUNKERS *Regular*   **AMT. OF BUNKERS** *Average*

PAR	YARDS	RATING	SLOPE	1992 GREEN FEES $
N/A	N/A	N/A	N/A	**HIGH** $9
31	2010	57.0	80	**LOW**
31	1685	56.5	79	**SPECIALS** *None*

THE COURSE COMMENTARY

This short executive course is great for seniors and beginners.

TOUGHEST HOLE	THE 330 YARD PAR-4 5TH HOLE IS A DOGLEG LEFT. STAY RIGHT OFF THE TEE TO HAVE A CLEAR SHOT TO THE GREEN.
BIRDIE HOLE	THE 110 YARD PAR-3 4TH HOLE PLAYS TO A LARGE UNGUARDED GREEN.
WATER IN PLAY ON...	5 HOLES
OVERALL STRATEGY	KEEP IT IN THE FAIRWAY OFF THE TEE ON THE FOUR PAR-4'S.
CART REQUIRED?	NO
PRACTICE FACILITIES?	N/A
COURSE IS OPEN...	YES
OVERSEEDING	N/A
RESTAURANT?	NO
ACCOMMODATIONS?	NO
DON'T FORGET YOUR..	3 WOOD
COURSE DESIGNER	N/A
# OF ROUNDS ANNUALLY	N/A
DIRECTIONS	A HALF MILE WEST OF MILL AVE. ON BASELINE RD.

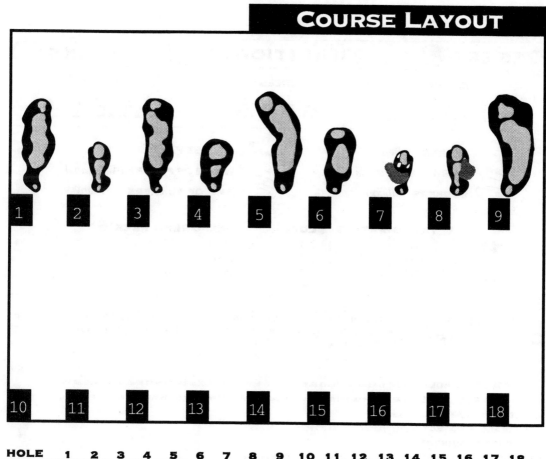

COURSE LAYOUT

HOLE	1	2	3	4	5	6	7	8	9	10	11	12	13	14	15	16	17	18
CHAMP	310	130	290	110	330	140	115	165	280									
MENS	325	150	305	125	340	155	125	185	300									
LADIES	295	115	275	95	320	125	90	105	265									
PAR	4	3	4	3	4	3	3	3	4									
M.HCP	2	8	4	9	1	7	6	3	5									
L.HCP	2	8	4	9	1	7	6	3	5									

149

PHOENICIAN G.C.

6000 E. Camelback Rd. Scottsdale, AZ 85251

602-423-2449

DESERT ●   TRADITIONAL ○   LINKS ○

TERRAIN	TREES	WATER

GREENS *Bent*	**COURSE FAVORS A...** *Mix*
FAIRWAYS *Bermuda*	**WIDTH OF FAIRWAYS** *Normal*
BUNKERS *Silicon*	**AMT. OF BUNKERS** *Many*

PAR	YARDS	RATING	SLOPE
71	6487	71.2	134
71	6033	68.7	128
71	5058	68.2	122

1992 GREEN FEES $

HIGH	$110
LOW	$70
SPECIALS	N/A

THE COURSE COMMENTARY

One of the premier golf resorts in the country. The front nine is very tropical with lush fairways and the back nine bends around Camelback Mountain in the desert. The signature hole is the 180 yard par-3 13th with a 100 foot drop to the green.

TOUGHEST HOLE	THE 591 YARD PAR-5 14TH IS SURROUNDED BY DESERT. THREE ISLANDS OF GRASS MAKE UP THE DOGLEG RIGHT.
BIRDIE HOLE	THE 487 YARD PAR-5 16TH HOLE IS THE COURSES SHORTEST PAR-5. IT COMES STRAIGHT OFF THE MOUNTAIN.
WATER IN PLAY ON...	9 HOLES
OVERALL STRATEGY	THIS IS "TARGET GOLF" AT ITS BEST.
CART REQUIRED?	YES
PRACTICE FACILITIES?	DRIVING RANGE PUTTING GREEN CHIPPING GREEN
COURSE IS OPEN...	YES
OVERSEEDING	SEPTEMBER FOR 1 WEEK. TEES AND FAIRWAYS.
RESTAURANT?	RESTAURANT AND BAR. "WINDOWS ON THE GREEN"
ACCOMMODATIONS?	THE PHOENICIAN, A 580 ROOM LUXURY RESORT IS ON PROPERTY.
DON'T FORGET YOUR..	CAMERA
COURSE DESIGNER	HOMER FLINT
# OF ROUNDS ANNUALLY	45,000
DIRECTIONS	NORTH OF CAMELBACK RD. ON 60TH ST.

HOLE	1	2	3	4	5	6	7	8	9	10	11	12	13	14	15	16	17	18
CHAMP	421	518	211	419	218	358	396	192	358	415	505	446	180	591	115	487	132	525
MENS	393	489	177	377	182	335	371	164	335	390	490	421	168	550	105	480	114	492
LADIES	352	451	122	325	125	312	304	128	309	375	442	355	114	409	75	412	70	378
PAR	4	5	3	4	3	4	4	3	4	4	5	4	4	5	3	5	3	5
M.HCP	7	1	13	3	15	11	5	17	9	12	6	8	14	2	18	10	16	4
L.HCP	7	1	13	3	15	11	5	17	9	12	6	8	14	2	18	10	16	4

POINTE HILTON G.C. AT LOOKOUT MTN.

PUBLIC   18 HOLES

11111 N. 7th St. Phoenix, AZ 85020   602-866-6356

DESERT ●   TRADITIONAL ○   LINKS ○

TERRAIN	TREES	WATER

GREENS Bent   **COURSE FAVORS A...** Fade

FAIRWAYS Bermuda   **WIDTH OF FAIRWAYS** Tight

BUNKERS Silicon   **AMT. OF BUNKERS** Many

PAR	YARDS	RATING	SLOPE	1992 GREEN FEES $	
72	6617	71.7	131	HIGH	$98
72	5834	69.1	126	LOW	$37
72	4552	65.3	113	SPECIALS	Varies

THE COURSE COMMENTARY

Home of the M.O.N.Y. Senior PGA Tour "MONY Arizona Classic." Located in the Phoenix Mountain Preserve, this course is beautiful to look at and requires almost pinpoint accuracy throughout the course. 10 yards in the wrong direction spells trouble.

TOUGHEST HOLE THE 419 YARD PAR-4 10TH HOLE COMES STRAIGHT DOWN OFF THE MOUNTAIN. THE SCARIEST TEE SHOT OF YOUR LIFE.

BIRDIE HOLE THE 492 YARD PAR-5 15TH HOLE HAS WATER TO THE LEFT BUT GOOD SHOTS TAKE IT OUT OF PLAY.

WATER IN PLAY ON... 4 HOLES

OVERALL STRATEGY THIS IS A DIFFICULT "TARGET STYLE" LAYOUT AND REQUIRES YOU TO REALLY THINK ON EVERY SHOT.

CART REQUIRED? YES

PRACTICE FACILITIES? DRIVING RANGE   PUTTING GREEN   CHIPPING GREEN

COURSE IS OPEN... YES

OVERSEEDING OCTOBER FOR 3 WEEKS. TEES AND FAIRWAYS.

RESTAURANT? THE POINTE IN TYME RESTAURANT.

ACCOMMODATIONS? THE POINTE HILTON RESORT IS ON PROPERTY AND BOASTS OVER 600 ROOMS AND THREE THEME RESTAURANTS.

DON'T FORGET YOUR.. ROCK IRON

COURSE DESIGNER BILL JOHNSTON & FOREST RICHARDSON

 # OF ROUNDS ANNUALLY 42,000

DIRECTIONS A HALF MILE SOUTH OF THUNDERBIRD RD. ON 7TH ST.

COURSE LAYOUT

HOLE	1	2	3	4	5	6	7	8	9	10	11	12	13	14	15	16	17	18
CHAMP	361	562	193	461	504	248	527	355	128	419	185	409	347	344	492	182	388	512
MENS	337	487	162	365	464	190	458	321	105	339	146	355	313	327	456	149	369	491
LADIES	310	400	117	304	400	132	386	209	100	278	108	258	230	205	326	96	310	383
PAR	4	5	3	4	5	3	5	4	3	4	3	4	4	4	5	3	4	5
M.HCP	3	11	17	1	7	13	5	9	15	8	18	2	6	10	14	16	4	12
L.HCP	9	3	15	7	1	13	5	11	17	14	16	6	10	12	4	18	8	2

POINTE HILTON G.C. ON SOUTH MTN.

PUBLIC / 18 HOLES

7777 S. Pointe Pkwy   Phoenix, AZ 85044   *602-438-1413*

DESERT ● TRADITIONAL ○ LINKS ○

TERRAIN	TREES	WATER

GREENS	*Bermuda*	COURSE FAVORS A...	*Draw*	
FAIRWAYS	*Bermuda*	WIDTH OF FAIRWAYS	*Tight*	
BUNKERS	*Regular*	AMT. OF BUNKERS	*Minimal*	

PAR	YARDS	RATING	SLOPE	1992 GREEN FEES $	
70	6003	68.9	115	HIGH	*$72*
70	5800	66.5	100	LOW	*$32*
70	5600	66.2	107	SPECIALS	*Seasonal rates*

THE COURSE COMMENTARY

This course is located on South Mountain offering some of the best views of the "Valley of the Sun" in Arizona. A high class facility and scenic layout make for an enjoyable round of golf.

TOUGHEST HOLE	THE 210 YARD PAR-3 8TH HOLE PLAYS INTO THE WIND, IS SURROUNDED BY WATER, AND HAS A DEEP SWALE IN THE GREEN.
BIRDIE HOLE	THE 461 YARD PAR-5 13TH IS A REACHABLE DOGLEG LEFT WITH AN ELEVATED GREEN OF 20 FEET.
WATER IN PLAY ON...	6 HOLES
OVERALL STRATEGY	BECAUSE THE BACK NINE IS SHORT AND NARROW YOU'LL WANT TO USE IRONS OFF THE TEE.
CART REQUIRED?	YES
PRACTICE FACILITIES?	PUTTING GREEN
COURSE IS OPEN...	YES
OVERSEEDING	OCTOBER FOR 2 WEEKS. INCLUDES EVERYTHING.
RESTAURANT?	FULL SERVICE RESTAURANT, BEVERAGE CART SERVICE
ACCOMMODATIONS?	THE POINTE HILTON IS ON PROPERTY.
DON'T FORGET YOUR..	ROCK IRON & CAMERA
COURSE DESIGNER	FOREST RICHARDSON
# OF ROUNDS ANNUALLY	37,000
DIRECTIONS	TAKE I-10 TO THE BASELINE EXIT, GO WEST. YOU WILL IMMEDIATELY SEE THE POINTE HILTON ON THE SOUTH SIDE. TURN LEFT AT THE POINTE PKWY (THE LIGHT). FOLLOW THE SIGNS.

COURSE LAYOUT

HOLE	1	2	3	4	5	6	7	8	9	10	11	12	13	14	15	16	17	18
CHAMP	343	170	529	371	161	553	379	208	380	374	535	132	461	157	395	275	280	230
MENS	300	145	474	308	121	467	345	154	331	307	474	107	412	120	317	202	230	185
LADIES	251	145	444	268	104	436	293	125	262	229	451	93	388	82	289	202	198	150
PAR	4	3	5	4	3	5	4	3	4	4	5	3	5	3	4	4	4	3
M.HCP	11	15	1	7	17	3	9	13	5	6	4	18	8	12	2	14	10	16
L.HCP	17	15	3	11	13	1	5	7	9	12	4	18	2	10	6	14	8	16

PUEBLO EL MIRAGE C.C.

SEMI PRIVATE 18 HOLES

11201 N. El Mirage Rd. El Mirage, AZ 85335   602-583-0425

DESERT ●   **TRADITIONAL** ○   **LINKS** ○

TERRAIN	TREES	WATER

GREENS Bermuda	**COURSE FAVORS A...** Draw	
FAIRWAYS Bermuda	**WIDTH OF FAIRWAYS** Normal	
BUNKERS Regular	**AMT. OF BUNKERS** Many	

	PAR	YARDS	RATING	SLOPE	1992 GREEN FEES $	
★	72	6521	70.0	119	**HIGH**	$20
	72	6125	68.1	114	**LOW**	$20
	72	5563	71.0	117	**SPECIALS**	$9 after 2pm to walk

THE COURSE COMMENTARY This could be the best kept secret on the west side of Phoenix. One of the best rounds of golf for the money.

TOUGHEST HOLE THE 423 YARD PAR-4 5TH HOLE IS LONG AND HAS A WELL PLACED FAIRWAY BUNKER AND TOUGH GREENSIDE BUNKERS.

BIRDIE HOLE THE 507 YARD PAR-5 9TH IS A SHORT PAR-5 AND IS REACHABLE IN TWO.

WATER IN PLAY ON... 12 HOLES

OVERALL STRATEGY PLACEMENT OF YOUR TEE SHOT IS CRITICAL TO SURVIVAL ON THIS COURSE.

CART REQUIRED? NO

PRACTICE FACILITIES? DRIVING RANGE   PUTTING GREEN   CHIPPING GREEN

COURSE IS OPEN... YES

OVERSEEDING OCTOBER FOR 3 WEEKS. INCLUDES EVERYTHING

RESTAURANT? FULL SERVICE RESTAURANT AND SNACK BAR.

ACCOMMODATIONS? ON PROPERTY

DON'T FORGET YOUR.. SUN TAN LOTION

COURSE DESIGNER FUZZY ZOELLER

 # OF ROUNDS ANNUALLY 65,000

DIRECTIONS 2 MILES NORTH OF OLIVE & EL MIRAGE RD. (123RD AVE)

COURSE LAYOUT

HOLE	1	2	3	4	5	6	7	8	9	10	11	12	13	14	15	16	17	18
CHAMP	377	492	118	390	423	405	148	324	507	389	535	144	386	383	409	173	534	384
MENS	362	481	103	366	402	376	135	308	482	364	522	119	366	353	379	148	509	350
LADIES	327	460	85	338	359	323	108	294	447	340	491	89	338	319	341	115	472	317
PAR	4	5	3	4	4	4	3	4	5	4	5	3	4	4	4	3	5	4
M.HCP	10	2	16	12	4	6	18	14	8	5	3	15	9	11	7	17	1	13
L.HCP	10	2	16	12	6	4	18	14	8	5	3	17	9	11	7	15	1	1

QUEEN VALLEY G.C.

SEMI PRIVATE 18 HOLES

600 N. Fairway Dr. Queen Valley, AZ 85219

602-463-2214

DESERT ● TRADITIONAL ○ LINKS ○

TERRAIN	TREES	WATER

GREENS *Bermuda*

FAIRWAYS *Bermuda*

BUNKERS *Other*

COURSE FAVORS A... *Mix*

WIDTH OF FAIRWAYS *Normal*

AMT. OF BUNKERS *Average*

	PAR	YARDS	RATING	SLOPE	1992 GREEN FEES $	
★	N/A	N/A	N/A	N/A	HIGH	$30
	66	4482	61.5	94	LOW	$12
	69	4136	63.4	101	SPECIALS	Call

THE COURSE COMMENTARY

This short 18 hole layout is cut into the eastern hills of Queen Valley. This is a great course for seniors. There are no bunkers.

TOUGHEST HOLE THE 377 YARD PAR-5 16TH HOLE IS A TOUGH DOGLEG RIGHT THROUGH THE HILLS.

BIRDIE HOLE THE 144 YARD PAR-3 4TH HOLE PLAYS TO A LARGE GREEN.

WATER IN PLAY ON... 6 HOLES

OVERALL STRATEGY STAY IN THE FAIRWAY OFF THE TEE OR THE DESERT WILL EAT YOU UP.

CART REQUIRED? NO

PRACTICE FACILITIES? N/A

COURSE IS OPEN... YES

OVERSEEDING OCTOBER FOR 2 WEEKS. INCLUDES EVERYTHING.

RESTAURANT? COFFEE SHOP

ACCOMMODATIONS? NO

DON'T FORGET YOUR.. ROCK IRON

COURSE DESIGNER N/A

 # OF ROUNDS ANNUALLY 44,000

DIRECTIONS 20 MILES EAST OF APACHE JUNCTION ON US 60, TAKE THE QUEEN VALLEY EXIT, GO 4 MILES NORTH.

COURSE LAYOUT

HOLE	1	2	3	4	5	6	7	8	9	10	11	12	13	14	15	16	17	18
CHAMP																		
MENS	316	403	285	144	195	251	309	146	182	91	253	426	143	260	352	377	203	146
LADIES	252	403	211	144	195	231	309	146	182	91	233	410	143	260	290	377	153	146
PAR	4	4	4	3	3	4	4	3	3	3	4	5	3	4	4	5	3	3
M.HCP	10	2	4	18	12	8	6	16	14	17	7	3	13	11	9	1	5	15
L.HCP	10	2	12	14	18	8	4	16	6	17	11	3	5	9	13	7	1	15

RANCHO DEL RAY G.C.

PUBLIC   18 HOLES

21515 Rancho del Ray Blvd.   Queen Creek, AZ 85242

602-987-3633

DESERT ○   **TRADITIONAL** ●   **LINKS** ○

TERRAIN	TREES	WATER

GREENS *Bermuda*	**COURSE FAVORS A...** *Mix*
FAIRWAYS *Bermuda*	**WIDTH OF FAIRWAYS** *Normal*
BUNKERS *Regular*	**AMT. OF BUNKERS** *Average*

PAR	YARDS	RATING	SLOPE	1992 GREEN FEES **$**	
N/A	N/A	N/A	N/A	HIGH	*$25*
71	5840	67.5	N/A	LOW	
71	5509	N/A	N/A	SPECIALS	*None*

THE COURSE COMMENTARY   This is one of Arizona's hidden gem's. Don't be fooled by the shorter layout; this is a challenging and well maintained course.

TOUGHEST HOLE	THE 404 YARD PAR-4 18TH HOLE IS A TOUGH, LONG DOGLEG RIGHT.
BIRDIE HOLE	THE 242 YARD PAR-4 15TH HOLE IS SHORT AND PLAYS TO A LARGE GREEN.
WATER IN PLAY ON...	4 HOLES
OVERALL STRATEGY	A LONG TEE SHOT WILL HELP YOU HIT SHORT IRONS ALL DAY.
CART REQUIRED?	No
PRACTICE FACILITIES?	DRIVING RANGE PUTTING GREEN
COURSE IS OPEN...	YES
OVERSEEDING	OCTOBER FOR 2 WEEKS. INCLUDES EVERYTHING.
RESTAURANT?	YES
ACCOMMODATIONS?	No
DON'T FORGET YOUR..	FAVORITE DRIVER
COURSE DESIGNER	N/A
# OF ROUNDS ANNUALLY	N/A
DIRECTIONS	1 MILE SOUTHEAST OF ELSWORTH RD. ON RITTENHOUSE RD.

HOLE	1	2	3	4	5	6	7	8	9	10	11	12	13	14	15	16	17	18
CHAMP																		
MENS	346	200	379	282	378	445	181	341	285	335	332	357	471	390	242	307	165	404
LADIES	327	185	357	269	364	430	165	329	267	315	310	329	452	368	229	283	143	387
PAR	4	3	4	4	4	5	3	4	4	4	4	4	5	4	4	4	3	4
M.HCP	6	3	4	12	7	17	10	8	15	9	11	15	13	2	18	16	14	1
L.HCP	7	2	6	15	5	9	13	10	16	12	11	8	4	3	17	14	18	1

RANDOLPH PARK G.C. - NORTH

PUBLIC   18 HOLES

600 S. Alveron Wy. Tucson, AZ 85711   *602-791-4336*

DESERT ○   TRADITIONAL ●   LINKS ○

TERRAIN	TREES	WATER

GREENS	Bermuda	COURSE FAVORS A...	Mix
FAIRWAYS	Bermuda	WIDTH OF FAIRWAYS	Normal
BUNKERS	Regular	AMT. OF BUNKERS	Many

PAR	YARDS	RATING	SLOPE	1992 GREEN FEES
72	6902	72.5	128	HIGH $20
72	6436	70.0	121	LOW $16
73	5972	73.7	124	SPECIALS $6 after 4pm

THE COURSE COMMENTARY

This course has hosted tournaments on the PGA Tour, the LPGA Tour, and the Senior PGA Tour.

TOUGHEST HOLE THE 440 YARD PAR-4 5TH HOLE IS LONG AND STRAIGHT. IF YOU MISS THE GREEN, MISS IT LEFT.

BIRDIE HOLE THE 480 YARD PAR-5 13TH HOLE IS A DOGLEG LEFT. HIT YOUR TEE SHOT LEFT OF THE FAIRWAY BUNKERS.

WATER IN PLAY ON... 6 HOLES

OVERALL STRATEGY HIT YOUR MIDDLE IRONS WELL.

CART REQUIRED? NO

PRACTICE FACILITIES? DRIVING RANGE   PUTTING GREEN   CHIPPING GREEN

COURSE IS OPEN... YES

OVERSEEDING SEPT./OCT. FOR 4 WEEKS. INCLUDES EVERYTHING.

RESTAURANT? YES

ACCOMMODATIONS? DOUBLETREE ACROSS THE STREET.

DON'T FORGET YOUR.. L-WEDGE

COURSE DESIGNER BILL BELL

 # OF ROUNDS ANNUALLY 200,000

DIRECTIONS 22ND ST. EAST TO ALVERON, THEN NORTH 1 MILE.

COURSE LAYOUT

HOLE	1	2	3	4	5	6	7	8	9	10	11	12	13	14	15	16	17	18
CHAMP	365	415	569	429	440	136	356	202	469	423	197	388	480	432	193	574	360	474
MENS	354	337	502	411	412	126	342	191	452	411	187	369	471	382	149	560	352	428
LADIES	341	326	474	375	407	111	320	144	451	351	177	363	467	375	131	478	349	332
PAR	4	4	5	4	4	3	4	3	5	4	3	5	5	4	3	5	4	4
M.HCP	15	17	9	3	1	13	5	7	11	6	12	10	18	8	14	2	16	4
L.HCP	10	8	6	2	14	16	12	18	4	7	15	9	11	5	17	1	13	3

RANDOLPH PARK G.C. - SOUTH

PUBLIC   18 HOLES

600 S. Alveron Wy. Tucson, AZ 85711   602-791-4336

DESERT ○   TRADITIONAL ●   LINKS ○

TERRAIN	TREES	WATER

GREENS	Bermuda	COURSE FAVORS A...	Mix
FAIRWAYS	Bermuda	WIDTH OF FAIRWAYS	Forgiving
BUNKERS	Regular	AMT. OF BUNKERS	Average

PAR	YARDS	RATING	SLOPE	1992 GREEN FEES $
70	6229	68.1	101	HIGH $20
70	5939	66.5	99	LOW $16
72	5568	69.6	108	SPECIALS $6 after 4pm

THE COURSE COMMENTARY

The South course is quite trouble-free. The fairways are wide and tree lined with little or no rough and only 2 lakes.

TOUGHEST HOLE	THE 438 YARD PAR-4 8TH HOLE IS A SLIGHT DOGLEG LEFT. HIT YOUR TEE SHOT LONG AND LEFT.
BIRDIE HOLE	THE 163 YARD PAR-3 17TH HOLE HAS A LOT OF ROOM FOR ERROR IF YOUR TEE SHOT MISSES THE GREEN.
WATER IN PLAY ON...	2 HOLES
OVERALL STRATEGY	HIT YOUR DRIVER LONG AND KEEP IT IN THE FAIRWAY.
CART REQUIRED?	NO
PRACTICE FACILITIES?	DRIVING RANGE PUTTING GREEN CHIPPING GREEN
COURSE IS OPEN...	YES
OVERSEEDING	SEPT./OCT. FOR 4 WEEKS. INCLUDES EVERYTHING.
RESTAURANT?	YES
ACCOMMODATIONS?	DOUBLETREE ACROSS THE STREET.
DON'T FORGET YOUR..	L-WEDGE
COURSE DESIGNER	BILL BELL
# OF ROUNDS ANNUALLY	200,000
DIRECTIONS	22ND ST. EAST TO ALVERON, THEN NORTH 1 MILE.

COURSE LAYOUT

HOLE	1	2	3	4	5	6	7	8	9	10	11	12	13	14	15	16	17	18
CHAMP	372	174	545	296	189	495	397	438	197	428	209	405	498	358	311	321	163	433
MENS	352	154	525	286	172	480	375	426	178	420	196	395	484	343	299	304	150	400
LADIES	339	144	439	277	158	475	366	407	153	406	169	380	470	322	293	264	136	370
PAR	4	3	5	4	3	5	4	4	3	4	3	4	5	4	4	4	3	4
M.HCP	5	15	7	17	13	9	3	1	11	2	6	8	14	10	12	16	18	4
L.HCP	9	17	3	11	13	1	7	5	15	4	16	6	2	10	12	14	18	8

RED MOUNTAIN RANCH C.C.

SEMI PRIVATE 18 HOLES

6425 E. Teton Mesa AZ 85205

602-985-0285

DESERT ● **TRADITIONAL** ○ **LINKS** ○

TERRAIN	TREES	WATER

GREENS *Bent*	**COURSE FAVORS A...** *Mix*	
FAIRWAYS *Bermuda*	**WIDTH OF FAIRWAYS** *Tight*	
BUNKERS *Regular*	**AMT. OF BUNKERS** *Many*	

PAR	YARDS	RATING	SLOPE
72	6797	74.1	135
72	6112	69.7	123
72	4982	65.1	116

1992 GREEN FEES $

HIGH *$99*
LOW
SPECIALS *$19 afetr 1pm (call for details)*

THE COURSE COMMENTARY *This is a classic Pete Dye layout set in the northern Mesa foothills . The rolling fairways and elevated undulating greens are highlighted with exaggerated railroad ties shooting out of the edge of the sand traps. This is a thinking man's course! It's in beautiful condition.*

TOUGHEST HOLE THE 452 YARD PAR-4 3RD HOLE IS A LONG DOGLEG LEFT TO A NARROW GREEN WITH TRAPS DOWN THE LEFT SIDE.

BIRDIE HOLE THE 385 YARD PAR-4 14TH HOLE. HIT AN IRON OFF THE TEE TO AVOID DRIVING THROUGH THE FAIRWAY.

WATER IN PLAY ON... 4 HOLES

OVERALL STRATEGY PLAY SMART AND MAKE SURE YOU IN THE FAIRWAY OFF THE TEE.

CART REQUIRED? YES

PRACTICE FACILITIES? DRIVING RANGE PUTTING GREEN CHIPPING GREEN

COURSE IS OPEN... YES

OVERSEEDING OCTOBER FOR 3 WEEKS. INCLUDES EVERYTHING.

RESTAURANT? YES

ACCOMMODATIONS? NO

DON'T FORGET YOUR.. EVERYTHING

COURSE DESIGNER PETE DYE

 # OF ROUNDS ANNUALLY 40,000

DIRECTIONS 1 MILE NORTH OF THOMAS RD. ON THE BUSH HWY. TAKE THE 2ND ENTRANCE TO RED MTN. RANCH.

COURSE LAYOUT

HOLE	1	2	3	4	5	6	7	8	9	10	11	12	13	14	15	16	17	18
CHAMP	455	393	452	178	539	164	404	386	480	540	201	363	397	385	201	415	490	354
MENS	418	339	417	151	512	118	362	347	454	505	175	329	329	323	173	370	452	338
LADIES	336	264	339	123	434	83	330	248	379	446	114	253	272	294	121	293	376	277
PAR	4	4	4	3	5	3	4	4	5	5	3	4	4	4	3	4	5	4
M.HCP	3	9	1	13	5	17	7	11	15	4	10	8	6	18	14	2	12	16
L.HCP	3	9	1	13	5	17	7	15	11	4	18	16	12	6	14	2	8	10

RIO SALADO G.C.

PUBLIC   18 HOLES

1490 E. Weber   Tempe, AZ 85281   602-990-1233

DESERT ○   **TRADITIONAL** ●   **LINKS** ○

| TERRAIN | TREES | WATER |

GREENS Bermuda	**COURSE FAVORS A...** Draw
FAIRWAYS Bermuda	**WIDTH OF FAIRWAYS** Normal
BUNKERS Regular	**AMT. OF BUNKERS** Average

PAR	YARDS	RATING	SLOPE	1992 GREEN FEES **$**	
N/A	N/A	N/A	N/A	HIGH	$10
34	2536	62.3	92	LOW	$10
34	2174	61.3	90	SPECIALS	$6.50 after 1pm

THE COURSE COMMENTARY   The signature hole is the 175 yard par-3 7th hole which stretches across the Rio Salado River. Hit your tee shot over the bunker that guards the left-front side of the green.

TOUGHEST HOLE	THE 175 YARD PAR-3 7TH HOLE REQUIRES A SOFT IRON SHOT OVER A BUNKER THAT GUARDS THE LEFT-FRONT OF THE GREEN.
BIRDIE HOLE	THE 425 YARD PAR-5 5TH IS SHORT AND REACHABLE IN TWO.
WATER IN PLAY ON...	2 HOLES
OVERALL STRATEGY	GOOD IRON PLAY IS A MUST.
CART REQUIRED?	NO
PRACTICE FACILITIES?	DRIVING RANGE PUTTING GREEN CHIPPING GREEN
COURSE IS OPEN...	YES
OVERSEEDING	OCTOBER FOR 2 WEEKS. INCLUDES EVERYTHING.
RESTAURANT?	OPEN FOR BREAKFAST AND LUNCH.
ACCOMMODATIONS?	SCOTTSDALE INN NEARBY.
DON'T FORGET YOUR..	FAVORITE WEDGE
COURSE DESIGNER	MIKE MORLEY
# OF ROUNDS ANNUALLY	50,000
DIRECTIONS	TAKE THE FIRST STREET SOUTH OF BIG SURF BETWEEN CURRY & MCKELLOPS OFF HAYDEN RD.

COURSE LAYOUT

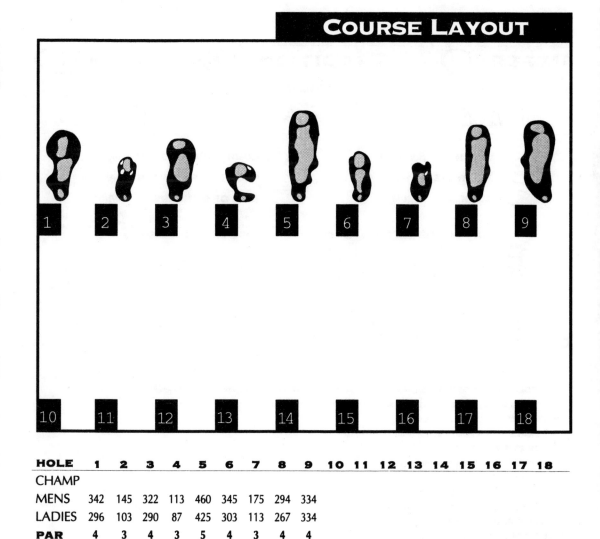

HOLE	1	2	3	4	5	6	7	8	9	10	11	12	13	14	15	16	17	18
CHAMP																		
MENS	342	145	322	113	460	345	175	294	334									
LADIES	296	103	290	87	425	303	113	267	334									
PAR	4	3	4	3	5	4	3	4	4									
M.HCP	2	8	5	9	1	3	7	6	4									
L.HCP	2	8	5	9	1	3	7	6	4									

RIO VERDE G.C. - QUAIL RUN

SEMI PRIVATE 18 HOLES

Four Peaks Blvd. Rio Verde, AZ 85263   *602-471-9420*

DESERT ⭕	TRADITIONAL ⬤	LINKS ⭕
TERRAIN	TREES	WATER

GREENS	Bermuda	COURSE FAVORS A...	Mix
FAIRWAYS	Bermuda	WIDTH OF FAIRWAYS	Forgiving
BUNKERS	Regular	AMT. OF BUNKERS	Minimal

PAR	YARDS	RATING	SLOPE	1992 GREEN FEES
72	6524	70.8	116	HIGH $75
72	6228	69.2	113	LOW $35
72	5558	70.2	113	SPECIALS Call

THE COURSE COMMENTARY

This is one of two 18 hole courses at Rio Verde G.C. recently re-designed by Gary Panks. Non-members need to make tee times well in advance in the winter months.

TOUGHEST HOLE	THE 406 YARD PAR-4 15TH HOLE. AN ACCURATE DRIVE WILL MAKE OR BREAK YOU HERE.
BIRDIE HOLE	THE 170 YARD PAR-3 17TH HOLE IS FORGIVING AROUND THE GREEN.
WATER IN PLAY ON...	4 HOLES
OVERALL STRATEGY	KEEP IT IN THE FAIRWAY.
CART REQUIRED?	YES
PRACTICE FACILITIES?	DRIVING RANGE PUTTING GREEN CHIPPING GREEN
COURSE IS OPEN...	YES
OVERSEEDING	OCTOBER FOR 3 WEEKS. GREENS AND FAIRWAYS.
RESTAURANT?	NEW CLUBHOUSE
ACCOMMODATIONS?	NO
DON'T FORGET YOUR..	EVERYTHING
COURSE DESIGNER	GARY PANKS
# OF ROUNDS ANNUALLY	N/A
DIRECTIONS	TAKE SHEA BLVD. TO FOUNTAIN HILLS BLVD. GO NORTH FOR 8 MILES.

COURSE LAYOUT

HOLE	1	2	3	4	5	6	7	8	9	10	11	12	13	14	15	16	17	18
CHAMP	384	200	435	195	394	468	389	344	459	194	383	345	373	511	406	170	391	483
MENS	368	193	412	160	376	455	376	336	441	184	347	334	357	497	395	155	377	465
LADIES	347	175	324	112	330	425	320	306	401	165	299	323	399	434	331	143	366	418
PAR	4	3	4	3	4	5	4	4	5	3	4	4	4	5	4	3	4	5
M.HCP	3	11	1	17	5	13	7	15	9	16	12	14	4	10	2	18	6	8
L.HCP	3	15	11	17	7	5	9	13	1	16	14	12	2	10	8	18	6	4

RIO VERDE G.C. - WHITE WING

SEMI PRIVATE 18 HOLES

Four Peaks Blvd. Rio Verde, AZ 85263

602-471-9420

DESERT ○   TRADITIONAL ●   LINKS ○

TERRAIN	TREES	WATER

GREENS	Bermuda	COURSE FAVORS A...	Mix
FAIRWAYS	Bermuda	WIDTH OF FAIRWAYS	Forgiving
BUNKERS	Regular	AMT. OF BUNKERS	Minimal

PAR	YARDS	RATING	SLOPE	1992 GREEN FEES $	
71	3378	70.5	123	HIGH	$75
71	3200	68.5	112	LOW	$35
71	2845	70.2	114	SPECIALS	Call

THE COURSE COMMENTARY

This is one of two 18 hole courses at Rio Verde G.C. recently re-designed by Gary Panks. This is the executive layout. Non-members need to make tee times well in advance in the winter months.

TOUGHEST HOLE	THE 435 YARD PAR-4 5TH HOLE. KEEP IT IN THE FAIRWAY OFF THE TEE.
BIRDIE HOLE	THE 205 YARD PAR-3 16TH HOLE PLAYS TO A LARGE GREEN AND IS FORGIVING WITH YOUR TEE SHOT.
WATER IN PLAY ON...	2 HOLES
OVERALL STRATEGY	KEEP IT IN THE FAIRWAY.
CART REQUIRED?	YES
PRACTICE FACILITIES?	DRIVING RANGE PUTTING GREEN CHIPPING GREEN
COURSE IS OPEN...	YES
OVERSEEDING	OCTOBER FOR 3 WEEKS. GREENS AND FAIRWAYS.
RESTAURANT?	NEW CLUBHOUSE
ACCOMMODATIONS?	No
DON'T FORGET YOUR..	EVERYTHING
COURSE DESIGNER	GARY PANKS
# OF ROUNDS ANNUALLY	N/A
DIRECTIONS	TAKE SHEA BLVD. TO FOUNTAIN HILLS BLVD. GO NORTH FOR 8 MILES.

COURSE LAYOUT

HOLE	1	2	3	4	5	6	7	8	9	10	11	12	13	14	15	16	17	18
CHAMP	364	518	220	477	435	158	383	200	323	521	363	351	435	190	414	205	533	366
MENS	342	494	200	457	389	131	363	169	308	505	350	333	405	175	384	184	511	353
LADIES	324	481	163	427	338	106	342	146	293	424	337	315	353	160	331	162	428	335
PAR	4	5	3	5	4	3	4	3	4	5	4	4	4	3	4	3	5	4
M.HCP	5	7	9	11	1	17	3	13	15	4	10	12	2	14	6	18	16	8
L.HCP	9	1	13	3	7	17	5	15	11	2	6	12	4	18	8	16	14	10

RIVERVIEW G.C. - MESA

PUBLIC 9 HOLES

2202 W. 8th St Mesa, AZ 85201   *602-644-3315*

DESERT ○   TRADITIONAL ●   LINKS ○

TERRAIN	TREES	WATER

GREENS	Bermuda	COURSE FAVORS A...	Draw
FAIRWAYS	Bermuda	WIDTH OF FAIRWAYS	Normal
BUNKERS	Regular	AMT. OF BUNKERS	Many

PAR	YARDS	RATING	SLOPE	1992 GREEN FEES	
36	3065	68.0	109	HIGH	$11
36	2790	65.6	104	LOW	$7
36	2560	67.8	108	SPECIALS	Seasonal afternoon rates

THE COURSE COMMENTARY

The signature hole is the 282 yard par-4 9th hole. Long hitters can go for the green but must carry the tee shot over water to the green. It's a big gamble but the dividend for a great shot could make for a great memory.

TOUGHEST HOLE THE 517 YARD PAR-4 4TH HOLE. THE FAIRWAY ZIGZAG'S AND WATER SURROUNDS THE GREEN.

BIRDIE HOLE THE 313 YARD PAR-4 5TH HOLE IS STRAIGHT AND THE BALL FEEDS BACK INTO FAIRWAY ON BOTH SIDES.

WATER IN PLAY ON... 0 HOLES

OVERALL STRATEGY KEEP IT STRAIGHT OFF THE TEE AND KEEP YOUR APPROACH SHOT BELOW THE HOLE.

CART REQUIRED? NO

PRACTICE FACILITIES? DRIVING RANGE   PUTTING GREEN   CHIPPING GREEN

COURSE IS OPEN... YES

OVERSEEDING OCTOBER FOR 3 WEEKS. TEES AND GREENS.

RESTAURANT? SNACKS AND SANDWICHES AVAILABLE INSIDE THE PRO SHOP.

ACCOMMODATIONS? THE SHERATON HOTEL IN MESA IS NEARBY.

DON'T FORGET YOUR.. THIRD WEDGE

COURSE DESIGNER GARY PANKS

 # OF ROUNDS ANNUALLY 75,000

DIRECTIONS LOCATED ACROSS THE PARK AT DOBSON & 8TH ST.

COURSE LAYOUT NOT AVAILABLE

HOLE	1	2	3	4	5	6	7	8	9	10	11	12	13	14	15	16	17	18
CHAMP																		
MENS																		
LADIES																		
PAR																		
M.HCP																		
L.HCP																		

ROLLING HILLS G.C.

PUBLIC   18 HOLES

1415 N. Mill Ave. Tempe, AZ 85281   602-350-5275

DESERT ○   **TRADITIONAL** ●   **LINKS** ○

TERRAIN	TREES	WATER

GREENS	Bermuda	**COURSE FAVORS A...** Draw
FAIRWAYS	Bermuda	**WIDTH OF FAIRWAYS** Normal
BUNKERS	Regular	**AMT. OF BUNKERS** Average

PAR	YARDS	RATING	SLOPE	1992 GREEN FEES $
62	3817	N/A	N/A	**HIGH** $16
62	3509	56.3	72	**LOW** $6
62	3296	57.1	89	**SPECIALS** All day fee available

THE COURSE COMMENTARY

The course is played as two separate nine hole courses. The older North Course has a minimum of rough and is more forgiving than the newer South Course which has a desert layout requiring more accuracy to elevated greens.

TOUGHEST HOLE	THE 411 YARD PAR-4 9TH HOLE ON THE SOUTH COURSE PLAYS DOWNHILL TO AN ELEVATED GREEN WITH 6 BUNKERS.
BIRDIE HOLE	THE 233 YARD PAR-4 1ST HOLE ON THE NORTH COURSE IS STRAIGHT & FLAT AND IS REACHABLE FROM THE TEE.
WATER IN PLAY ON...	0 HOLES
OVERALL STRATEGY	CLUB DOWN TO HIT THE ELEVATED GREENS.
CART REQUIRED?	NO
PRACTICE FACILITIES?	DRIVING RANGE PUTTING GREEN CHIPPING GREEN
COURSE IS OPEN...	YES
OVERSEEDING	OCTOBER FOR 3 WEEKS. INCLUDES EVERYTHING.
RESTAURANT?	FULL SERVICE RESTAURANT WITH A GREAT VIEW OVERLOOKING THE COURSE.
ACCOMMODATIONS?	HOTELS ARE PLENTIFUL WITHIN 2-3 MILES
DON'T FORGET YOUR..	PLAY FOR POSITION OFF THE TEE, NOT LENGTH.
COURSE DESIGNER	GARY PANKS
# OF ROUNDS ANNUALLY	130,000
DIRECTIONS	1 MILE NORTH OF THE MILL AVE BRIDGE ON MILL.

COURSE LAYOUT

SOUTH HILLS

| 1 | 2 | 3 | 4 | 5 | 6 | 7 | 8 | 9 |

NORTH HILLS

| 10 | 11 | 12 | 13 | 14 | 15 | 16 | 17 | 18 |

HOLE	1	2	3	4	5	6	7	8	9	10	11	12	13	14	15	16	17	18
CHAMP										300	307	275	137	190	285	153	172	411
MENS	233	164	266	113	132	118	152	138	271	369	392	250	104	163	270	136	134	304
LADIES	222	1645	255	113	126	107	152	116	259	247	277	228	85	140	248	126	127	304
PAR	4	3	4	3	3	3	3	3	4	4	4	4	3	3	4	3	3	4
M.HCP	3	5	1	7	8	6	2	9	4	3	2	5	9	6	4	8	7	1
L.HCP	3	5	1	7	8	6	2	9	4	3	2	5	9	6	4	8	7	1

SANTA RITA C.C.

SEMI PRIVATE 18 HOLES

16461 S. Houghton Rd. Tucson, AZ 85747   602-762-5620

DESERT ●   **TRADITIONAL** ○   **LINKS** ○

TERRAIN	TREES	WATER

GREENS	Bent	**COURSE FAVORS A...**	Mix
FAIRWAYS	Bermuda	**WIDTH OF FAIRWAYS**	Tight
BUNKERS	Regular	**AMT. OF BUNKERS**	Average

PAR	YARDS	RATING	SLOPE	1992 GREEN FEES $	
71	6396	69.4	115	**HIGH**	$16
71	6042	68.3	113	**LOW**	$12
72	5539	70.9	117	**SPECIALS**	$6 after 2pm

THE COURSE COMMENTARY Santa Rita sports excellent bent grass greens with beautiful views from most of the 18 hole layout. It's also a lot higher and cooler than nearby Tucson.

TOUGHEST HOLE	THE 250 YARD PAR-3 12TH HOLE IS A VERY LONG PAR-3 AND HAS TROUBLE ON BOTH SIDES.
BIRDIE HOLE	THE 471 YARD PAR-5 10TH HOLE IS STRAIGHTAWAY AND IS REACHABLE IN TWO SHOTS.
WATER IN PLAY ON...	3 HOLES
OVERALL STRATEGY	KEEP IT IN THE FAIRWAY AND OUT OF THE DESERT.
CART REQUIRED?	NO
PRACTICE FACILITIES?	DRIVING RANGE PUTTING GREEN CHIPPING GREEN
COURSE IS OPEN...	YES
OVERSEEDING	SEPTEMBER FOR 2 WEEKS. TEES AND FAIRWAYS
RESTAURANT?	FULL BAR & RESTAURANT. LUNCH SERVED EVERY DAY.
ACCOMMODATIONS?	N/A
DON'T FORGET YOUR..	ROCK IRON
COURSE DESIGNER	RED LAWRENCE
# OF ROUNDS ANNUALLY	N/A
DIRECTIONS	TAKE EXIT 275 OFF OF I-10, THEN GO SOUTH ON HOUGHTON RD. FOR 2 MILES.

COURSE LAYOUT

HOLE	1	2	3	4	5	6	7	8	9	10	11	12	13	14	15	16	17	18
CHAMP	420	193	469	413	185	512	403	401	346	471	183	250	368	198	484	409	328	363
MENS	406	166	462	395	171	499	390	392	328	454	168	231	359	190	457	328	312	334
LADIES	346	150	447	361	151	439	358	381	318	436	113	207	308	180	411	324	303	306
PAR	4	3	5	4	3	5	4	4	4	5	3	3	4	3	5	4	4	4
M.HCP	3	9	7	1	17	5	11	13	15	4	18	2	12	14	6	8	10	16
L.HCP	9	11	5	1	13	3	15	7	17	2	18	16	12	6	4	8	14	10

SCOTTSDALE C. C. - NE

PUBLIC   18 HOLES

7702 E. Shea Blvd. Scottsdale, AZ 85260   *602-951-2535*

DESERT ○   **TRADITIONAL** ●   **LINKS** ○

TERRAIN	TREES	WATER

GREENS	*Bermuda*	**COURSE FAVORS A...**	*Fade*
FAIRWAYS	*Bermuda*	**WIDTH OF FAIRWAYS**	*Normal*
BUNKERS	*Regular*	**AMT. OF BUNKERS**	*Many*

PAR	YARDS	RATING	SLOPE
71	6292	69.7	119
71	5881	67.9	115
71	5339	69.4	108

1992 GREEN FEES $

HIGH	*$75*
LOW	*$32*
SPECIALS	*Afternoon rates*

THE COURSE COMMENTARY

Arnold Palmer re-designed this course in 1984 and took advantage of the mature eucalyptus and pine trees. The course has beautiful lakes that provide both difficulty in play and a garden type look.

TOUGHEST HOLE THE 201 YARD PAR-3 8TH HOLE ON THE EAST COURSE IS A LONG CARRY OVER A LAKE TO AN ELEVATED GREEN.

BIRDIE HOLE THE 484 YARD PAR-5 6TH HOLE ON THE NORTH COURSE IS STRAIGHTAWAY WITH A DEEP NARROW GREEN.

WATER IN PLAY ON... 10 HOLES

OVERALL STRATEGY YOU NEED TO KEEP THE BALL IN THE FAIRWAY; THE ROUGH IS THICK AND CAN TAKE YOU OUT OF ANY GIVEN HOLE.

CART REQUIRED? YES

PRACTICE FACILITIES? PUTTING GREEN   CHIPPING GREEN

COURSE IS OPEN... YES

OVERSEEDING SEPT/OCT FOR 6 WEEKS. INCLUDES EVERYTHING.

RESTAURANT? FULL SERVICE RESTAURANT AND LOUNGE WITH BANQUET FACILITIES.

ACCOMMODATIONS? NUMEROUS RESORTS IN SCOTTSDALE WITHIN 10 MINUTES FROM COURSE.

DON'T FORGET YOUR.. BALL RETRIEVER

COURSE DESIGNER ARNOLD PALMER

 # OF ROUNDS ANNUALLY 70,000

DIRECTIONS HALF MILE WEST OF SCOTTSDALE RD. ON SHEA BLVD.

COURSE LAYOUT

HOLE	1	2	3	4	5	6	7	8	9	10	11	12	13	14	15	16	17	18
CHAMP	316	189	529	400	111	484	409	172	411	545	187	424	130	357	506	410	201	511
MENS	301	171	518	395	103	475	392	165	380	515	161	376	115	324	468	372	179	471
LADIES	293	134	486	367	87	413	367	140	360	438	140	353	100	305	435	350	140	431
PAR	4	3	5	4	3	5	4	3	4	5	3	4	3	4	5	4	3	5
M.HCP	6	8	2	4	9	7	1	5	3	3	7	1	9	8	4	5	6	2
L.HCP	7	8	1	5	9	3	2	6	4	3	8	2	9	7	1	4	6	5

SCOTTSDALE C.C. - NS

PUBLIC   18 HOLES

7702 E. Shea Blvd. Scottsdale, AZ 85260   602-951-2535

DESERT ○   **TRADITIONAL** ●   **LINKS** ○

TERRAIN	TREES	WATER

GREENS	Bermuda	COURSE FAVORS A...	Fade
FAIRWAYS	Bermuda	WIDTH OF FAIRWAYS	Normal
BUNKERS	Regular	AMT. OF BUNKERS	Many

PAR	YARDS	RATING	SLOPE	1992 GREEN FEES $	
70	6085	68.8	118	HIGH	$75
70	5785	67.2	115	LOW	$32
70	5101	69.0	111	SPECIALS	Afternoon rates

THE COURSE COMMENTARY Arnold Palmer re-designed this course in 1984 and took advantage of the mature eucalyptus and pine trees. The course has beautiful lakes that provide both difficulty in play and a garden type look.

TOUGHEST HOLE THE 402 YARD PAR-4 4TH HOLE ON THE SOUTH COURSE IS AN EXTREME DOGLEG LEFT WITH WATER GUARDING THE GREEN.

BIRDIE HOLE THE 111 YARD PAR-3 5TH HOLE ON THE NORTH COURSE. BUNKERS ALL AROUND SHOULDN'T COME INTO PLAY.

WATER IN PLAY ON... 7 HOLES

OVERALL STRATEGY YOU NEED TO KEEP THE BALL IN THE FAIRWAY; THE ROUGH IS THICK AND CAN TAKE YOU OUT OF ANY GIVEN HOLE.

CART REQUIRED? YES

PRACTICE FACILITIES? PUTTING GREEN   CHIPPING GREEN

COURSE IS OPEN... YES

OVERSEEDING SEPT/OCT FOR 6 WEEKS. INCLUDES EVERYTHING.

RESTAURANT? FULL SERVICE RESTAURANT AND LOUNGE WITH BANQUET FACILITIES.

ACCOMMODATIONS? NUMEROUS RESORTS IN SCOTTSDALE WITHIN 10 MINUTES FROM COURSE.

DON'T FORGET YOUR.. BALL RETRIEVER

COURSE DESIGNER ARNOLD PALMER

 # OF ROUNDS ANNUALLY 70,000

DIRECTIONS HALF MILE WEST OF SCOTTSDALE RD. ON SHEA BLVD.

COURSE LAYOUT

HOLE	1	2	3	4	5	6	7	8	9	10	11	12	13	14	15	16	17	18
CHAMP	316	189	529	400	111	484	409	172	411	502	175	405	402	149	364	197	524	346
MENS	301	171	518	395	103	475	392	165	380	488	154	373	376	140	361	192	476	325
LADIES	293	134	486	367	87	413	367	140	360	456	127	337	342	112	317	166	401	296
PAR	4	3	5	4	3	5	4	3	4	5	3	4	4	3	4	3	5	4
M.HCP	6	8	2	4	9	7	1	5	3	6	8	4	1	7	9	3	2	5
L.HCP	7	8	1	5	9	3	2	6	4	3	9	4	1	8	6	7	2	5

SCOTTSDALE C.C. - SE

PUBLIC   18 HOLES

7702 E. Shea Blvd. Scottsdale, AZ 85260   *602-951-2535*

DESERT ○   TRADITIONAL ●   LINKS ○

TERRAIN   **TREES**   **WATER**

GREENS	*Bermuda*	**COURSE FAVORS A...** *Fade*
FAIRWAYS	*Bermuda*	**WIDTH OF FAIRWAYS** *Normal*
BUNKERS	*Regular*	**AMT. OF BUNKERS** *Many*

PAR	YARDS	RATING	SLOPE	1992 GREEN FEES $	
71	6335	69.6	118	**HIGH**	*$75*
71	5866	67.4	114	**LOW**	*$32*
71	5246	68.8	109	**SPECIALS**	*Afternoon rates*

THE COURSE COMMENTARY

Arnold Palmer re-designed this course in 1984 and took advantage of the mature eucalyptus and pine trees. The course has beautiful lakes that provide both difficulty in play and a garden type look.

TOUGHEST HOLE	THE 402 YARD PAR-4 4TH HOLE ON THE SOUTH COURSE IS AN EXTREME DOGLEG LEFT WITH WATER GUARDING THE GREEN.
BIRDIE HOLE	THE 502 YARD PAR-5 1ST HOLE ON THE SOUTH COURSE IS STRAIGHTAWAY WITH A LARGE GREEN.
WATER IN PLAY ON...	9 HOLES
OVERALL STRATEGY	YOU NEED TO KEEP THE BALL IN THE FAIRWAY; THE ROUGH IS THICK AND CAN TAKE YOU OUT OF ANY GIVEN HOLE.
CART REQUIRED?	YES
PRACTICE FACILITIES?	PUTTING GREEN CHIPPING GREEN
COURSE IS OPEN...	YES
OVERSEEDING	SEPT/OCT FOR 6 WEEKS. INCLUDES EVERYTHING.
RESTAURANT?	FULL SERVICE RESTAURANT AND LOUNGE WITH BANQUET FACILITIES.
ACCOMMODATIONS?	NUMEROUS RESORTS IN SCOTTSDALE WITHIN 10 MINUTES FROM COURSE.
DON'T FORGET YOUR..	BALL RETRIEVER
COURSE DESIGNER	ARNOLD PALMER
# OF ROUNDS ANNUALLY	70,000
DIRECTIONS	HALF MILE WEST OF SCOTTSDALE RD. ON SHEA BLVD.

COURSE LAYOUT

HOLE	1	2	3	4	5	6	7	8	9	10	11	12	13	14	15	16	17	18
CHAMP	502	175	405	402	149	364	197	524	346	545	187	424	130	357	506	410	201	511
MENS	488	154	373	376	140	361	192	476	325	515	161	376	115	324	468	372	179	471
LADIES	456	127	337	342	112	317	166	401	296	438	140	353	100	305	435	350	140	431
PAR	5	3	4	4	3	4	3	5	4	5	3	4	3	4	5	4	3	5
M.HCP	6	8	4	1	7	9	3	2	5	3	7	1	9	8	4	5	6	2
L.HCP	3	9	4	1	8	6	7	2	5	3	8	2	9	7	1	4	6	5

SEDONA G.R.

PUBLIC   18 HOLES

7256 Highway 179 Sedona, AZ 86336   *602-284-9355*

DESERT ○   **TRADITIONAL** ●   **LINKS** ○

TERRAIN	TREES	WATER

GREENS	*Bent*	COURSE FAVORS A...	*Draw*
FAIRWAYS	*Other*	WIDTH OF FAIRWAYS	*Normal*
BUNKERS	*Regular*	AMT. OF BUNKERS	*Many*

PAR	YARDS	RATING	SLOPE	1992 GREEN FEES
71	6642	70.3	129	HIGH *$50*
71	6126	67.8	121	LOW *$40*
71	5030	67.0	109	SPECIALS *$35 - please call*

THE COURSE COMMENTARY

Wow! One of the most beautiful and challenging courses in all of the Southwest. If you don't bring your camera you will shoot yourself. This course blends wonderfully with the surrounding red rock vistas. The view at the 10th green will take your breath away.

TOUGHEST HOLE	THE 623 YARD PAR-5 5TH HOLE WILL TAKE EVERYTHING YOU'VE GOT.
BIRDIE HOLE	THE 326 YARD PAR-4 1ST HOLE IS SHORT ENOUGH TO GET YOU OFF TO A GOOD START.
WATER IN PLAY ON...	6 HOLES
OVERALL STRATEGY	NO MATTER HOW GOOD OR BAD YOUR ROUND IS, FEEL LUCKY THAT YOUR PLAYING GOLF IN SUCH BEAUTIFUL SCENERY.
CART REQUIRED?	NO
PRACTICE FACILITIES?	DRIVING RANGE PUTTING GREEN CHIPPING GREEN
COURSE IS OPEN...	YES
OVERSEEDING	NO
RESTAURANT?	GOLFERS GRILL
ACCOMMODATIONS?	NONE
DON'T FORGET YOUR..	CAMERA
COURSE DESIGNER	GARY PANKS
# OF ROUNDS ANNUALLY	35,000
DIRECTIONS	TAKE I-17 NORTH TO EXIT 298 TO HWY. 179, GO 7 MILES NORTH, GO LEFT AT THE RIDGE AT SEDONA MAIN GATE.

COURSE LAYOUT NOT AVAILABLE

HOLE	1	2	3	4	5	6	7	8	9	10	11	12	13	14	15	16	17	18
CHAMP	326	183	506	404	623	397	176	448	522	210	380	559	394	157	449	417	155	336
MENS	308	169	474	362	586	365	144	420	491	171	341	533	373	144	427	390	131	297
LADIES	240	119	398	304	486	335	111	338	412	149	284	439	284	84	341	343	95	268
PAR	4	3	5	4	5	4	3	4	5	3	4	5	4	3	4	4	3	4
M.HCP	13	17	15	9	1	7	11	5	3	10	8	4	12	16	2	6	18	14
L.HCP	13	17	15	9	1	7	11	5	3	10	8	4	12	16	2	6	18	14

SHALIMAR C.C.

PUBLIC 9 HOLES

2032 E. Golf Ave. Tempe, AZ 85282   602-838-0488

DESERT ◯   **TRADITIONAL** ●   **LINKS** ◯

TERRAIN	TREES	WATER

🚩 **GREENS** *Bermuda*   ↖ **COURSE FAVORS A...** *Mix*

🥖 **FAIRWAYS** *Bermuda*   🥖 **WIDTH OF FAIRWAYS** *Normal*

⬭ **BUNKERS** *Regular*   ⬭ **AMT. OF BUNKERS** *Minimal*

	PAR	YARDS	RATING	SLOPE	1992 GREEN FEES $	
⭐	33	2400	61.7	95	**HIGH**	*$10*
🧍	33	2100	60.0	92	**LOW**	*$5*
🧍	33	1900	64.7	93	**SPECIALS**	*None*

THE COURSE COMMENTARY

Shalimar C.C. is located in the heart of Tempe. It has a very warm mid-west feel around the clubhouse and on the course. This 9 hole course plays to two sets of tees for 18 holes.

TOUGHEST HOLE THE 223 YARD PAR-4 9TH HOLE HAS A NARROW FAIRWAY AND AN ISLAND GREEN.

BIRDIE HOLE THE 257 YARD PAR-4 3RD HOLE. HIT YOUR DRIVE OVER A WASH. PLAYS TO A LARGE GREEN.

WATER IN PLAY ON... 3 HOLES

OVERALL STRATEGY THE COURSE IS NOT LONG SO ACCURACY IS AT A PREMIUM.

CART REQUIRED? NO

PRACTICE FACILITIES? DRIVING RANGE   PUTTING GREEN   CHIPPING GREEN

COURSE IS OPEN... YES

OVERSEEDING OCTOBER FOR 3 WEEKS. INCLUDES EVERYTHING.

RESTAURANT? FULL SERVICE RESTAURANT.

ACCOMMODATIONS? NO

DON'T FORGET YOUR.. THIRD WEDGE

COURSE DESIGNER N/A

 # OF ROUNDS ANNUALLY 60,000

DIRECTIONS 1 BLOCK NORTH OF SOUTHERN OFF COUNTRY CLUB WY. BETWEEN PRICE & MCCLINTOCK.

HOLE	1	2	3	4	5	6	7	8	9	10	11	12	13	14	15	16	17	18
CHAMP	352	128	257	286	100	345	149	294	223	369	165	267	311	127	381	155	314	300
MENS	352	128	257	286	100	345	149	294	223	369	165	267	311	127	381	155	314	300
LADIES	291	99	235	275	72	292	139	276	180	352	128	257	286	100	345	149	294	223
PAR	4	3	4	4	3	4	3	4	4	4	3	4	4	3	4	3	4	4
M.HCP	2	18	10	12	16	4	14	8	6	1	17	9	11	15	3	13	7	5
L.HCP	2	18	10	12	16	4	14	8	6	1	17	9	11	15	3	13	7	5

SHERATON EL CONQUISTADOR G.C.

HOTEL GUEST PRIORITY 9 HOLES

10000 N. Oracle Rd. Tucson, AZ 85737　　　602-544-1770

DESERT ● 　　TRADITIONAL ○ 　　LINKS ○

TERRAIN	TREES	WATER

GREENS	Bermuda	**COURSE FAVORS A...**	Fade
FAIRWAYS	Bermuda	**WIDTH OF FAIRWAYS**	Tight
BUNKERS	Regular	**AMT. OF BUNKERS**	Many

PAR	YARDS	RATING	SLOPE	1992 GREEN FEES $	
34	2759	65.6	110	**HIGH**	$55
34	2552	63.7	107	**LOW**	$25
35	2322	N/A	N/A	**SPECIALS**	None

THE COURSE COMMENTARY

The 9 hole course is relatively short but very narrow. The greens are very undulated and fast. The course is very demanding even for the best golfers. The green fees listed are for playing 18 holes.

TOUGHEST HOLE	THE 529 YARD PAR-5 3RD HOLE IS UPHILL AND WELL BUNKERED. THE GREEN IS VERY UNDULATED AND FAST.
BIRDIE HOLE	THE 111 YARD PAR-3 7TH HOLE IS ALL OVER DESERT TO A WIDE OPEN GREEN.
WATER IN PLAY ON...	1 HOLES
OVERALL STRATEGY	HIT YOUR DRIVES TO THE MIDDLE OF THE FAIRWAY.
CART REQUIRED?	YES
PRACTICE FACILITIES?	PUTTING GREEN　CHIPPING GREEN
COURSE IS OPEN...	YES
OVERSEEDING	SEPT/OCT FOR 5 WEEKS. INCLUDES EVERYTHING.
RESTAURANT?	FULL SNACK BAR.
ACCOMMODATIONS?	THE SHERATON RESORT IS ON PROPERTY.
DON'T FORGET YOUR..	LONG IRONS - YOU CAN LEAVE YOUR WOODS AT HOME.
COURSE DESIGNER	JEFF HARDEN AND GREG NASH
# OF ROUNDS ANNUALLY	25,000
DIRECTIONS	GO NORTH ON ORACLE RD. FOR 4 MILES FROM INA RD. IT IS LOCATED IN THE SHERATON EL CONQUISTADOR RESORT.

HOLE	1	2	3	4	5	6	7	8	9	10	11	12	13	14	15	16	17	18
CHAMP	421	284	529	191	371	366	111	320	166	421	284	529	191	371	366	111	320	166
MENS	403	260	497	155	349	334	99	299	156	403	260	497	155	349	334	99	299	156
LADIES	386	232	491	107	334	319	84	245	124	386	232	491	107	334	319	84	245	124
PAR	4	4	5	3	4	4	3	4	3	4	4	5	3	4	4	3	4	3
M.HCP	3	13	1	9	5	7	17	11	15	4	14	2	10	6	8	18	12	16
L.HCP	3	13	1	17	5	7	15	9	11	4	14	2	18	6	8	16	10	12

SHERATON SAN MARCOS G.R.

PUBLIC   18 HOLES

1 San Marcos Pl. Chandler, AZ 85224   *602-963-3358*

DESERT ○   **TRADITIONAL** ●   **LINKS** ○

TERRAIN   **TREES**   **WATER**

GREENS *Bermuda*	**COURSE FAVORS A...** *Draw*
FAIRWAYS *Bermuda*	**WIDTH OF FAIRWAYS** *Normal*
BUNKERS *Regular*	**AMT. OF BUNKERS** *Many*

PAR	YARDS	RATING	SLOPE		1992 GREEN FEES
72	6501	70.0	117	**HIGH**	*$70*
72	6172	68.5	114	**LOW**	*$24*
72	5386	69.4	112	**SPECIALS**	*Twilight rates*

THE COURSE COMMENTARY

This course overseeds twice a year and is always in top shape. It's a beautiful course with wide fairways and a lot of mature trees.

TOUGHEST HOLE	THE 434 YARD PAR-4 4TH HOLE HAS TREES ON THE LEFT AND O.B. ON THE RIGHT.
BIRDIE HOLE	THE 490 YARD PAR-5 9TH HOLE IS SHORT WITH NO DANGER FOR A WHOPPING DRIVE.
WATER IN PLAY ON...	2 HOLES
OVERALL STRATEGY	STAY OUT OF THE TREES.
CART REQUIRED?	JAN. THRU APRIL AND FRI.-SUN. UNTIL NOON.
PRACTICE FACILITIES?	DRIVING RANGE PUTTING GREEN CHIPPING GREEN
COURSE IS OPEN...	YES
OVERSEEDING	OCTOBER FOR 2 WEEKS. INCLUDES EVERYTHING.
RESTAURANT?	YES
ACCOMMODATIONS?	THE SHERATON RESORT AND CONFERENCE CENTER IS ON PROPERTY.
DON'T FORGET YOUR..	SUN SCREEN
COURSE DESIGNER	N/A
# OF ROUNDS ANNUALLY	65,000
DIRECTIONS	1 MILE EAST OF CHANDLER BLVD., GO SOUTH ON DAKOTA FOR 1 BLOCK.

COURSE LAYOUT

HOLE	1	2	3	4	5	6	7	8	9	10	11	12	13	14	15	16	17	18
CHAMP	353	360	211	434	504	373	398	156	490	454	403	314	117	330	213	376	492	523
MENS	337	341	176	427	487	346	376	144	475	440	392	297	112	320	195	336	475	496
LADIES	324	325	165	412	410	318	308	130	378	340	359	271	95	305	123	290	448	385
PAR	4	4	3	4	5	4	4	3	5	4	4	4	3	4	3	4	5	5
M.HCP	8	12	10	2	14	6	4	18	16	1	5	15	17	13	7	11	9	3
L.HCP	2	4	12	18	16	6	8	14	10	3	1	13	15	9	17	7	5	11

SILVERBELL G.C.

PUBLIC   18 HOLES

3600 N. Silverbell Rd.   Tucson, AZ 85745   *602-791-4336*

DESERT ○   TRADITIONAL ●   LINKS ○

TERRAIN	TREES	WATER

GREENS	Bermuda	**COURSE FAVORS A...**	Mix
FAIRWAYS	Bermuda	**WIDTH OF FAIRWAYS**	Forgiving
BUNKERS	Regular	**AMT. OF BUNKERS**	Average

PAR	YARDS	RATING	SLOPE	1992 GREEN FEES $
72	6756	71.2	114	**HIGH** $18
72	6284	68.8	110	**LOW** $15
73	5751	70.3	N/A	**SPECIALS** $6 all you can play

THE COURSE COMMENTARY

The 551 yard par-5 17th hole has been voted one of the "Best 18 Holes in Southern Arizona." Home of the Tucson City Amateur.

TOUGHEST HOLE	THE 411 YARD PAR-4 16TH HOLE IS AN UPHILL DOGLEG RIGHT. YOUR DRIVE IS OVER WATER. HIT A DRAW INTO THE GREEN.
BIRDIE HOLE	THE 511 YARD PAR-5 1ST HOLE IS SHORT AND STAIGHTAWAY. HIT A FADE INTO THE GREEN.
WATER IN PLAY ON...	13 HOLES
OVERALL STRATEGY	SET YOUR APPROACH SHOT UP VERY CAREFULLY FROM THE TEE.
CART REQUIRED?	NO
PRACTICE FACILITIES?	DRIVING RANGE
COURSE IS OPEN...	YES
OVERSEEDING	OCTOBER FOR 2 WEEKS. INCLUDES EVERYTHING.
RESTAURANT?	COFFEE SHOP
ACCOMMODATIONS?	MANY HOTELS & MOTELS NEARBY.
DON'T FORGET YOUR..	THIRD WEDGE
COURSE DESIGNER	ARTHUR SNYDER
# OF ROUNDS ANNUALLY	85,000
DIRECTIONS	TAKE GRANT RD. WEST TO SILVERBELL RD., THEN GO NORTH FOR 1 MILE.

COURSE LAYOUT

HOLE	1	2	3	4	5	6	7	8	9	10	11	12	13	14	15	16	17	18
CHAMP	511	427	381	181	415	383	524	400	197	360	360	176	528	363	154	411	551	434
MENS	491	405	357	157	397	359	504	365	173	317	336	152	504	345	137	387	529	369
LADIES	463	303	331	134	380	332	469	357	130	288	293	131	471	303	120	403	500	343
PAR	5	4	4	3	4	4	5	4	3	4	4	3	5	4	3	4	5	4
M.HCP	10	2	14	12	4	18	16	6	8	17	11	13	5	9	15	3	1	7
L.HCP	4	16	10	12	6	14	8	2	18	15	7	13	5	11	17	1	3	9

STONECREEK, THE G.C.

SEMI PRIVATE 18 HOLES

4435 E. Paradise Village Pkwy. S Paradise Valley, AZ 85032

602-953-9110

DESERT ○   **TRADITIONAL** ○   **LINKS** ●

TERRAIN	TREES	WATER

GREENS	Bent	**COURSE FAVORS A...** Draw
FAIRWAYS	Bermuda	**WIDTH OF FAIRWAYS** Forgiving
BUNKERS	Regular	**AMT. OF BUNKERS** Average

PAR	YARDS	RATING	SLOPE	1992 GREEN FEES $	
71	6839	73.5	133	**HIGH**	$85
71	6280	70.2	126	**LOW**	$20
71	5098	69.2	118	**SPECIALS**	Seasonal

THE COURSE COMMENTARY

This course features a "Scottish links" style with many grass bunkers and elevated greens. A gorgeous new full service pro shop and restaurant compliment this upscale environment.

TOUGHEST HOLE	THE 389 YARD PAR-4 6TH HOLE FEATURES A LOT OF SAND, OUT-OF-BOUNDS TO THE LEFT AND A CREEK GUARDING THE PIN.
BIRDIE HOLE	THE 227 YARD PAR-3 15TH HOLE HAS A DEEP GREEN THAT FORGIVES ERRANT SHOTS.
WATER IN PLAY ON...	7 HOLES
OVERALL STRATEGY	WATCH OUT FOR THE NATURAL STONE FILLED CREEK THAT RUNS ALONG THE RIGHT SIDE OF MANY OF THE HOLES.
CART REQUIRED?	YES
PRACTICE FACILITIES?	DRIVING RANGE PUTTING GREEN CHIPPING GREEN
COURSE IS OPEN...	YES
OVERSEEDING	SEPT/OCT FOR 2 WEEKS. TEES AND GREENS.
RESTAURANT?	FULL SERVICE RESTAURANT SERVES BREAKFAST AND LUNCH.
ACCOMMODATIONS?	MANY SCOTTSDALE RESORTS NEARBY.
DON'T FORGET YOUR..	FAVORITE DRIVER
COURSE DESIGNER	ARTHUR HILLS
# OF ROUNDS ANNUALLY	55,000
DIRECTIONS	HALF MILE SOUTH OF TATUM BLVD. AND CACTUS., TURN WEST ON PARADISE PKWY.

COURSE LAYOUT

HOLE	1	2	3	4	5	6	7	8	9	10	11	12	13	14	15	16	17	18
CHAMP	364	399	181	426	186	389	548	370	410	350	402	197	548	378	227	609	419	436
MENS	340	381	165	373	156	359	529	325	379	328	377	183	513	348	166	547	397	414
LADIES	282	316	106	300	119	284	405	262	356	269	287	165	457	222	125	453	369	321
PAR	4	4	3	4	3	4	5	4	4	4	4	3	5	4	3	5	4	4
M.HCP	15	3	17	13	9	1	5	7	11	16	6	8	12	4	18	2	14	10
L.HCP	15	3	17	13	9	1	5	7	11	16	6	8	12	4	18	2	14	10

SUN CITY VISTOSO G.C.

SEMI PRIVATE 18 HOLES

1495A E. Rancho Vistoso Blvd.   Tucson, AZ 85737   602-825-0428

DESERT ●   **TRADITIONAL** ○   **LINKS** ○

TERRAIN	TREES	WATER

GREENS *Bent*	**COURSE FAVORS A...** *Draw*
FAIRWAYS *Bent*	**WIDTH OF FAIRWAYS** *Tight*
BUNKERS *Regular*	**AMT. OF BUNKERS** *Many*

PAR	YARDS	RATING	SLOPE	1992 GREEN FEES $	
72	6723	72.2	143	**HIGH**	*$58*
72	6163	69.9	135	**LOW**	*$30*
72	5109	68.3	110	**SPECIALS**	*None*

THE COURSE COMMENTARY *This course is carved in the hills of northern Tucson. The gorgeous undulating bent grass greens and fairways make for a challenging up and down on each hole. The greens are in perfect condition and are very slick.*

TOUGHEST HOLE THE 437 YARD PAR-4 5TH HOLE HAS AN LARGE BUNKER TO THE LEFT OFF THE FAIRWAY SO KEEP YOUR TEE SHOT RIGHT.

BIRDIE HOLE THE 171 YARD PAR-3 12TH HOLE HAS A LARGE GREEN WITH THE ONLY BUNKERS IN BACK OF THE GREEN.

WATER IN PLAY ON... 2 HOLES

OVERALL STRATEGY HIT FOR ACCURACY OFF THE TEE.

CART REQUIRED? YES

PRACTICE FACILITIES? DRIVING RANGE   PUTTING GREEN   CHIPPING GREEN

COURSE IS OPEN... YES

OVERSEEDING OCTOBER FOR 2 WEEKS. INCLUDES EVERYTHING.

RESTAURANT? YES

ACCOMMODATIONS? NO

DON'T FORGET YOUR.. FAVORITE PUTTER

COURSE DESIGNER N/A

 # OF ROUNDS ANNUALLY 54,000

DIRECTIONS TAKE ORACLE RD. 5 MILES NORTH OF EL CONQUISTADOR. TURN LEFT AT THE SUN CITY VISTOSO ENTRANCE.

COURSE LAYOUT

HOLE	1	2	3	4	5	6	7	8	9	10	11	12	13	14	15	16	17	18
CHAMP	406	502	200	386	437	358	523	161	348	386	519	171	446	490	411	189	390	400
MENS	387	462	175	360	404	310	505	140	326	339	465	144	403	462	384	170	357	370
LADIES	321	422	150	292	340	253	421	101	220	240	401	116	371	387	346	117	304	307
PAR	4	5	3	4	4	4	5	3	4	4	5	3	4	5	4	3	4	4
M.HCP	5	7	11	9	1	15	3	17	13	14	10	18	2	8	4	16	12	6
L.HCP	9	1	15	7	5	13	3	17	11	12	10	18	4	2	6	16	14	8

SUN VILLAGE RESORT & G.C.

SEMI PRIVATE   18 HOLES

14300 W. Bell Rd.   Suprise AZ 85374   602-584-5774

DESERT ○   TRADITIONAL ●   LINKS ○

TERRAIN	TREES	WATER

	GREENS	Bermuda		COURSE FAVORS A...	Mix
	FAIRWAYS	Bermuda		WIDTH OF FAIRWAYS	Forgiving
	BUNKERS	Regular		AMT. OF BUNKERS	Many

	PAR	YARDS	RATING	SLOPE	1992 GREEN FEES $	
	54	1977	N/A	N/A	HIGH	$15
	54	1876	50.4	N/A	LOW	$9
	54	1610	50.0	N/A	SPECIALS	None

THE COURSE COMMENTARY   This is a hilly executive 18 hole layout with water coming into play on 8 of 9 holes on the back nine. Pull carts are available.

TOUGHEST HOLE	THE SHORT 123 YARD PAR-3 9TH HOLE. PLAY A DRAW TO THIS VERY UNDULATING GREEN.
BIRDIE HOLE	THE 87 YARD PAR-3 4TH HOLE IS VERY SHORT AND PLAYS TO A LARGE GREEN.
WATER IN PLAY ON...	8 HOLES
OVERALL STRATEGY	HIT IT STRAIGHT!
CART REQUIRED?	NO
PRACTICE FACILITIES?	PUTTING GREEN CHIPPING GREEN
COURSE IS OPEN...	YES
OVERSEEDING	OCTOBER FOR 2 WEEKS. INCLUDES EVERYTHING.
RESTAURANT?	RESTAURANT, COFFEE SHOP, LOUNGE, AND SNACK BAR.
ACCOMMODATIONS?	NO
DON'T FORGET YOUR..	FAVORITE PUTTER
COURSE DESIGNER	N/A
# OF ROUNDS ANNUALLY	N/A
DIRECTIONS	1 MILE WEST OF GRANDE AVE. ON BELL RD.

HOLE	1	2	3	4	5	6	7	8	9	10	11	12	13	14	15	16	17	18
CHAMP	113	85	114	87	118	90	125	93	123	135	142	88	82	112	111	103	141	115
MENS	113	85	114	87	118	90	125	93	123	120	113	88	82	82	111	103	114	115
LADIES	101	75	82	87	118	71	102	93	115	120	78	79	82	82	82	75	101	67
PAR	3	3	3	3	3	3	3	3	3	3	3	3	3	3	3	3	3	3
M.HCP	14	10	6	18	4	8	2	16	15	12	1	17	11	7	9	3	5	13
L.HCP	8	12	6	14	2	18	4	10	16	5	15	13	7	9	17	1	3	11

SUNBIRD G.R.

SEMI PRIVATE 18 HOLES

6250 Sunbird Blvd. Chandler, AZ 85249   602-732-1001

DESERT ●   **TRADITIONAL ○**   **LINKS ○**

TERRAIN	TREES	WATER

GREENS	Bermuda		COURSE FAVORS A...	Mix
FAIRWAYS	Bermuda		WIDTH OF FAIRWAYS	Tight
BUNKERS	Regular		AMT. OF BUNKERS	Average

PAR	YARDS	RATING	SLOPE		1992 GREEN FEES $
65	4084	59.3	93	HIGH	$23
65	3820	58.3	91	LOW	$12
65	3394	58.1	85	SPECIALS	None

THE COURSE COMMENTARY This short 18 hole executive layout is one of Arizona's hidden gem's. This course is in great condition. Great course for seniors.

TOUGHEST HOLE THE 469 YARD PAR-5 7TH HOLE IS GUARDED BY BUNKERS AND LAKES ALL THE WAY TO THE GREEN.

BIRDIE HOLE THE 120 YARD PAR-3 17TH HOLE PLAYS TO A WIDE GREEN. A BUNKER AND LAKE WILL NOT AFFECT YOU.

WATER IN PLAY ON... 8 HOLES

OVERALL STRATEGY CONSIDER HITTING YOUR LONG IRONS OFF THE TEE TO KEEP IT IN THE FAIRWAY.

CART REQUIRED? NO

PRACTICE FACILITIES? DRIVING RANGE   PUTTING GREEN   CHIPPING GREEN

COURSE IS OPEN... YES

OVERSEEDING OCTOBER FOR 5 WEEKS. INCLUDES EVERYTHING.

RESTAURANT? YES

ACCOMMODATIONS? NO

DON'T FORGET YOUR.. 1 IRON

COURSE DESIGNER GARY PANKS

 # OF ROUNDS ANNUALLY N/A

DIRECTIONS 1.5 MILES EAST OF ARIZONA AVE. ON RIGGS RD.

COURSE LAYOUT

HOLE	1	2	3	4	5	6	7	8	9	10	11	12	13	14	15	16	17	18
CHAMP	273	162	174	368	137	273	469	115	323	263	94	276	137	121	219	275	120	285
MENS	262	150	168	360	107	261	458	103	297	255	83	268	110	112	210	266	86	264
LADIES	239	129	148	332	82	240	441	78	277	235	52	235	88	89	186	232	69	242
PAR	4	3	3	4	3	4	5	3	4	4	3	4	3	3	4	4	3	4
M.HCP	9	13	7	3	17	11	1	15	5	8	16	4	10	12	14	6	18	2
L.HCP	9	13	7	3	17	11	1	15	5	8	16	4	10	12	14	6	18	2

SUNLAND VILLAGE G.C.

SEMI PRIVATE 18 HOLES

725 S. Rochester Mesa, AZ 85206   602-832-3691

DESERT ○   TRADITIONAL ●   LINKS ○

TERRAIN	TREES	WATER

GREENS	Bermuda	COURSE FAVORS A...	Fade
FAIRWAYS	Bermuda	WIDTH OF FAIRWAYS	Forgiving
BUNKERS	Regular	AMT. OF BUNKERS	Minimal

	PAR	YARDS	RATING	SLOPE	1992 GREEN FEES $	
	N/A	N/A	N/A	N/A	HIGH	$18
	62	3579	56.6	80	LOW	$10
	62	3178	56.6	78	SPECIALS	None

THE COURSE COMMENTARY

This executive style layout is in excellent condition.

TOUGHEST HOLE	THE 149 YARD PAR-3 9TH HOLE IS LONG AND TIGHT WITH ROLLING HILLS THROUGH THE FAIRWAY.
BIRDIE HOLE	THE 287 YARD PAR-4 4TH HOLE IS SHORT AND HAS NO TROUBLE.
WATER IN PLAY ON...	9 HOLES
OVERALL STRATEGY	KEEP IT IN PLAY OFF THE TEE.
CART REQUIRED?	NO
PRACTICE FACILITIES?	DRIVING RANGE PUTTING GREEN CHIPPING GREEN
COURSE IS OPEN...	YES
OVERSEEDING	OCTOBER FOR 2 WEEKS. INCLUDES EVERYTHING.
RESTAURANT?	FULL SERVICE RESTAURANT
ACCOMMODATIONS?	THE REGIS INN IS NEARBY
DON'T FORGET YOUR..	BALL RETRIEVER
COURSE DESIGNER	FARNSWORTH
# OF ROUNDS ANNUALLY	35,000
DIRECTIONS	GO EAST OF GREENFIELD ON DIAMOND.

COURSE LAYOUT

HOLE	1	2	3	4	5	6	7	8	9	10	11	12	13	14	15	16	17	18
CHAMP																		
MENS	319	139	117	287	114	142	311	307	149	312	251	133	130	281	112	337	116	132
LADIES	289	128	112	269	72	126	296	282	84	291	219	109	113	266	90	311	100	113
PAR	4	3	3	4	3	3	4	4	3	4	4	3	3	4	3	4	3	3
M.HCP	1	13	15	7	17	11	3	5	9	4	8	10	14	6	18	2	16	12
L.HCP	1	13	15	7	17	11	3	5	9	4	8	10	14	6	18	2	16	12

SUPERSTITION SPRINGS G.C.

PUBLIC   18 HOLES

6542 E. Baseline Rd. Mesa AZ 85206   602-890-9009

DESERT ○   **TRADITIONAL** ●   **LINKS** ○

TERRAIN   **TREES**   **WATER**

GREENS Bermuda	**COURSE FAVORS A...** Mix	
FAIRWAYS Bermuda	**WIDTH OF FAIRWAYS** Forgiving	
BUNKERS Silicon	**AMT. OF BUNKERS** Many	

PAR	YARDS	RATING	SLOPE	1992 GREEN FEES $	
72	7005	74.1	135	**HIGH**	$69
72	6405	71.0	132	**LOW**	$29
72	5328	70.9	120	**SPECIALS**	None

THE COURSE COMMENTARY

This course features mounding grass bunkers and large white silicon sand bunkers. The 425 yard par-4 9th hole has been voted as "Arizona's Most Popular Hole" for 2 years. It is the site for regional qualifying for the PGA Tour. Great golf shop!!!

TOUGHEST HOLE THE 455 YARD PAR-4 18TH HAS A CREEK THAT WINDS ALONG SIDE THE FAIRWAY.

BIRDIE HOLE THE 489 YARD PAR-5 11TH HOLE IS SHORT AND POSES LITTLE DANGER TO A BIRDIE POSSIBILITY.

WATER IN PLAY ON... 9 HOLES

OVERALL STRATEGY MAKE SURE YOU HIT THE GREENS... RECOVERY IS DIFFICULT AT BEST AROUND THEM.

CART REQUIRED? YES

PRACTICE FACILITIES? DRIVING RANGE   PUTTING GREEN   CHIPPING GREEN

COURSE IS OPEN... YES

OVERSEEDING OCTOBER FOR 2 WEEKS. INCLUDES EVERYTHING.

RESTAURANT? FULL SERVICE RESTAURANT AND LOUNGE. LOCKER ROOMS AVAILABLE.

ACCOMMODATIONS? THE HILTON PAVILION IS NEARBY.

DON'T FORGET YOUR.. FAVORITE SAND WEDGE AND L-WEDGE.

COURSE DESIGNER GREG NASH

 # OF ROUNDS ANNUALLY 45,000

DIRECTIONS EXIT STATE 360 AT POWER RD., THEN GO SOUTH 1 MILE TO BASELINE, THEN TRAVEL WEST TO THE CLUBHOUSE.

COURSE LAYOUT

HOLE	1	2	3	4	5	6	7	8	9	10	11	12	13	14	15	16	17	18
CHAMP	391	432	205	332	325	610	228	597	425	360	489	161	402	401	231	424	537	455
MENS	362	383	153	304	293	571	190	569	391	318	457	143	380	361	209	391	500	430
LADIES	328	305	93	221	252	501	140	475	318	289	413	117	308	292	158	329	469	320
PAR	4	4	3	4	4	5	3	5	4	4	5	3	4	4	3	4	5	4
M.HCP	13	7	11	15	17	1	5	9	3	12	14	18	16	8	4	10	2	6
L.HCP	13	7	11	15	17	1	5	9	3	12	14	18	16	8	4	10	2	6

TATUM RANCH G.C.

PUBLIC   18 HOLES

29888 N. Tatum Ranch Dr. Cave Creek, AZ 85331   602-585-4909

DESERT ● TRADITIONAL ○ LINKS ○

TERRAIN	TREES	WATER

GREENS Bermuda   **COURSE FAVORS A...** Mix

FAIRWAYS Bermuda   **WIDTH OF FAIRWAYS** Normal

BUNKERS Regular   **AMT. OF BUNKERS** Average

PAR	YARDS	RATING	SLOPE	1992 GREEN FEES $	
72	6870	73.4	128	HIGH	$70
72	6357	71.0	123	LOW	$25
72	5609	71.5	116	SPECIALS	Varies

THE COURSE COMMENTARY

A forgiving but challenging layout. Always in pretty good shape and very green. This course is nestled north of the valley in the quiet desert of Tatum Ranch. A great course for the money.

TOUGHEST HOLE THE 467 YARD PAR-4 18TH. HIT A LONG DRIVE DOWN THE LEFT SIDE TO SET UP YOUR APPROACH.

BIRDIE HOLE THE 181 YARD PAR-3 16TH HOLE PLAYS TO A LARGE GREEN THAT SLOPES DOWN FROM BACK TO FRONT.

WATER IN PLAY ON... 1 HOLE

OVERALL STRATEGY STAY OUT OF THE "RAKED DESERT WASH AREAS"... IT'S AN AUTOMATIC BOGEY.

CART REQUIRED? YES

PRACTICE FACILITIES? DRIVING RANGE   PUTTING GREEN   CHIPPING GREEN

COURSE IS OPEN... YES

OVERSEEDING OCTOBER FOR 4 WEEKS. INCLUDES EVERYTHING.

RESTAURANT? BREAKFAST AND LUNCH.

ACCOMMODATIONS? RESORT SUITES ON PROPERTY.

DON'T FORGET YOUR.. ROCK IRON.

COURSE DESIGNER ROBERT CUPP

 # OF ROUNDS ANNUALLY 55,000

DIRECTIONS TAKE TATUM BLVD NORTH APPROX. 7 MILES PAST UNION HILLS RD.

HOLE	1	2	3	4	5	6	7	8	9	10	11	12	13	14	15	16	17	18
CHAMP	402	341	185	544	446	483	351	204	393	448	152	330	371	540	473	181	559	467
MENS	374	329	166	470	406	467	331	184	354	413	141	307	352	513	428	160	512	450
LADIES	327	293	136	417	349	417	305	164	315	388	118	273	307	441	382	138	452	387
PAR	4	4	3	5	4	5	4	3	4	4	3	4	4	5	4	3	5	4
M.HCP	7	17	5	3	1	15	13	9	11	6	12	16	10	14	4	18	8	2
L.HCP	3	17	7	5	1	11	15	9	13	8	12	18	14	10	4	16	6	2

THUNDERBIRD C.C.

PUBLIC   18 HOLES

701 E. Thunderbird Trl. Phoenix, AZ 85040   602-243-1262

DESERT ○   TRADITIONAL ○   LINKS ●

TERRAIN	TREES	WATER

GREENS	Bent	COURSE FAVORS A...	Mix
FAIRWAYS	Bent	WIDTH OF FAIRWAYS	Normal
BUNKERS	Regular	AMT. OF BUNKERS	Many

PAR	YARDS	RATING	SLOPE	1992 GREEN FEES $	
72	6459	70.2	110	HIGH	$35
72	6271	68.9	107	LOW	$24
74	5853	72.8	115	SPECIALS	Call

THE COURSE COMMENTARY

This course has a spectacular view of the valley from the base of South Mountain.

TOUGHEST HOLE	THE 450 YARD PAR-4 8TH HOLE IS LONG AND STRAIGHTAWAY!
BIRDIE HOLE	THE 524 YARD PAR-5 18TH HOLE IS A DOGLEG LEFT AND PLAYS TO A LARGE GREEN.
WATER IN PLAY ON...	3 HOLES
OVERALL STRATEGY	KEEP IT IN THE FAIRWAY OFF THE TEE.
CART REQUIRED?	NO
PRACTICE FACILITIES?	DRIVING RANGE PUTTING GREEN CHIPPING GREEN
COURSE IS OPEN...	YES
OVERSEEDING	OCT. FOR 2 WEEKS. INCLUDES EVERYTHING.
RESTAURANT?	YES
ACCOMMODATIONS?	YES
DON'T FORGET YOUR..	EVERYTHING
COURSE DESIGNER	N/A
# OF ROUNDS ANNUALLY	N/A
DIRECTIONS	GO SOUTH ON 7TH ST. FROM BASELINE RD. FOR 1.5 MILES.

HOLE	1	2	3	4	5	6	7	8	9	10	11	12	13	14	15	16	17	18
CHAMP	486	345	336	413	138	340	212	450	496	572	195	371	170	385	475	380	181	524
MENS	450	333	334	370	133	338	204	441	489	542	192	369	167	370	469	377	172	459
LADIES	439	348	331	359	121	331	215	411	351	525	185	362	158	337	413	371	152	443
PAR	5	4	4	4	3	4	3	4	5	5	3	4	3	4	5	4	3	5
M.HCP	15	5	9	3	13	11	7	1	17	4	6	10	14	8	16	2	12	18
L.HCP	3	5	11	9	13	15	17	7	1	2	16	8	18	12	4	6	14	10

TOM WEISKOPF'S FOOTHILLS G.C.

PUBLIC   18 HOLES

2201 E. Clubhouse Dr.   Phoenix, AZ 85044

602-460-8337

DESERT ●   TRADITIONAL ○   LINKS ○

TERRAIN	TREES	WATER

GREENS Bermuda
FAIRWAYS Bermuda
BUNKERS Regular

COURSE FAVORS A... Mix
WIDTH OF FAIRWAYS Normal
AMT. OF BUNKERS Many

PAR	YARDS	RATING	SLOPE	1992 GREEN FEES $	
72	6967	72.7	125	HIGH	$69
72	6406	69.9	115	LOW	$25
72	5213	64.5	102	SPECIALS	None

THE COURSE COMMENTARY

The team of Tom Weiskopf and Jay Morrish have designed both a beautiful and challenging layout in a foothill setting. These greens are some of the toughest in the entire state. If you putt well you will score well.

TOUGHEST HOLE THE 451 YARD PAR-4 15TH HOLE PLAYS TO A SMALL GREEN WITH WATER TO THE RIGHT OFF THE TEE.

BIRDIE HOLE THE 152 YARD PAR-3 4TH HOLE HAS BUNKERS FRONT AND LEFT OF A DEEP GREEN.

WATER IN PLAY ON... 4 HOLES

OVERALL STRATEGY KEEP IT IN THE FAIRWAY OFF THE TEE!!!

CART REQUIRED? NO

PRACTICE FACILITIES? DRIVING RANGE   PUTTING GREEN   CHIPPING GREEN

COURSE IS OPEN... YES

OVERSEEDING OCT. FOR 2 WEEKS. INCLUDES EVERYTHING.

RESTAURANT? DOUBLE EAGLE BAR & GRILL ALSO SERVES BREAKFAST ON SATURDAY'S.

ACCOMMODATIONS? NO

DON'T FORGET YOUR.. 1 IRON

COURSE DESIGNER TOM WEISKOPF AND JAY MORRISH

 # OF ROUNDS ANNUALLY N/A

DIRECTIONS TAKE I-10 SOUTH TO CHANDLER BLVD., THEN GO 4 MILES WEST TO THE 24TH ST. ENTRANCE.

COURSE LAYOUT

HOLE	1	2	3	4	5	6	7	8	9	10	11	12	13	14	15	16	17	18
CHAMP	421	513	410	152	382	311	217	510	417	432	437	526	202	385	451	187	557	457
MENS	368	473	384	135	367	292	196	480	380	399	381	500	195	357	421	149	512	420
LADIES	321	427	266	108	305	258	163	434	335	336	263	450	167	323	340	119	446	337
PAR	4	5	4	3	4	4	3	5	4	4	4	5	3	4	4	3	5	4
M.HCP	8	2	6	18	12	16	14	10	4	7	3	11	13	15	1	17	9	5
L.HCP	8	2	6	18	12	16	14	10	4	7	3	11	13	15	1	17	9	5

TPC AT STARPASS

3645 W. 22nd St. Tucson , AZ 85745   602-622-6060

DESERT ●   **TRADITIONAL** ○   **LINKS** ○

TERRAIN	**TREES**	**WATER**

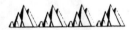

	GREENS	Bent		COURSE FAVORS A...	Draw
	FAIRWAYS	Bermuda		WIDTH OF FAIRWAYS	Tight
	BUNKERS	Regular		AMT. OF BUNKERS	Many

PAR	YARDS	RATING	SLOPE
72	7010	74.6	139
72	6383	71.3	127
72	5210	70.7	121

1992 GREEN FEES $

HIGH	$79
LOW	$39
SPECIALS	Discount cards honored

THE COURSE COMMENTARY

Co-home of the PGA Tour Northern Telecom Tucson Open. This course is cut through the mountains of western Tucson... watch for wildlife. The front nine requires superb accuracy, not length. This is a beautiful layout.

TOUGHEST HOLE THE 506 YARD PAR-5 5TH HOLE. YOU CAN LAY-UP LEFT OR RIGHT BUT NOT IN THE MIDDLE... A WASH GUARDS THE FRONT.

BIRDIE HOLE THE 155 YARD PAR-3 14TH HOLE. A SMALL BUNKER GUARDS THE FRONT OF THE GREEN. HIT TO THE RIGHT SIDE.

WATER IN PLAY ON... 0 HOLES

OVERALL STRATEGY HIT FOR ACCURACY. THE FAIRWAYS AND GREENS ARE VERY UNDULATED.

CART REQUIRED? YES

PRACTICE FACILITIES? DRIVING RANGE   PUTTING GREEN   CHIPPING GREEN

COURSE IS OPEN... YES

OVERSEEDING OCTOBER FOR 3 WEEKS. TEES AND FAIRWAYS.

RESTAURANT? FULL RESTAURANT AND PRO SHOP

ACCOMMODATIONS? MANY HOTELS NEARBY IN TUCSON

DON'T FORGET YOUR.. ROCK IRON AND YOUR LUCKY PUTTER.

COURSE DESIGNER ROBERT CUPP AND CRAIG STADLER

 # OF ROUNDS ANNUALLY 44,000

DIRECTIONS TAKE I-10 SOUTH TO THE 22ND ST. EXIT, THEN GO WEST FOR 3.5 MILES.

COURSE LAYOUT

HOLE	1	2	3	4	5	6	7	8	9	10	11	12	13	14	15	16	17	18
CHAMP	380	522	430	396	506	199	433	203	454	439	427	502	437	155	350	197	543	437
MENS	323	494	394	365	478	170	405	168	429	427	377	486	323	145	325	190	506	378
LADIES	266	428	330	308	420	118	316	129	347	345	329	421	276	81	267	96	421	312
PAR	4	5	4	4	5	3	4	3	4	4	4	5	4	3	4	3	5	4
M.HCP	13	7	5	9	1	15	11	17	3	8	12	4	14	18	6	16	2	10
L.HCP	13	7	5	9	1	15	11	17	3	8	12	4	14	18	6	16	2	10

TPC SCOTTSDALE - DESERT COURSE

PUBLIC   18 HOLES

17020 N. Hayden Rd. Scottsdale, AZ 85260   602-585-3600

DESERT ●   TRADITIONAL ○   LINKS ○

TERRAIN	**TREES**	**WATER**

GREENS	Bermuda		**COURSE FAVORS A...**	Draw
FAIRWAYS	Bermuda		**WIDTH OF FAIRWAYS**	Normal
BUNKERS	Regular		**AMT. OF BUNKERS**	Many

	PAR	YARDS	RATING	SLOPE	1992 GREEN FEES $	
★	71	6552	71.4	112	**HIGH**	$30
	71	5908	67.4	109	**LOW**	$11
	71	4715	66.3	109	**SPECIALS**	Afternoon rates

THE COURSE COMMENTARY

This is the sister course to the Stadium Course (home of the PGA Tour Phoenix Open.) This course has generous landing areas off most tees but is tough around the greens. This is another outstanding Weiskopf & Morrish design. Great course for the money.

TOUGHEST HOLE	THE 465 YARD PAR-4 17TH HOLE IS LONG, LONG, LONG, AND STRAIGHTAWAY. LEAVE YOUR IRONS IN THE BAG.
BIRDIE HOLE	THE 160 YARD PAR-3 4TH HOLE PLAYS TO A LARGE GREEN WITH A SMALL BUNKER TO THE LEFT.
WATER IN PLAY ON...	2 HOLES
OVERALL STRATEGY	KEEP IT IN THE FAIRWAY OFF THE TEE OR YOU'LL BE HITTING YOUR APPROACH'S WITH YOUR ROCK IRON ALL DAY.
CART REQUIRED?	NO
PRACTICE FACILITIES?	DRIVING RANGE PUTTING GREEN CHIPPING GREEN
COURSE IS OPEN...	YES
OVERSEEDING	OCT. FOR 2 WEEKS. INCLUDES EVERYTHING.
RESTAURANT?	SNACK BAR
ACCOMMODATIONS?	THE AAA 5 STAR, 5 DIAMOND LUXURY SCOTTSDALE PRINCESS RESORT IS ON PROPERTY.
DON'T FORGET YOUR..	ROCK IRON
COURSE DESIGNER	TOM WEISKOPF & JAY MORRISH
# OF ROUNDS ANNUALLY	250,000 (DESERT & STADIUM)
DIRECTIONS	ON SCOTTSDALE RD. 1 MILE NORTH OF BELL RD. FOLLOW THE ENTRANCE ROAD ALL THE WAY TO THE END.

COURSE LAYOUT

HOLE	1	2	3	4	5	6	7	8	9	10	11	12	13	14	15	16	17	18
CHAMP	521	383	439	160	417	193	376	351	515	313	392	205	510	418	370	154	465	370
MENS	492	344	393	129	385	157	332	313	481	285	344	165	468	382	343	125	429	341
LADIES	375	276	330	94	318	102	263	255	427	243	273	90	396	270	277	77	373	276
PAR	5	4	4	3	4	3	4	4	5	4	4	3	5	4	4	3	4	4
M.HCP	2	10	6	18	8	16	12	14	4	11	7	15	5	3	13	17	1	9
L.HCP	2	10	6	17	8	16	12	14	4	11	7	15	5	3	13	17	1	9

TPC SCOTTSDALE - STADIUM COURSE

PUBLIC   18 HOLES

17020 N. Hayden Rd. Scottsdale, AZ 85260   602-585-3600

DESERT ●   TRADITIONAL ○   LINKS ○

| TERRAIN | TREES | WATER |

GREENS *Bent*	**COURSE FAVORS A...** *Draw*
FAIRWAYS *Bermuda*	**WIDTH OF FAIRWAYS** *Tight*
BUNKERS *Silicon*	**AMT. OF BUNKERS** *Many*

PAR	YARDS	RATING	SLOPE	1992 GREEN FEES $
71	6992	73.9	131	**HIGH** *$87*
71	6508	71	124	**LOW** *$43*
71	5567	71.6	123	**SPECIALS** *Guest specials*

THE COURSE COMMENTARY

Easily one of the best courses in all of Arizona. The Stadium Course is home to the PGA Tour Phoenix Open. Stay in the fairway off the tee and away from the mounds. The greens are fast and undulated. Get ready for the best 4 finishing holes in the state.

TOUGHEST HOLE	THE 554 YARD PAR-5 3RD HOLE. LAY UP WELL SHORT OF THE WASH ON YOUR 2ND SHOT TO AVOID A SURE DISASTER.
BIRDIE HOLE	THE 150 YARD PAR-3 4TH HOLE. MAKE SURE THAT YOU DON'T UNDER-CLUB HERE OR YOU'LL END UP IN THE TRAPS.
WATER IN PLAY ON...	6 HOLES
OVERALL STRATEGY	STAY IN THE FAIRWAY OFF THE TEE. IT'S TOUGH TO GET UP & DOWN AROUND THESE GREENS.
CART REQUIRED?	YES
PRACTICE FACILITIES?	DRIVING RANGE PUTTING GREEN CHIPPING GREEN
COURSE IS OPEN...	YES
OVERSEEDING	OCTOBER FOR 2 WEEKS. INCLUDES EVERYTHING.
RESTAURANT?	EVERYTHING YOUR HEART DESIRES.
ACCOMMODATIONS?	THE AAA 5 STAR, 5 DIAMOND LUXURY SCOTTSDALE PRINCESS RESORT IS ON PROPERTY.
DON'T FORGET YOUR..	YOUR FAVORITE DRIVER AND PUTTER AND A 3RD WEDGE.
COURSE DESIGNER	TOM WEISKOPF & JAY MORRISH
# OF ROUNDS ANNUALLY	250,000 (DESERT & STADIUM)
DIRECTIONS	ON SCOTTSDALE RD. 1 MILE NORTH OF BELL RD. FOLLOW THE ENTRANCE ROAD ALL THE WAY TO THE END.

COURSE LAYOUT

HOLE	1	2	3	4	5	6	7	8	9	10	11	12	13	14	15	16	17	18
CHAMP	410	416	554	150	453	389	215	470	415	403	469	195	576	444	501	162	332	438
MENS	366	393	537	133	416	365	190	446	383	385	439	170	552	419	468	143	292	411
LADIES	311	340	489	98	350	322	137	395	329	340	372	124	486	361	403	100	246	364
PAR	4	4	5	3	4	4	3	4	4	4	4	3	5	4	5	3	4	4
M.HCP	14	8	4	18	6	12	16	2	10	11	1	15	5	7	9	17	13	3
L.HCP	14	8	4	18	6	12	16	2	10	11	1	15	5	7	9	17	13	3

TROON NORTH G.C.

SEMI PRIVATE 18 HOLES

10320 E. Dynamite Blvd. Scottsdale, AZ 85255

602-585-5300

DESERT ●   **TRADITIONAL** ○   **LINKS** ○

TERRAIN	TREES	WATER

GREENS *Bent*
FAIRWAYS *Bermuda*
BUNKERS *Regular*

COURSE FAVORS A... *Draw*
WIDTH OF FAIRWAYS *Tight*
AMT. OF BUNKERS *Many*

PAR	YARDS	RATING	SLOPE	1992 GREEN FEES $	
72	7008	73.1	146	**HIGH**	$115
72	6474	70.0	131	**LOW**	$80
72	6026	68.8	127	**SPECIALS**	None

THE COURSE COMMENTARY

Troon North is ranked #85 in "America's Top 100 Golf Courses" by Golf Magazine and ranked #1 in Arizona by Golfweek Magazine. This "desert-links" style layout is unique. Each hole has it's own name and personality.

TOUGHEST HOLE THE 464 YARD PAR-4 5TH HOLE. THE GREEN SLOPES DOWN DRASTICALLY FROM FRONT TO BACK.

BIRDIE HOLE THE 306 YARD PAR-4 6TH HOLE. DRIVER COULD GET YOU ON THE GREEN OR OUT OF PLAY.

WATER IN PLAY ON... 2 HOLES

OVERALL STRATEGY KEEP YOUR DRIVES IN THE FAIRWAY!!! MAKE SURE YOU HAVE A GOOD IDEA WHERE YOUR PUTT IS GOING.

CART REQUIRED? YES

PRACTICE FACILITIES? DRIVING RANGE PUTTING GREEN CHIPPING GREEN

COURSE IS OPEN... YES

OVERSEEDING SEPTEMBER FOR 2 WEEKS. TEES AND FAIRWAYS.

RESTAURANT? YES.

ACCOMMODATIONS? TWO FIVE-STAR RESORTS ARE NEARBY; THE SCOTTSDALE PRINCESS AND THE BOULDERS.

DON'T FORGET YOUR.. ROCK IRON AND EXTRA BALLS

COURSE DESIGNER TOM WEISKOPF AND JAY MORRISH

 # OF ROUNDS ANNUALLY N/A

DIRECTIONS GO NORTH ON PIMA RD. TO DYNAMITE, THEN GO EAST FOR 2 MILES.

HOLE	1	2	3	4	5	6	7	8	9	10	11	12	13	14	15	16	17	18
CHAMP	444	172	544	420	464	306	205	408	530	342	539	414	176	604	368	140	438	444
MENS	411	165	502	340	425	295	190	352	515	378	528	350	161	565	352	132	409	414
LADIES	300	114	456	256	335	261	105	308	415	284	419	289	113	454	263	95	293	290
PAR	4	3	5	4	4	4	3	4	5	4	5	4	3	5	4	3	4	4
M.HCP	5	17	3	11	1	13	15	9	7	10	6	12	16	2	14	18	4	8
L.HCP	5	17	3	11	1	13	15	9	7	10	6	12	16	2	14	18	4	8

TUCSON NATIONAL - GREEN/GOLD

PUBLIC · 18 HOLES

2727 West Club Drive Tucson, AZ 85741

602-575-7540

DESERT ○ **TRADITIONAL** ● **LINKS** ○

TERRAIN	TREES	WATER

GREENS	Bent		COURSE FAVORS A...	Mix
FAIRWAYS	Bermuda		WIDTH OF FAIRWAYS	Normal
BUNKERS	Regular		AMT. OF BUNKERS	Many

	PAR	YARDS	RATING	SLOPE	1992 GREEN FEES $	
	73	6850	74.7	135	HIGH	$95
	73	6388	70.9	120	LOW	$45
	73	5442	71.0	117	SPECIALS	None

THE COURSE COMMENTARY

The distinctively traditional layout hosts the PGA Tour Northern Telecom Tucson Open. This is a fair test for all skill levels. Relaxed southwestern hospitality and charm are their specialty.

TOUGHEST HOLE	THE 439 YARD PAR-4 9TH HOLE AT GOLD IS RANKED AS ONE OF THE TOUGHEST FINISHING HOLES ON THE PGA TOUR.
BIRDIE HOLE	THE 512 YARD PAR-5 2ND HOLE AT GOLD IS SHORT BUT STAY IN THE FAIRWAY TO GET YOUR BIRDIE.
WATER IN PLAY ON...	8 HOLES
OVERALL STRATEGY	THE PREMIUM IS PLACED ON APPROACH SHOTS AND REMEMBER TO STAY OUT OF THE ROUGH!!!
CART REQUIRED?	YES
PRACTICE FACILITIES?	DRIVING RANGE PUTTING GREEN CHIPPING GREEN
COURSE IS OPEN...	YES
OVERSEEDING	SEPT/OCT FOR 5 WEEKS. TEES AND FAIRWAYS.
RESTAURANT?	SNACK BAR
ACCOMMODATIONS?	CONFERENCE RESORT ON PROPERTY HAS 170 BEAUTIFUL SPACIOUS VILLAS WITH VIEWS OF THE SURROUNDING DESERT..
DON'T FORGET YOUR..	SPOUSE. TUCSON NATIONAL HAS A WORLD CLASS SPA TO PAMPER THE NON-GOLFER.
COURSE DESIGNER	ROBERT BRUCE HARRIS
# OF ROUNDS ANNUALLY	54,000
DIRECTIONS	TAKE I-10 SOUTH TO CORTARO RD., THEN GO EAST FOR 3.5 MILES AND THEN GO NORTH ON SHANNON DR.

COURSE LAYOUT

HOLE	1	2	3	4	5	6	7	8	9	10	11	12	13	14	15	16	17	18
CHAMP	501	512	178	399	386	622	421	180	439	337	356	542	375	168	500	374	152	418
MENS	476	495	163	347	373	570	361	162	414	324	344	527	363	144	460	350	136	379
LADIES	410	438	142	275	348	462	297	142	345	313	287	440	358	95	351	341	116	282
PAR	5	5	3	4	4	5	4	3	4	4	4	5	4	3	5	4	3	4
M.HCP	2	1	8	5	7	3	6	9	4	8	2	1	4	7	3	6	9	5
L.HCP	5	1	8	6	4	2	7	9	3	7	6	2	3	9	1	4	8	5

TUCSON NATIONAL - GREEN/ORANGE

PUBLIC   18 HOLES

2727 West Club Drive   Tucson, AZ 85741   602-575-7540

DESERT ○   **TRADITIONAL** ●   **LINKS** ○

TERRAIN	TREES	WATER

GREENS Bent	**COURSE FAVORS A...** Mix	
FAIRWAYS Bermuda	**WIDTH OF FAIRWAYS** Normal	
BUNKERS Regular	**AMT. OF BUNKERS** Many	

PAR	YARDS	RATING	SLOPE	1992 GREEN FEES
72	6692	74.6	134	HIGH $95
72	6115	70.2	120	LOW $45
72	5371	70.3	117	SPECIALS None

THE COURSE COMMENTARY

The distinctively traditional layout hosts the PGA Tour Northern Telecom Tucson Open. This is a fair test for all skill levels. Relaxed southwestern hospitality and charm are their specialty.

TOUGHEST HOLE	THE 542 YARD PAR-5 3RD HOLE AT GREEN IS STRAIGHTAWAY WITH FAIRWAY BUNKERS TO BOTH SIDES.
BIRDIE HOLE	THE 374 YARD PAR-4 6TH HOLE AT GREEN IS A DOGLEG LEFT OVER WATER TO A LARGE GREEN.
WATER IN PLAY ON...	6 HOLES
OVERALL STRATEGY	THE PREMIUM IS PLACED ON APPROACH SHOTS AND REMEMBER TO STAY OUT OF THE ROUGH!!!
CART REQUIRED?	YES
PRACTICE FACILITIES?	DRIVING RANGE PUTTING GREEN CHIPPING GREEN
COURSE IS OPEN...	YES
OVERSEEDING	SEPT/OCT FOR 5 WEEKS. TEES AND FAIRWAYS.
RESTAURANT?	SNACK BAR
ACCOMMODATIONS?	CONFERENCE RESORT ON PROPERTY HAS 170 BEAUTIFULL SPACIOUS VILLAS WITH VIEWS OF THE SURROUNDING DESERT..
DON'T FORGET YOUR..	SPOUSE. TUCSON NATIONAL HAS A WORLD CLASS SPA TO PAMPER THE NON-GOLFER.
COURSE DESIGNER	ROBERT BRUCE HARRIS
# OF ROUNDS ANNUALLY	54,000
DIRECTIONS	TAKE I-10 SOUTH TO CORTARO RD., THEN GO EAST FOR 3.5 MILES AND THEN GO NORTH ON SHANNON DR.

COURSE LAYOUT

HOLE	1	2	3	4	5	6	7	8	9	10	11	12	13	14	15	16	17	18
CHAMP	337	356	542	375	168	500	374	152	418	410	500	390	175	398	434	201	524	438
MENS	324	344	527	363	144	460	350	136	379	390	470	340	150	370	400	168	500	400
LADIES	313	287	440	358	95	351	341	116	282	345	441	307	102	340	357	129	462	305
PAR	4	4	5	4	3	5	4	3	4	4	5	4	3	4	4	3	5	4
M.HCP	8	2	1	4	7	3	6	9	5	5	2	6	8	7	4	9	1	3
L.HCP	7	6	2	3	9	1	4	8	5	6	5	7	9	4	1	8	2	3

TUCSON NATIONAL - ORANGE/GOLD

PUBLIC   18 HOLES

2727 W. Club Dr. Tucson, AZ 85741   602-575-7540

DESERT ○   TRADITIONAL ●   LINKS ○

TERRAIN   **TREES**   **WATER**

GREENS *Bent*   **COURSE FAVORS A...** *Mix*
FAIRWAYS *Bermuda*   **WIDTH OF FAIRWAYS** *Normal*
BUNKERS *Regular*   **AMT. OF BUNKERS** *Many*

PAR	YARDS	RATING	SLOPE		1992 GREEN FEES
73	7108	74.9	136	**HIGH**	$95
73	6549	71.0	122	**LOW**	$45
73	5647	72.4	123	**SPECIALS**	None

THE COURSE COMMENTARY

The distinctively traditional layout hosts the PGA Tour Northern Telecom Tucson Open. This is a fair test for all skill levels. Relaxed southwestern hospitality and charm are their specialty.

TOUGHEST HOLE THE 622 YARD PAR-5 6TH HOLE AT GOLD. FAIRWAY BUNKERS TO THE LEFT GUARD A LONG TEE SHOT.

BIRDIE HOLE THE 201 YARD PAR-3 7TH HOLE AT ORANGE IS A LONG PAR-3 BUT PLAYS TO A VERY LARGE GREEN.

WATER IN PLAY ON... 9 HOLES

OVERALL STRATEGY THE PREMIUM IS PLACED ON APPROACH SHOTS AND REMEMBER TO STAY OUT OF THE ROUGH!!!

CART REQUIRED? YES

PRACTICE FACILITIES? DRIVING RANGE   PUTTING GREEN   CHIPPING GREEN

COURSE IS OPEN... YES

OVERSEEDING SEPT/OCT FOR 5 WEEKS. TEES AND FAIRWAYS.

RESTAURANT? SNACK BAR

ACCOMMODATIONS? CONFERENCE RESORT ON PROPERTY HAS 170 BEAUTIFULL SPACIOUS VILLAS WITH VIEWS OF THE SURROUNDING DESERT..

DON'T FORGET YOUR.. SPOUSE. TUCSON NATIONAL HAS A WORLD CLASS SPA TO PAMPER THE NON-GOLFER.

COURSE DESIGNER ROBERT BRUCE HARRIS

 # OF ROUNDS ANNUALLY 54,000

DIRECTIONS TAKE I-10 SOUTH TO CORTARO RD., THEN GO EAST FOR 3.5 MILES AND THEN GO NORTH ON SHANNON DR.

COURSE LAYOUT

HOLE	1	2	3	4	5	6	7	8	9	10	11	12	13	14	15	16	17	18
CHAMP	410	500	390	175	398	434	201	524	438	501	512	178	399	386	622	421	180	439
MENS	390	470	340	150	370	400	168	500	400	476	495	163	347	373	570	361	162	414
LADIES	345	441	307	102	340	357	129	462	305	410	438	142	275	348	462	297	142	345
PAR	4	5	4	3	4	4	3	5	4	5	5	3	4	4	5	4	3	4
M.HCP	5	2	6	8	7	4	9	1	3	2	1	8	5	7	3	6	9	4
L.HCP	6	5	7	9	4	1	8	2	3	5	1	8	6	4	2	7	9	3

VALLEY CLUB G.C.

PUBLIC   9 HOLES

5200 E. Camelback Rd.   Phoenix, AZ 85018

602-840-3610

DESERT ◯   **TRADITIONAL** ⬤   **LINKS** ◯

TERRAIN	TREES	WATER

 GREENS   *Bermuda*   COURSE FAVORS A... *Mix*

 FAIRWAYS *Bermuda*   WIDTH OF FAIRWAYS *Forgiving*

BUNKERS *Other*   AMT. OF BUNKERS *Average*

	PAR	YARDS	RATING	SLOPE	1992 GREEN FEES $
⭐	N/A	N/A	N/A	N/A	HIGH $8
🧍	72	4920	N/A	N/A	LOW $8
🧍‍♀️	N/	N/A	N/A	N/A	SPECIALS None

THE COURSE COMMENTARY

This course sets at the foot of Camelback Mountain with beautiful views from every hole.

TOUGHEST HOLE	THE 305 YARD PAR-4 4TH HOLE IS A SHARP DOGLEG LEFT. HIT AN IRON OFF THE TEE FOR A SHOT AT THE GREEN.
BIRDIE HOLE	THE 245 YARD PAR-4 5TH HOLE IS A DOGLEG RIGHT. HIT A FAIWAY WOOD TO THE FRONT OF THE GREEN.
WATER IN PLAY ON...	3 HOLES
OVERALL STRATEGY	PLAY TO THE MIDDLE OF THE FAIRWAY AND SHOOT FOR THE PIN.
CART REQUIRED?	NO
PRACTICE FACILITIES?	PUTTING GREEN
COURSE IS OPEN...	YES
OVERSEEDING	OCTOBER FOR 2 WEEKS. INCLUDES EVERYTHING.
RESTAURANT?	THE ROYAL PALMS INN HAS A RESTAURANT.
ACCOMMODATIONS?	THE ROYAL PALMS INN IS ON PROPERTY.
DON'T FORGET YOUR..	THIRD WEDGE
COURSE DESIGNER	DAVID GILL
# OF ROUNDS ANNUALLY	N/A
DIRECTIONS	LOCATED JUST WEST OF 52ND ST. AND CAMELBACK RD.

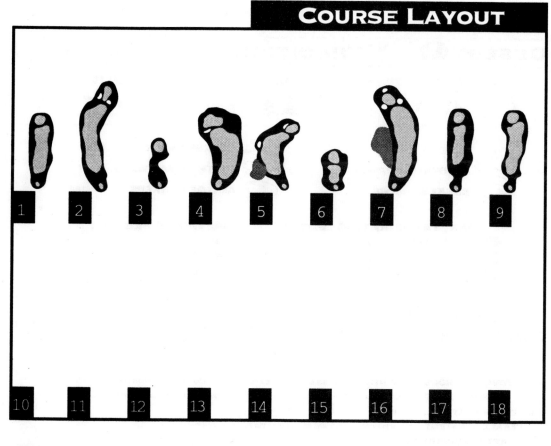

HOLE	1	2	3	4	5	6	7	8	9	10	11	12	13	14	15	16	17	18
CHAMP																		
MENS	265	400	135	305	245	125	400	285	300									
LADIES																		
PAR	4	5	3	4	4	3	5	4	4									
M.HCP																		
L.HCP																		

VENTANA CANYON G.C. - MTN. COURSE

HOTEL GUEST PRIORITY 18 HOLES

6200 N. Clubhouse Ln. Tucson, AZ 85715   602-577-2115

DESERT ●   **TRADITIONAL** ○   **LINKS** ○

TERRAIN	TREES	WATER

GREENS Bent	**COURSE FAVORS A...** Fade
FAIRWAYS Bermuda	**WIDTH OF FAIRWAYS** Tight
BUNKERS Regular	**AMT. OF BUNKERS** Average

PAR	YARDS	RATING	SLOPE	1992 GREEN FEES $
72	6948	73.6	149	**HIGH** $89
72	6356	71.2	139	**LOW** $40
72	4709	68.3	117	**SPECIALS** None

THE COURSE COMMENTARY This course is ranked #1 "Resort Course in Arizona" by Golf Digest. The signature hole is the 107 yard par-3 3rd hole. Drive off an elevated tee across a canyon to a green protected by desert on all sides.

TOUGHEST HOLE THE 548 YARD PAR-5 12TH HOLE. YOUR DRIVE NEEDS TO CARRY 230 YARDS TO A TIGHT FAIRWAY.

BIRDIE HOLE THE 107 YARD PAR-3 3RD HOLE PLAYS DOWNHILL ACROSS A CANYON TO A VERY LARGE GREEN.

WATER IN PLAY ON... 2 HOLES

OVERALL STRATEGY STAY IN PLAY OFF THE TEE AND BE AWARE OF PIN PLACEMENT ON THE GREENS.

CART REQUIRED? YES

PRACTICE FACILITIES? DRIVING RANGE   PUTTING GREEN   CHIPPING GREEN

COURSE IS OPEN... YES

OVERSEEDING OCTOBER FOR 6 WEEKS. TEES AND FAIRWAYS.

RESTAURANT? 2 DINING FACILITIES, A SNACK BAR, AND A LOCKER ROOM.

ACCOMMODATIONS? 48 CONDO-STYLE SUITES ON PROPERTY.

DON'T FORGET YOUR.. SUNSCREEN

COURSE DESIGNER TOM FAZIO

 # OF ROUNDS ANNUALLY 40,000

DIRECTIONS GO NORTH ON KOLB RD. FOR A MILE AND A HALF AT SUNRISE DR.

COURSE LAYOUT

HOLE	1	2	3	4	5	6	7	8	9	10	11	12	13	14	15	16	17	18
CHAMP	422	347	107	598	392	239	454	517	414	362	445	548	324	183	435	169	403	589
MENS	386	336	104	512	361	230	416	474	364	337	406	509	281	150	413	139	374	564
LADIES	299	240	67	432	280	141	252	404	260	220	286	411	209	102	263	100	295	448
PAR	4	4	3	5	4	3	4	5	4	4	4	5	4	3	4	3	4	5
M.HCP	7	15	17	3	11	9	1	5	13	16	6	4	12	14	2	18	8	10
L.HCP	9	17	17	3	5	15	11	1	13	14	10	2	12	16	8	18	6	4

VIEWPOINT R.V. & G. R.

SEMI PRIVATE 9 HOLES

8700 E. University Dr. Mesa, AZ 85207   602-373-8715

DESERT ○   TRADITIONAL ○   LINKS ●

TERRAIN	TREES	WATER

	GREENS	Bermuda		COURSE FAVORS A...	Mix
	FAIRWAYS	Bermuda		WIDTH OF FAIRWAYS	Tight
	BUNKERS	Regular		AMT. OF BUNKERS	Average

	PAR	YARDS	RATING	SLOPE	1992 GREEN FEES $	
	N/A	N/A	N/A	N/A	HIGH	$8
	34	2217	60.8	88	LOW	$4
	35	1829	58.3	82	SPECIALS	None

THE COURSE COMMENTARY

This is an executive style layout with two tees for each hole playing 18 holes. Most of the greens are large and have plenty of greenside bunkers to afflict your short game.

TOUGHEST HOLE	THE PAR-5 411-YARD 1ST HOLE IS WIDE OPEN OFF THE TEE WITH GREENSIDE BUNKERS TO THE LEFT.
BIRDIE HOLE	THE 108 YARD PAR-3 17TH HOLE PLAYS TO A HUGE GREEN.
WATER IN PLAY ON...	0 HOLES
OVERALL STRATEGY	MAKE YOUR APPROACH COUNT BECAUSE MOST OF THE GREENS A LARGE AND YOU COULD HAVE SOME LONG PUTTS.
CART REQUIRED?	NO
PRACTICE FACILITIES?	DRIVING RANGE PUTTING GREEN
COURSE IS OPEN...	YES
OVERSEEDING	OCTOBER FOR 3 WEEKS. INCLUDES EVERYTHING.
RESTAURANT?	NO
ACCOMMODATIONS?	R.V. RESORT COMMUNITY ON PROPERTY.
DON'T FORGET YOUR..	THIRD WEDGE
COURSE DESIGNER	N/A
# OF ROUNDS ANNUALLY	40,000 +
DIRECTIONS	2 MILES EAST OF BUSH HWY. ON UNIVERSITY DR.

COURSE LAYOUT

HOLE	1	2	3	4	5	6	7	8	9	10	11	12	13	14	15	16	17	18
CHAMP																		
MENS	411	229	124	188	146	200	322	93	274	487	244	151	235	159	216	330	108	287
LADIES	382	199	113	145	105	166	305	78	222	384	216	120	167	123	187	317	85	230
PAR	5	4	3	4	3	4	4	3	4	5	4	3	4	3	4	4	3	4
M.HCP	1	13	15	3	7	9	5	17	11	2	14	16	4	8	10	6	18	12
L.HCP	1	13	9	5	7	15	3	17	11	2	14	10	6	8	16	4	18	12

VILLA DE PAZ G.C.

PUBLIC   18 HOLES

4220 N. 103rd Ave. Phoenix, AZ 85039   602-877-1171

DESERT ○   **TRADITIONAL** ●   **LINKS** ○

TERRAIN	TREES	WATER

	GREENS	Bermuda		COURSE FAVORS A...	Mix
	FAIRWAYS	Bermuda		WIDTH OF FAIRWAYS	Tight
	BUNKERS	Regular		AMT. OF BUNKERS	Many

	PAR	YARDS	RATING	SLOPE	1992 GREEN FEES $	
	72	6140	68.6	N/A	HIGH	$34
	72	5868	67.2	N/A	LOW	$23
	72	5288	69.1	N/A	SPECIALS	$24 after 12pm to walk.

THE COURSE COMMENTARY
This course is very easy to walk.

TOUGHEST HOLE	THE 475 YARD PAR-5 4TH HOLE IS A SHARP DOGLEG RIGHT THAT FORCES YOU TO LAY-UP SHORT OF THE WATER.
BIRDIE HOLE	THE 142 YARD PAR-3 11TH HOLE PLAYS TO A WIDE GREEN WITH LEFT AND TO THE BACK. AIM CENTER-RIGHT.
WATER IN PLAY ON...	8 HOLES
OVERALL STRATEGY	HIT FOR ACCURACY OFF THE TEE TO KEEP FROM DRIVING THRU THE FAIRWAY.
CART REQUIRED?	No
PRACTICE FACILITIES?	DRIVING RANGE PUTTING GREEN
COURSE IS OPEN...	YES
OVERSEEDING	OCTOBER FOR 2 WEEKS. INCLUDES EVERYTHING.
RESTAURANT?	COFFEE SHOP
ACCOMMODATIONS?	No
DON'T FORGET YOUR..	N/A
COURSE DESIGNER	N/A
# OF ROUNDS ANNUALLY	N/A
DIRECTIONS	103RD AVE. AND INDIAN SCHOOL RD.

HOLE	1	2	3	4	5	6	7	8	9	10	11	12	13	14	15	16	17	18
CHAMP	383	165	475	475	326	200	305	334	515	490	142	325	360	373	300	237	345	390
MENS	369	136	457	457	310	176	288	315	488	475	125	325	340	357	300	232	345	373
LADIES	317	85	410	431	296	164	240	282	432	444	102	305	312	341	260	189	326	352
PAR	4	3	5	5	4	3	4	4	5	5	3	4	4	4	4	3	4	4
M.HCP	7	15	5	1	11	17	13	9	3	2	18	6	14	8	16	12	10	4
L.HCP	7	17	5	1	11	13	15	9	3	6	18	2	14	8	16	10	12	4

VILLA MONTEREY G.C.

PUBLIC   9 HOLES

8100 E. Camelback Rd. Scottsdale, AZ 85251   *602-990-7100*

DESERT ○   TRADITIONAL ●   LINKS ○

TERRAIN	TREES	WATER

GREENS *Bermuda*	**COURSE FAVORS A...** *Draw*
FAIRWAYS *Bermuda*	**WIDTH OF FAIRWAYS** *Normal*
BUNKERS *Regular*	**AMT. OF BUNKERS** *Average*

PAR	YARDS	RATING	SLOPE	1992 GREEN FEES $	
31	2035	56.7	85	**HIGH**	*$9*
31	2100	55.7	82	**LOW**	
31	1505	54.6	78	**SPECIALS**	*None*

THE COURSE COMMENTARY

This executive course is located in the heart of Scottsdale at Hayden & Camelback Rd. At least nine shots are effected by water. The pro shop has a low price guarantee on equipment.

TOUGHEST HOLE	THE 179 YARD PAR-3 7TH HOLE PLAYS OVER WATER TO A NARROW GREEN WELL GUARDED BY FOUR BUNKERS.
BIRDIE HOLE	THE 135 YARD PAR-3 5TH HOLE PLAYS TO A LARGE UNGUARDED FORGIVING GREEN.
WATER IN PLAY ON...	7 HOLES
OVERALL STRATEGY	AIM FOR THE PIN AND DON'T UNDERCLUB.
CART REQUIRED?	NO
PRACTICE FACILITIES?	N/A
COURSE IS OPEN...	YES
OVERSEEDING	OCTOBER FOR 2 WEEKS. INCLUDES EVERYTHING.
RESTAURANT?	NO
ACCOMMODATIONS?	NO
DON'T FORGET YOUR..	BALL RETRIEVER
COURSE DESIGNER	ARTHUR JACK SNYDER
# OF ROUNDS ANNUALLY	N/A
DIRECTIONS	THE NORTHEAST CORNER OF HAYDEN RD. AND CAMELBACK RD.

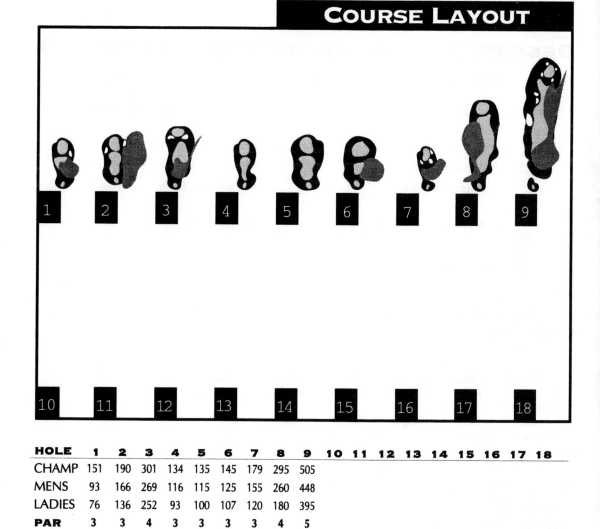

HOLE	1	2	3	4	5	6	7	8	9	10	11	12	13	14	15	16	17	18
CHAMP	151	190	301	134	135	145	179	295	505									
MENS	93	166	269	116	115	125	155	260	448									
LADIES	76	136	252	93	100	107	120	180	395									
PAR	3	3	4	3	3	3	3	4	5									
M.HCP	7	6	4	8	9	5	3	2	1									
L.HCP	7	6	4	8	9	5	3	2	1									

VISTAS CLUB

PUBLIC   18 HOLES

18823 N. Country Club Pkwy.   Peoria, AZ 85382   602-566-1633

DESERT ○   **TRADITIONAL** ●   **LINKS** ○

TERRAIN	TREES	WATER

GREENS *Bent*   **COURSE FAVORS A...** *Mix*

FAIRWAYS *Bermuda*   **WIDTH OF FAIRWAYS** *Normal*

BUNKERS *Regular*   **AMT. OF BUNKERS** *Average*

PAR	YARDS	RATING	SLOPE	1992 GREEN FEES $
72	6493	70.6	114	**HIGH** *$24*
72	6001	68.2	111	**LOW**
72	5222	68.1	105	**SPECIALS** *None*

THE COURSE COMMENTARY
A UDC planned community.

TOUGHEST HOLE THE 482 YARD PAR-5 5TH HOLE IS THE #1 HANDICAP HOLE ON THE COURSE.

BIRDIE HOLE THE 172 YARD PAR-3 13TH HOLE. SHOOT FOR THE PIN.

WATER IN PLAY ON... HOLES

OVERALL STRATEGY A LONG DRIVE WILL BE A GREAT BENEFIT ON THIS COURSE.

CART REQUIRED? No

PRACTICE FACILITIES? DRIVING RANGE   PUTTING GREEN   CHIPPING GREEN

COURSE IS OPEN... YES

OVERSEEDING OCTOBER FOR 2 WEEKS. INCLUDES EVERYTHING.

RESTAURANT? YES

ACCOMMODATIONS? PLANNED COMMUNITY ON PROPERTY

DON'T FORGET YOUR.. FAVORITE DRIVER

COURSE DESIGNER N/A

 # OF ROUNDS ANNUALLY N/A

DIRECTIONS 87TH AVE. AND UNION HILLS DR. TURN WEST TO COUNTRY CLUB DR. INTO WESTBROOKE VILLAGE.

COURSE LAYOUT NOT AVAILABLE

HOLE	1	2	3	4	5	6	7	8	9	10	11	12	13	14	15	16	17	18
CHAMP	362	150	413	351	482	291	215	537	362	382	166	419	172	486	464	401	495	345
MENS	321	130	377	338	456	264	194	503	320	354	144	387	152	466	428	370	474	323
LADIES	294	117	264	277	401	233	172	459	290	311	107	340	126	406	390	330	423	282
PAR	4	3	4	4	5	4	3	5	4	4	3	4	3	5	4	4	5	4
M.HCP	7	17	5	9	1	13	15	3	11	12	16	8	18	4	2	10	6	14
L.HCP	7	17	5	9	1	13	15	3	11	12	16	8	18	4	2	10	6	14

WESTBROOK VILLAGE C.C.

SEMI PRIVATE 18 HOLES

19260 N. Westbrook Pkwy Peoria, AZ 85345   602-933-0174

DESERT ○   TRADITIONAL ●   LINKS ○

TERRAIN	TREES	WATER

GREENS	Bermuda		COURSE FAVORS A...	Mix
FAIRWAYS	Bermuda		WIDTH OF FAIRWAYS	Normal
BUNKERS	Regular		AMT. OF BUNKERS	Average

PAR	YARDS	RATING	SLOPE	1992 GREEN FEES
71	6412	69.2	112	HIGH $40
71	6033	67.0	107	LOW $14
71	5388	69.5	112	SPECIALS None

THE COURSE COMMENTARY

The signature hole is the 530 yard par-5 18th hole. It is a dogleg right with water down the right side and in front of a narrow green. This hole is considered one of Arizona's best hole's.

TOUGHEST HOLE	THE 534 YARD PAR-5 5TH HOLE IS A DOGLEG RIGHT. YOUR TEE SHOT PLAYS TO A TIGHT FAIRWAY WITH WATER ON THE LEFT.
BIRDIE HOLE	THE 350 YARD PAR-4 14TH HOLE IS STRAIGHTAWAY TO A LARGE GREEN.
WATER IN PLAY ON...	6 HOLES
OVERALL STRATEGY	THE FAIRWAYS ARE TIGHT SO BE SMART ON THE TEE.
CART REQUIRED?	NO
PRACTICE FACILITIES?	DRIVING RANGE PUTTING GREEN CHIPPING GREEN
COURSE IS OPEN...	YES
OVERSEEDING	OCTOBER FOR 2 WEEKS. INCLUDES EVERYTHING.
RESTAURANT?	FULL SERVICE RESTAURANT.
ACCOMMODATIONS?	NO
DON'T FORGET YOUR..	1 IRON AND FAIRWAY WOODS.
COURSE DESIGNER	TED ROBINSON
# OF ROUNDS ANNUALLY	70,000
DIRECTIONS	LOCATED AT 96TH AVE AND UNION HILLS DR.

COURSE LAYOUT

HOLE	1	2	3	4	5	6	7	8	9	10	11	12	13	14	15	16	17	18
CHAMP	360	377	160	500	534	337	208	364	384	413	390	164	390	350	372	394	185	530
MENS	347	367	140	480	514	327	157	347	364	388	370	145	362	331	348	378	157	494
LADIES	327	327	127	427	447	300	115	314	329	354	328	124	332	306	322	338	115	438
PAR	4	4	3	5	5	4	3	4	4	4	4	3	4	4	4	4	3	5
M.HCP	13	5	17	3	1	9	15	7	11	4	8	18	10	12	14	6	16	2
L.HCP	7	9	15	3	1	5	17	13	11	4	8	18	10	12	14	6	16	2

WIGWAM - BLUE COURSE

HOTEL GUEST PRIORITY 18 HOLES

451 N. Litchfield Rd. Litchfield Park, AZ 85340   602-272-4653

DESERT ○   TRADITIONAL ●   LINKS ○

| TERRAIN | TREES | WATER |

GREENS	Bermuda	COURSE FAVORS A...	Fade
FAIRWAYS	Bermuda	WIDTH OF FAIRWAYS	Tight
BUNKERS	Regular	AMT. OF BUNKERS	Many

PAR	YARDS	RATING	SLOPE
N/A	N/A	N/A	N/A
70	6030	68.0	118
70	5178	69.8	118

1992 GREEN FEES

HIGH	$80
LOW	$55
SPECIALS	Hotel guest special

THE COURSE COMMENTARY

The Wigwam is a 54 hole resort course. The Blue course is the shortest of the three courses yet it is more challenging because of tighter fairways and more water. A colored coded flag system denotes placement of the flagstick on each green.

TOUGHEST HOLE THE 422 YARD PAR-4 8TH HOLE IS A DOGLEG RIGHT WITH A FAIRWAY BUNKER AT THE BEND AND A VERY SMALL GREEN.

BIRDIE HOLE THE 462 YARD PAR-5 10TH HOLE IS STRAIGHTAWAY AND REACHABLE IN TWO SHOTS.

WATER IN PLAY ON... 8 HOLES

OVERALL STRATEGY RESPECT THE YARDAGE OF THE COURSE. WATCH OUT FOR THESE POSTAGE STAMP GREENS.

CART REQUIRED? YES

PRACTICE FACILITIES? DRIVING RANGE   PUTTING GREEN   CHIPPING GREEN

COURSE IS OPEN... YES

OVERSEEDING OCTOBER FOR 3 WEEKS. INCLUDES EVERYTHING.

RESTAURANT? HALFWAY HOUSE AT THE TURN AND A 5 STAR DINING ROOM AT THE WIGWAM.

ACCOMMODATIONS? THE 5 STAR WIGWAM RESORT, CONSISTENTLY RATED AS ONE OF THE NATIONS FINEST GOLF DESTINATIONS, IS ON PROPERTY.

DON'T FORGET YOUR.. 1 IRON

COURSE DESIGNER ROBERT TRENT JONES SR.

 # OF ROUNDS ANNUALLY 35,000

DIRECTIONS 1 MILE NORTH OF THE INTERSECTION AT INDIAN SCHOOL RD. AND LITCHFIELD RD.

COURSE LAYOUT

HOLE	1	2	3	4	5	6	7	8	9	10	11	12	13	14	15	16	17	18
CHAMP																		
MENS	502	202	505	149	420	396	351	426	161	464	322	329	192	328	391	334	409	149
LADIES	459	148	459	127	375	347	296	392	113	427	263	284	121	291	355	283	376	119
PAR	5	3	5	3	4	4	4	4	3	5	4	4	3	4	4	4	4	3
M.HCP	3	13	1	15	7	9	11	5	17	2	12	6	16	10	4	14	8	18
L.HCP	3	15	1	13	7	9	11	5	17	2	14	12	16	8	6	10	4	18

WIGWAM - GOLD COURSE

HOTEL GUEST PRIORITY 18 HOLES

451 N. Litchfield Rd.   Litchfield Park, AZ 85340

602-272-4653

DESERT ◯   TRADITIONAL ⬤   LINKS ◯

TERRAIN	TREES	WATER

 GREENS *Bermuda*

 FAIRWAYS *Bermuda*

BUNKERS *Regular*

 COURSE FAVORS A... *Mix*

WIDTH OF FAIRWAYS *Normal*

AMT. OF BUNKERS *Many*

PAR	YARDS	RATING	SLOPE
72	7074	74.5	133
72	6504	71.7	129
72	5657	71.9	128

1992 GREEN FEES $

HIGH	*$95*
LOW	*$60*
SPECIALS	*Hotel guest special*

THE COURSE COMMENTARY

The Wigwam is a 54 hole resort course. This is Robert Trent Jones Sr. at his best. This course is the annual host of The World Champions of Golf, The Wigwam Classic, and The Wigwam Interclub Challenge.

TOUGHEST HOLE THE 228 PAR-3 3RD HOLE HAS A SMALL ELEVATED GREEN. THE LOCALS SAY THAT THIS HOLE WILL GET YOU EVERY TIME.

BIRDIE HOLE THE 369 YARD PAR-4 18TH HAS A LARGE FAIRWAY WITH A LARGE WELL-BUNKERED GREEN.

WATER IN PLAY ON... 11 HOLES

OVERALL STRATEGY HIT IT LONG AND HIT IT HIGH. GIVE YOURSELF AN EXTRA CLUB ON THE ELEVATED GREENS.

CART REQUIRED? No

PRACTICE FACILITIES? DRIVING RANGE   PUTTING GREEN   CHIPPING GREEN

COURSE IS OPEN... YES

OVERSEEDING SEPT. FOR 3 WEEKS. INCLUDES EVERYTHING.

RESTAURANT? HALFWAY HOUSE AT THE TURN AND A 5 STAR DINING ROOM AT THE WIGWAM.

ACCOMMODATIONS? THE 5 STAR WIGWAM RESORT, CONSISTENTLY RATED AS ONE OF THE NATIONS FINEST GOLF DESTINATIONS, IS ON PROPERTY.

DON'T FORGET YOUR.. 1 IRON

COURSE DESIGNER ROBERT TRENT JONES SR.

 # OF ROUNDS ANNUALLY 35,000

DIRECTIONS 1 MILE NORTH OF THE INTERSECTION AT INDIAN SCHOOL RD. AND LITCHFIELD RD.

COURSE LAYOUT

HOLE	1	2	3	4	5	6	7	8	9	10	11	12	13	14	15	16	17	18
CHAMP	549	385	231	573	395	208	420	441	421	593	179	381	420	526	368	159	405	367
MENS	523	352	205	532	358	179	400	398	380	559	141	332	371	489	342	143	366	358
LADIES	483	322	161	476	328	152	320	330	341	519	123	307	300	454	307	126	343	281
PAR	5	4	3	5	4	3	4	4	4	5	3	4	4	5	4	3	4	4
M.HCP	5	13	15	3	11	17	9	1	7	2	16	12	8	4	10	18	6	14
L.HCP	3	7	15	1	13	17	11	5	9	2	18	10	12	4	8	16	6	14

WIGWAM - WEST COURSE

HOTEL GUEST PRIORITY 18 HOLES

451 N. Litchfield Rd. Litchfield Park, AZ 85340   602-272-4653

DESERT ○   TRADITIONAL ●   LINKS ○

| TERRAIN | TREES | WATER |

GREENS *Bent*   **COURSE FAVORS A...** *Fade*
FAIRWAYS *Bermuda*   **WIDTH OF FAIRWAYS** *Normal*
BUNKERS *Regular*   **AMT. OF BUNKERS** *Average*

PAR	YARDS	RATING	SLOPE
72	6865	72.1	119
72	6307	69.3	114
72	5808	71.9	117

1992 GREEN FEES $
HIGH   *$80*
LOW   *$55*
SPECIALS *Hotel guest special*

THE COURSE COMMENTARY

The Wigwam is a 54 hole resort course. The West Course offers the most challenging trio of finishing holes of the three courses. If you can play these final 1299 yards in 12 strokes than you've done well.

TOUGHEST HOLE THE 454 YARD PAR-4 16TH HOLE IS A DOGLEG LEFT WITH WATER, A TIGHT LANDING AREA, AND A WELL-BUNKERED GREEN.

BIRDIE HOLE THE 499 YARD PAR-5 4TH HOLE PLAYS DOWNWIND TO A DOGLEG LEFT.

WATER IN PLAY ON... 10 HOLES

OVERALL STRATEGY THE TROUBLE IS MOSTLY TO THE LEFT.

CART REQUIRED? YES

PRACTICE FACILITIES? DRIVING RANGE PUTTING GREEN CHIPPING GREEN

COURSE IS OPEN... YES

OVERSEEDING OCT. FOR 3 WEEKS. INCLUDES EVERYTHING.

RESTAURANT? HALFWAY HOUSE AT THE TURN AND A 5 STAR DINING ROOM AT THE WIGWAM.

ACCOMMODATIONS? THE 5 STAR WIGWAM RESORT, CONSTENTLY RATED AS ONE OF THE NATIONS FINEST GOLF DESTINATIONS, IS ON PROPERTY.

DON'T FORGET YOUR.. 1 IRON

COURSE DESIGNER "RED" LAWRENCE

 # OF ROUNDS ANNUALLY 30,000

DIRECTIONS 1 MILE NORTH OF THE INTERSECTION AT INDIAN SCHOOL RD. AND LITCHFIELD RD.

COURSE LAYOUT

HOLE	1	2	3	4	5	6	7	8	9	10	11	12	13	14	15	16	17	18
CHAMP	390	208	405	494	170	568	384	348	409	376	380	147	513	382	410	445	252	586
MENS	370	155	380	474	157	540	343	328	365	344	356	128	479	358	372	419	161	548
LADIES	347	129	337	448	136	513	293	317	349	314	323	104	465	355	362	389	141	510
PAR	4	3	4	5	3	5	4	4	4	4	4	3	5	4	4	4	3	5
M.HCP	9	15	11	3	17	1	7	13	5	14	12	18	4	10	8	6	16	2
L.HCP	9	17	11	3	15	1	7	13	5	14	12	18	4	10	8	6	16	2

OUTLYING AREAS
Courses open to the public

AJO C.C.

TRADITIONAL, 9 HOLES, SEMI PRIVATE

M.PAR: 36   **M.RATING:** 68.4
M.YARDS: 3096   **M.SLOPE:** 113
HIGH SEASON: $15
77 W. Mead Rd., Ajo, AZ 85321
602-387-5011
On Mead Rd., 7 miles north of town.

ALPINE C.C.

TRADITIONAL, 18 HOLES, SEMI PRIVATE

M.PAR: 70   **M.RATING:** 65.7
M.YARDS: 5595   **M.SLOPE:** 107
HIGH SEASON: $13
100 Country Club Ln., Alpine, AZ 85920
602-339-4944
2 miles east of town on the highway.

ARIZONA G.R.

TRADITIONAL, 18 HOLES, SEMI PRIVATE

M.PAR: 71   **M.RATING:** 69.4
M.YARDS: 6195   **M.SLOPE:** 117
HIGH SEASON: $50
425 S. Power Rd., Mesa, AZ 85206
602-832-1661
On the southeast corner of Power & Broadway Rds.

ARIZONA SUNSITES C.C.

TRADITIONAL, 18 HOLES, SEMI PRIVATE

M.PAR: 72   **M.RATING:** 68.8
M.YARDS: 6324   **M.SLOPE:** N/A
HIGH SEASON: $17
Box 384, Pearce, AZ 85625
602-826-3412
20 miles south of I-10 on US 666

BEAVER CREEK G.R.

TRADITIONAL, 18 HOLES, SEMI PRIVATE

M.PAR: 71   **M.RATING:** 69.2
M.YARDS: 6386   **M.SLOPE:** 114
HIGH SEASON: $58
Montezuma Ave. & Lakeshore Dr., Lake Montezuma, AZ 86342
602-567-4487
Go east 4 miles off exit 293 on I17.

CANOA HILLS G.C.

DESERT, 18 HOLES, PUBLIC

M.PAR: 72   **M.RATING:** 69.7
M.YARDS: 6600   **M.SLOPE:** 117
HIGH SEASON: $40
1401 Calle Urbano, Green Valley, AZ 85614
602-648-1880
Go south on I-19 to exit 63, then go south on the frontage road to Camino Encanto, then south to Calle Urbano.

CHAPARRAL C.C.

TRADITIONAL, 9 HOLES, SEMI PRIVATE

M.PAR: 64   **M.RATING:** 61.5
M.YARDS: 4663   **M.SLOPE:** N/A
HIGH SEASON: $15
1260 E. Mohave Dr., Riviera, AZ 86442
602-758-3939
5 miles south of Bulhead City on State rd. 95

COBRE VALLEY C.C.

TRADITIONAL, 9 HOLES, SEMI PRIVATE

M.PAR: 72   **M.RATING:** 69.9
M.YARDS: 6641   **M.SLOPE:** N/A
HIGH SEASON: $15
Box 2629, Globe, AZ 85502
602-473-2542
3 miles east on Globe on US 60.

Concho Valley C.C.

Traditional, 18 Holes, Public
M.Par: 36   **M.Rating:** 67.6
M.Yards: 3014   **M.Slope:** 109
High Season: $12
HC 30, Box 900, Concho, AZ 85924
602-337-4644
North of Showlow on US 60. Look for the signs

Country Meadows G.C.

Traditional, 18 Holes, Semi Private
M.Par: 63   **M.Rating:** 59.4
M.Yards: 4292   **M.Slope:** 88
High Season: $20
8411 N. 107th Ave., Peoria, AZ 85345
602-972-1364
At 107th Ave between Olive Ave and Northern Ave

Coyote Hills G.C.

Desert, 9 Holes, Public
M.Par: 36   **M.Rating:** 64.7
M.Yards: 2845   **M.Slope:** 96
High Season: $6
800 E. Country Club Dr., Benson, AZ 85602
602-586-2323
Leave Benson on US Hwy. 80 toward Tombstone, then go east on Country Club Dr. to the end.

Dave White Regional Municple G.C.

Desert, 18 Holes, Public
M.Par: 72   **M.Rating:** 68.8
M.Yards: 6316   **M.Slope:** 115
High Season: $22
2121 N. Thornton Rd., Casa Grande, AZ 85222
602-836-9216
Go north from Pinal Rd. to Cottonwood Ln., west 1 mile to Thornton Rd., go north to the end of the road

Desert Fairways G.C.

Traditional, 9 Holes, Public
M.Par: 35   **M.Rating:** 31
M.Yards: 2386   **M.Slope:** N/A
High Season: $12
813 W. Calle Rosa, Casa Grande, AZ 85222
602-723-9717
Take exit 190 off of I-10. Go east 7 miles.

Desert Lakes G.C.

Traditional, 18 Holes, Public
M.Par: 72   **M.Rating:** 69.5
M.Yards: 6537   **M.Slope:** 106
High Season: $10
5835 Desert Lakes Dr., Ft. Mohave, AZ 86427
602-625-5090
On U.S. Hwy. 95 go 13 miles from the bridge to Laughlin to Joy Ln., go East 1 mile.

Douglass G.C.

Desert, 9 Holes, Public
M.Par: 35   **M.Rating:** 68.3
M.Yards: 3070   **M.Slope:** 112
High Season: $9
P.O. Box 1220, Douglas, AZ 85608
602-364-3722
A mile and a half north of Douglas on Leslie Canyon Rd.

Dove Valley G.C.

Traditional, 9 Holes, Public
M.Par: 35   **M.Rating:** 68.4
M.Yards: 3000   **M.Slope:** 113
High Season: $9
220 N. Marshall Loop Rd., Somerton, AZ 85350
602-627-3262
South of Somerton on Hwy. 95.

ELEPHANT ROCKS G.C.

TRADITIONAL, 9 HOLES, PUBLIC
M.PAR: 70   **M.RATING: 66.3**
M.YARDS: 5937   **M.SLOPE: 109**
HIGH SEASON: $25
2200 Country Club Dr., Williams, AZ 86046
602-635-4936
Go 1 mile of Williams on Country Club Dr.

EMERALD CANYON G.C.

DESERT, 18 HOLES, PUBLIC
M.PAR: 72   **M.RATING: 72.0**
M.YARDS: 6657   **M.SLOPE: 127**
HIGH SEASON: $25
72 Emerald Canyon Dr., Parker, AZ 85344
602-667-3366
7 miles north of Parker on Hwy 95.

FRANCISCO GRANDE R. & G.C.

TRADITIONAL, 18 HOLES, PUBLIC
M.PAR: 72   **M.RATING: 71.7**
M.YARDS: 6975   **M.SLOPE: 119**
HIGH SEASON: $50
26000 Gila Bend Hwy., Casa Grande, AZ 85222
602-426-9205
5 miles west of Casa Grande on State Rd. 84.

GLEN CANYON G.C.

DESERT, 9 HOLES, PUBLIC
M.PAR: 36   **M.RATING: 69.3**
M.YARDS: 3259   **M.SLOPE: 110**
HIGH SEASON: $11
Highway 89, P.O. Box 1333, Page, AZ 86040
602-645-2715
1 mile west of town, take the access road from US 89A.

GREENLEE C.C.

TRADITIONAL, 9 HOLES, SEMI PRIVATE
M.PAR: 36   **M.RATING: 69.4**
M.YARDS: 3400   **M.SLOPE: 111**
HIGH SEASON: $12
HCR Box 306, Duncan, AZ 85534
602-687-1099
12 miles south of Clifton on State Rd. 75

HAVEN G.C.

TRADITIONAL, 18 HOLES, PUBLIC
M.PAR: 72   **M.RATING: 69.2**
M.YARDS: 6336   **M.SLOPE: 111**
HIGH SEASON: $22
110 N. Abrego, Green Valley, AZ 85614
602-625-4281
Go east off the Esperanza exit off I-19 to Abrego, then
north 1 half block.

HAYDEN MUNICIPAL G.C.

TRADITIONAL, 9 HOLES, PUBLIC
M.PAR: 70   **M.RATING: 67.1**
M.YARDS: 5675   **M.SLOPE: N/A**
HIGH SEASON: $9
Golf Course Rd., Hayden, AZ 85235
602-356-7801
Go south off Highway 177

HIDDEN COVE G.C.

TRADITIONAL, 9 HOLES, PUBLIC
M.PAR: 72   **M.RATING: 67.8**
M.YARDS: 5814   **M.SLOPE: 110**
HIGH SEASON: $10
Hidden Cove Rd, P.O. Box 70, Holbrook, AZ 86025
602-524-3097
Take the 283 exit off of I-40, then go north for 1 mile.

HOHOKAM G.C.

DESERT, 18 HOLES, SEMI PRIVATE
M.PAR: 70 **M.RATING: 70.1**
M.YARDS: 5967 **M.SLOPE: 110**
HIGH SEASON: $21
P.O. Box 1565, Coolidge, AZ 85228
602-723-7192
2 miles north of Douglas off Leslie Canyon Rd.

KEARNY G.C.

TRADITIONAL, 9 HOLES, SEMI PRIVATE
M.PAR: 70 **M.RATING: 69.1**
M.YARDS: 6336 **M.SLOPE: 110**
HIGH SEASON: $10
301 Airport Rd., P.O. Box 927, Kearny, AZ 85237
602-363-7441
Cross the RR tracks on State Rd. 177, then go north on
Airport Rd. for 1 block.

KINGMAN MUNICIPAL G.C.

TRADITIONAL, 9 HOLES, PUBLIC
M.PAR: 72 **M.RATING: 69.4**
M.YARDS: 6292 **M.SLOPE: 121**
HIGH SEASON: $15
1001 Gates Ave., Kingman, AZ 86401
602-753-6593
Take I40 to Stockton Hill, then go south to Gates Ave.

KINO SPRINGS C.C.

TRADITIONAL, 18 HOLES, PUBLIC
M.PAR: 72 **M.RATING: 67.5**
M.YARDS: 5974 **M.SLOPE: 116**
HIGH SEASON: $20
1 Kino Springs Dr., Nogales, AZ 85621
1-800-732-5751/602-287-8701
On State Rd. 82 at milepost 6.

LONDON BRIDGE G.C.

TRADITIONAL, 18 HOLES, SEMI PRIVATE
M.PAR: 71 **M.RATING: 69.5**
M.YARDS: 6298 **M.SLOPE: 120**
HIGH SEASON: $46
2400 Clubhouse Dr., Lake Havasu, AZ 86403
602-855-2719
Take State Rd. 95 to Acoma, then go east for 2 miles.

LOS CABALLEROS G.C.

DESERT, 18 HOLES, SEMI PRIVATE
M.PAR: 72 **M.RATING: 71.6**
M.YARDS: 6554 **M.SLOPE: 128**
HIGH SEASON: $75
Vulture Mine Rd., P.O. Box QQ, Wickenburg, AZ 85358
602-684-2704
Take US 60 west for 2 miles south to South Vulture Mine
Rd., then go south for 2 miles.

MEADOW HILLS MUNI. G.C.

LINKS 9 HOLES, PUBLIC
M.PAR: 36 **M.RATING: 68.9**
M.YARDS: 3441 **M.SLOPE: N/A**
HIGH SEASON: $8
3425 Country Club Rd., Nogales, AZ 85621
602-281-0011
Take the first Nogales exit off I-19 for a half mile, then go
east to Country Club Rd.

MESA VIEW G.C.

TRADITIONAL, 9 HOLES, PUBLIC
M.PAR: 60 **M.RATING: 55.4**
M.YARDS: 3318 **M.SLOPE: 75**
HIGH SEASON: $12
4 Ash St., Bagdad, AZ 86321
602-633-2818
Go 2 blocks north of Main at the corner of Lindahl & Ash.

MORRY CANOA HILLS G.C.

DESERT, 18 HOLES, SEMI PRIVATE
M.PAR: 72   **M.RATING:** 67.3
M.YARDS: 6077   **M.SLOPE:** 112
HIGH SEASON: $44
1401 W. Calle Urbano, Green Valley, AZ 85614
602-648-1880
Go south on I-19 to the Continental exit 63, then go south
to the frontage road to Camino Encanto, then south to
Calle Urbano.

MOUNT GRAHAM G.C.

TRADITIONAL, 18 HOLES, SEMI PRIVATE
M.PAR: 72   **M.RATING:** 69.5
M.YARDS: 6354   **M.SLOPE:** 116
HIGH SEASON: $10.50
Box 592, Safford, AZ 85546
602-428-1260
2 miles south of Safford on Golf Course Rd., in Daily
Estates

NAUTICAL INN G.C.

TRADITIONAL, 18 HOLES, PUBLIC
M.PAR: 61   **M.RATING:** 57.4
M.YARDS: 4012   **M.SLOPE:** 79
HIGH SEASON: $18
1000 McCulloch Blvd., Lake Havasu, AZ 86403
602-855-2131
Between the airport and the London Bridge off State Rd.
95.

PALO VERDE G.C.

TRADITIONAL, 9 HOLES, PUBLIC
M.PAR: 30   **M.RATING:** 55.3
M.YARDS: 1820   **M.SLOPE:** 74
HIGH SEASON: $6.50
6215 N. 15th Ave., Phoenix, AZ 85015
602-249-9930
At 15th Ave. and Maryland.

PAYSON G.C.

TRADITIONAL, 18 HOLES, PUBLIC
M.PAR: 71   **M.RATING:** 66.5
M.YARDS: 5842   **M.SLOPE:** 109
HIGH SEASON: $25
1504 W. Country Club Dr., Payson, AZ 85541
602-474-2273
West from state 87 on Main St. to the end.

PINE MEADOWS C.C.

TRADITIONAL, 9 HOLES, SEMI PRIVATE
M.PAR: 34   **M.RATING:** 64.4
M.YARDS: 2631   **M.SLOPE:** 113
HIGH SEASON: $20
Country Club Dr.., P.O. Box 562, Overgaard, AZ 85933
602-535-4220
Hwy. 260 to milepost 308 in Overgaard.

PINETOP LAKES G. & C.C.

TRADITIONAL, 18 HOLES, PUBLIC
M.PAR: 63   **M.RATING:** 60.6
M.YARDS: 4558   **M.SLOPE:** 94
HIGH SEASON: $24
Bucksprings Rd., Box 1699D, Pinetop, AZ 85935
602-369-4531
2 miles south of Pinetop on State Rd. 260, then east on
Bucksprings Rd,

PINEWOOD C.C.

TRADITIONAL, 18 HOLES, SEMI PRIVATE
M.PAR: 72   **M.RATING:** 69.2
M.YARDS: 6434   **M.SLOPE:** 112
HIGH SEASON: $40
P.O. Box 584, Munds Park, AZ 86017
602-286-1110
15 miles south of Flagstaff on I-17, take the Pinewood-
Munds Park.

POCO DIABLO RESORT

TRADITIONAL, 9 HOLES, PUBLIC

M.PAR: 27   **M.RATING:** N/A

M.YARDS: 720   **M.SLOPE:** N/A

HIGH SEASON: $12

So. Highway 179, Box 1709, Sedona, AZ 86336
602-282-7333
Exit I-17 north on State Rd. 179, go 12 miles.

PRESCOTT C.C.

TRADITIONAL, 18 HOLES, SEMI PRIVATE

M.PAR: 72   **M.RATING:** 71.4

M.YARDS: 6783   **M.SLOPE:** 123

HIGH SEASON: $22

1030 Prescott Countyr Club Blvd., Dewey, AZ 86327
602-772-8984
14 miles south of Prescott on State Rd. 69.

PUEBLO DEL SOL G.C.

TRADITIONAL, 18 HOLES, PUBLIC

M.PAR: 72   **M.RATING:** 70.0

M.YARDS: 6599   **M.SLOPE:** 118

HIGH SEASON: $20

2770 St. Andrews Dr., Sierra Vista, AZ 85635
602-378-6444
South on State Rd. 92. Go 2.5 miles beyond Fry Blvd. to
Country Club Estates, then west on St. Andrews.

QUAILWOOD GREENS G.C.

LINKS 9 HOLES, PUBLIC

M.PAR: 34   **M.RATING:** N/A

M.YARDS: 2083   **M.SLOPE:** N/A

HIGH SEASON: $17

12200 Highway 69, Dewey, AZ 86327
602-772-0130
14 miles south of Prescott on State Rd. 69, go north at The
Villages @ Links Creek, to the end.

QUEENS BAY C.C.

DESERT, 9 HOLES, PUBLIC

M.PAR: 27   **M.RATING:** 51.2

M.YARDS: 1373   **M.SLOPE:** 61

HIGH SEASON: $10

1480 Queens Bay, Lake Havasu City, AZ 86403
602-855-4777 or 1-800-624-7939
Located next to the Ramada London Bridge Resort.

RIO RICO RESORT & C.C.

TRADITIONAL, 18 HOLES, SEMI PRIVATE

M.PAR: 72   **M.RATING:** 73.3

M.YARDS: 7119   **M.SLOPE:** 127

HIGH SEASON: $20

1550 Camino a la Posada, Rio Rico, AZ 85621
602-281-8567
Take the Rio Rico exit from I-19, and go east 3 miles

ROYAL PALMS G. C.

TRADITIONAL, 9 HOLES, PUBLIC

M.PAR: 30   **M.RATING:** 52.2

M.YARDS: 1501   **M.SLOPE:** N/A

HIGH SEASON: $8

1415 E. McKellips Rd., Mesa, AZ 85203
602-964-1709
On McKellops 1 mile east of Stapley.

SADDLEBROOKE C.C.

TRADITIONAL, 18 HOLES, PUBLIC

M.PAR: 72   **M.RATING:** 70.2

M.YARDS: 6494   **M.SLOPE:** 119

HIGH SEASON: $35

64500 E. Saddlebrooke Blvd., Tucson, AZ 85737
602-825-2505
14 miles north of Ina Rd. off Oracle Rd.

San Ignacio G. C.

Desert, 18 Holes, Public
M.Par: 71   **M.Rating: 69.8**
M.Yards: 6228 **M.Slope: 126**
High Season: $45
24245 S. Camino del Sol, Green Valley, AZ 85614
602-648-3468
Take I-10 south to Continental Rd., go south on the west
frontage road to Camino Encanto, then south to Camino
del Sol.

San Manuel G.C.

Traditional, 9 Holes, Public
M.Par: 72   **M.Rating: 69.3**
M.Yards: 6500 **M.Slope: 108**
High Season: $10
1.5 miles North of Hwy. 76, San Manuel, AZ 85631
602-385-2224
A mile and a half north of Hwy. 76

Show Low C.C.

Traditional, 18 Holes, Public
M.Par: 70   **M.Rating: 65.2**
M.Yards: 5572 **M.Slope: 104**
High Season: $20
860 N. 36th Dr., Show Low, AZ 85901
602-537-4564
Go 2 miles west of Show Low on State rd. 260 to Linden
Rd. Look for the signs.

Silver Creek G.C.

Links 18 Holes, Public
M.Par: 71   **M.Rating: 68.2**
M.Yards: 6075 **M.Slope: 119**
High Season: $38
2051 Silver Lake Blvd., Box 965, White Mountains Lake,
AZ 85912
602-537-2744
7 miles north of Showlow on Hwy. 77, then go 5 miles east
on White Mountain Lake Rd.

Snowflake Muni. G.C.

Traditional, 9 Holes, Public
M.Par: 36   **M.Rating: 68.2**
M.Yards: 3112 **M.Slope: 103**
High Season: $13
Box 1116, Highway 277 West, Snowflake, AZ 85937
602-536-7233
2 miles west of town on State Rd. 277.

Stone Bridge G.C.

Traditional, 18 Holes, Semi Private
M.Par: 71   **M.Rating: 66.8**
M.Yards: 5766 **M.Slope: 109**
High Season: $36
2400 Clubhouse Dr., Lake Havasu, AZ 86403
602-855-2719
Take State Rd. 95 to Acoma, then go east for 2 miles.

Tubac G.R.

Traditional, 18 Holes, Public
M.Par: 72   **M.Rating: 70.2**
M.Yards: 6408 **M.Slope: 120**
High Season: $36
#1 Otera Rd., P.O. Box 1297, Tubac, AZ 85646
602-398-2211
Take I-19 42 miles south of Tucson to exit 40, go south on
the frontage road for 2 miles to archway.

Turquoise Valley G.C.

Traditional, 9 Holes, Public
M.Par: 72   **M.Rating: 69.4**
M.Yards: 6730 **M.Slope: 115**
High Season: $12
N. Newell Rd., Naco, AZ 85620
602-432-3091
8 miles north of Bisbee on Naco Hwy.

Twin Lakes G. C.

DESERT, 9 HOLES, PUBLIC

M.PAR: 72 **M.RATING: 69.1**
M.YARDS: 6384 **M.SLOPE: N/A**
HIGH SEASON: $10
Rex Allen Jr. Dr., Willcox, AZ 85643
602-384-2720
Go east on Maley Rd. over the RR tracks for a half mile.

VALLE VISTA C.C.

TRADITIONAL, 18 HOLES, SEMI PRIVATE

M.PAR: 72 **M.RATING: 69.6**
M.YARDS: 6266 **M.SLOPE: 109**
HIGH SEASON: $10
9686 Concho Dr., Kingman, AZ 86401
602-757-8744
Exit I-40 to Rte. 66, go east to milepost 71, turn left, go 3 miles.

WICKENBURG C.C.

DESERT, 9 HOLES, SEMI PRIVATE

M.PAR: 72 **M.RATING: 69.3**
M.YARDS: 6386 **M.SLOPE: 110**
HIGH SEASON: $35
Country Club Dr., Wickenburg, AZ 85358
602-684-2011
2 miles west of Wickenburg on US 60

WINSLOW MUNI. G.C.

DESERT, 9 HOLES, PUBLIC

M.PAR: 36 **M.RATING: 68.8**
M.YARDS: 3214 **M.SLOPE: 113**
HIGH SEASON: $12
North Road, Winslow, AZ 86047
602-289-4915
Take the I-40 exit at 253. Follow the signs.

PRIVATE COURSES
Entire state of Arizona

ALTA MESA C.C.

TRADITIONAL, 18 HOLES, PRIVATE
M.PAR: 72   **M.RATING:** 73.9
M.YARDS: 7132   **M.SLOPE:** 135
HIGH SEASON: $50
1460 E Alta Mesa Dr., Mesa, AZ 85205
602-827-9411
At Brown & Higley go east for 1 mile, then go north on Alta Mesa for a half mile.

ANCALA C.C.

DESERT, 18 HOLES, PRIVATE
M.PAR: 72   **M.RATING:** 73.5
M.YARDS: 6961   **M.SLOPE:** 134
HIGH SEASON: $59
11700 E. Via Linda, Scottsdale, AZ 85259
602-391-2777
At Scottsdale Rd and Shea Blvd. go east 5 miles to Via Linda. Go north to the gate.

ARIZONA C.C.

TRADITIONAL, 18 HOLES, PRIVATE
M.PAR: 72   **M.RATING:** 69.8
M.YARDS: 6273   **M.SLOPE:** 121
HIGH SEASON: $75
5668 E. Orange Blossom Ln., Phoenix, AZ 85018
602-947-7666
1 block north of Thomas and east of 56th st. Look for the small sign at the entrance because the clubhouse is not visible.

BRIARWOOD C.C.

TRADITIONAL, 18 HOLES, PRIVATE
M.PAR: 72   **M.RATING:** 67.9
M.YARDS: 6005   **M.SLOPE:** 112
HIGH SEASON: $25
20800 135th Ave., Sun City West, AZ 85375
602-584-5301
Take Bell Rd. to R.H. Johnson Blvd., then go north to Meeker to 135th Ave.

COTTONWOOD C.C.

TRADITIONAL, 18 HOLES, PRIVATE
M.PAR: 72   **M.RATING:** 71.2
M.YARDS: 6737   **M.SLOPE:** 122
HIGH SEASON: $57
25621 E. J. Robson Blvd., Sun Lakes, AZ 85248
602-895-9449
Take the Riggs Rd. exit aoff I-10 and go east for 3 miles.

DESERT FOREST G.C.

DESERT, 18 HOLES, PRIVATE
M.PAR: 72   **M.RATING:** 74.7
M.YARDS: 6981   **M.SLOPE:** 144
HIGH SEASON: $40
37207 N. Mule Train Rd., Carefree, AZ 85377
602-971-2121
At Pima Rd. and Cave Creek Rd. go west for 2 miles and north on Mule Train Rd. for 2 blocks.

DESERT HIGHLANDS

DESERT, 18 HOLES, PRIVATE
M.PAR: 72   **M.RATING:** 71.9
M.YARDS: 7099   **M.SLOPE:** 137
HIGH SEASON: $55
10040 E. Happy Valley Rd., Scottsdale, AZ 85255
602-585-8521
Go north on Pima Rd. from Pinnacle Peak Rd., then go east on Happy Valley Rd.

DESERT HILLS G.C. OF GREEN VALLEY

TRADITIONAL, 18 HOLES, PRIVATE
M.PAR: 72   **M.RATING:** 69.0
M.YARDS: 6094   **M.SLOPE:** 119
HIGH SEASON: $40
2500 Circulo de las Lomas, Green Valley, AZ 85614
602-625-5090
Take the Continental exit off I-19. take the frontage road south 2 miles, turn right on Camino Encanto, turn right on Camino del Sol, then take your first right.

DESERT MOUNTAIN G.C. - COCHISE

DESERT, 18 HOLES, PRIVATE
M.PAR: 72   M.RATING: 73.8
M.YARDS: 7045   M.SLOPE: 136
HIGH SEASON: $150
10333 Rockaway Hills, Scottsdale, AZ 85262
602-258-4084
1 mile east of the Carefree Airport.

DESERT MOUNTAIN G.C. - GERONIMO

DESERT, 18 HOLES, PRIVATE
M.PAR: 72   M.RATING: 74.9
M.YARDS: 7437   M.SLOPE: 139
HIGH SEASON: $150
10333 Rockaway Hills, Scottsdale, AZ 85262
602-258-4084
1 mile east of the Carefree Airport.

DESERT MOUNTAIN G.C. - RENAGADE

DESERT, 18 HOLES, PRIVATE
M.PAR: 72   M.RATING: 76.6
M.YARDS: 7515   M.SLOPE: 138
HIGH SEASON: $150
10333 Rockaway Hills, Scottsdale, AZ 85262
602-258-4084
1 mile east of the Carefree Airport.

ECHO MESA G.C.

TRADITIONAL, 18 HOLES, PRIVATE
M.PAR: 60   M.RATING: 60.2
M.YARDS: 4140   M.SLOPE: 91
HIGH SEASON: $22
20349 Echo Mesa Dr., Sun City West, AZ 85375
602-584-0666
Take Bell Rd. west to R.H. Johnson Blvd and go north to
Meeker then right to Echo Mesa Dr.

FAIRFIELD FLAGSTAFF RESORT - ASPEN VALLEY C.C.

TRADITIONAL, 18 HOLES, PRIVATE
M.PAR: 72   M.RATING: 70.1
M.YARDS: 6579   M.SLOPE: 121
HIGH SEASON: $47
1855 Continental Dr., Flagstaff, AZ 86004
602-527-7995
Take the Country Club Dr. exit off I-40 and go south for 3
miles to Continental Dr.

FOREST HIGHLANDS

TRADITIONAL, 18 HOLES, PRIVATE
M.PAR: 72   M.RATING: 73.1
M.YARDS: 7051   M.SLOPE: 134
HIGH SEASON: $N/A
657 Forest Highlands, Flagstaff, AZ 86001
602-525-9000
2 miles north of the Flagstaff Airport on US 89.

FORT HUACHUCA G.C.

TRADITIONAL, 18 HOLES, PRIVATE
M.PAR: 72   M.RATING: 69.6
M.YARDS: 6449   M.SLOPE: 112
HIGH SEASON: $12
Bldg. 15479, Fort Huachuca, AZ 85613
602-538-7160
Take a left turn after entering the main gate at the Fort
Huachuca Army Base.

FOUNTAIN OF THE SUN C.C.

TRADITIONAL, 18 HOLES, PRIVATE
M.PAR: 62   M.RATING: 59.3
M.YARDS: 4097   M.SLOPE: 89
HIGH SEASON: $N/A
500 S. 80th St., Mesa, AZ 85208
602-986-3128
A mile and a half east of Power Rd. on Broadway.

GRANDVIEW G.C.

TRADITIONAL, 18 HOLES, PRIVATE
M.PAR: 72   **M.RATING: 72.8**
M.YARDS: 6862   **M.SLOPE: 128**
HIGH SEASON: $25
14260 Meeker Blvd., Sun City West, AZ 85375
602-584-2998
Take Bell Rd. to R.H. Johnson Blvd. and then go north to Meeker Blvd.

GREEN VALLEY C.C.

DESERT, 18 HOLES, PRIVATE
M.PAR: 72   **M.RATING: 69.0**
M.YARDS: 6281   **M.SLOPE: 113**
HIGH SEASON: $25
77 Paseo de Golf, Green Valley, AZ 85614
602-625-8831
Exit off I-19 at Esperanza and go east then north on Abrego for 1.5 miles.

LAKES EAST G.C.

TRADITIONAL, 18 HOLES, PRIVATE
M.PAR: 60   **M.RATING: 56.3**
M.YARDS: 3244   **M.SLOPE: 76**
HIGH SEASON: $N/A
10433 Talisman Rd., Sun City, AZ 85351
602-876-3023
Go north on Del Webb Blvd. from Grand Ave. for 1 mile, then go east on Talisman Rd.

LAKES WEST G.C.

TRADITIONAL, 18 HOLES, PRIVATE
M.PAR: 72   **M.RATING: 68.5**
M.YARDS: 6251   **M.SLOPE: 112**
HIGH SEASON: $N/A
10433 Talisman Rd., Sun City, AZ 85351
602-876-3020
Go north on Del Webb Blvd. from Grand Ave. for 1 mile, then go east on Talisman Rd.

LEISURE WORLD C.C. - CHAMP.

TRADITIONAL, 18 HOLES, PRIVATE
M.PAR: 73   **M.RATING: 70.7**
M.YARDS: 6545   **M.SLOPE: 120**
HIGH SEASON: $33
908 S. Power Rd, Mesa, AZ 85206
602-844-8785
Half mile north of Southern on Power Rd.

LEISURE WORLD C.C. - EXEC.

LINKS 18 HOLES, PRIVATE
M.PAR: 62   **M.RATING: 58.6**
M.YARDS: 4024   **M.SLOPE: 93**
HIGH SEASON: $22
908 S. Power Rd, Mesa, AZ 85206
602-844-8785
Half mile north of Southern on Power Rd.

MESA C.C.

TRADITIONAL, 18 HOLES, PRIVATE
M.PAR: 72   **M.RATING: 70.9**
M.YARDS: 6599   **M.SLOPE: 125**
HIGH SEASON: $N/A
660 W. Fairway Dr., Mesa, AZ 85201
602-964-3514
1 block north of Brown on Country Club Dr.

MOON VALLEY C.C.

TRADITIONAL, 18 HOLES, PRIVATE
M.PAR: 73   **M.RATING: 74.8**
M.YARDS: 7298   **M.SLOPE: 131**
HIGH SEASON: $N/A
151 W. Moon valley Dr., Phoenix, AZ 85023
602-942-1278
At Thunderbird and Coral Gables go north for 2 miles.

ORO VALLEY C.C.

TRADITIONAL, 18 HOLES, PRIVATE
M.PAR: 72   **M.RATING:** 73.1
M.YARDS: 6964   **M.SLOPE:** 125
HIGH SEASON: $N/A
10200 N. Oracle Dr., Oro Valley, AZ 85737
602-297-3322
15 miles north of Tucson on Oracle Rd.

PALMBROOK C.C.

TRADITIONAL, 18 HOLES, PRIVATE
M.PAR: 72   **M.RATING:** 69.7
M.YARDS: 6529   **M.SLOPE:** 113
HIGH SEASON: $N/A
9350 W. Greenway Rd., Sun City, AZ 85357
602-977-8383
6 blocks east of 99th Ave. on Greenway Rd.

PALO VERDE C.C.

TRADITIONAL, 18 HOLES, PRIVATE
M.PAR: 62   **M.RATING:** 56.7
M.YARDS: 3811   **M.SLOPE:** 87
HIGH SEASON: $N/A
10841 E. San Tan Blvd., Sun Lakes, AZ 85248
602-895-0300
Take the Riggs Rd. Exit off I-10 and go east 4 miles

PARADISE PEAK WEST

TRADITIONAL, 9 HOLES, PRIVATE
M.PAR: 29   **M.RATING:** 55.0
M.YARDS: 1437   **M.SLOPE:** N/A
HIGH SEASON: $8
3901 E. Pinnacle Peak Rd., Phoenix, AZ 85024
602-946-2299
1 mile east of Cave Creek Rd. on Pinnacle Peak Rd.

PARADISE VALLEY C.C.

TRADITIONAL, 18 HOLES, PRIVATE
M.PAR: 72   **M.RATING:** 72.2
M.YARDS: 6680   **M.SLOPE:** 121
HIGH SEASON: $N/A
7101 N. Tatum Blvd., Paradise Valley, AZ 85253
602-840-8100
On Tatum Blvd. 1 mile north of Lincoln.

PEBBLEBROOK G.C.

TRADITIONAL, 18 HOLES, PRIVATE
M.PAR: 72   **M.RATING:** 69.9
M.YARDS: 6451   **M.SLOPE:** 116
HIGH SEASON: $25
18836 128th Ave., Sun City West, AZ 85375
602-584-2401
Take Bell Rd. to R.H. Johnson Blvd and go east on 128th
Ave.

PHOENIX C.C.

TRADITIONAL, 18 HOLES, PRIVATE
M.PAR: 71   **M.RATING:** 71.7
M.YARDS: 6742   **M.SLOPE:** 125
HIGH SEASON: $75
2901 N. 7th St., Phoenix, AZ 85014
602-263-5208
NWC of 7th St. and Thomas Rd.

PINETOP C.C.

TRADITIONAL, 18 HOLES, PRIVATE
M.PAR: 71   **M.RATING:** 67.3
M.YARDS: 6258   **M.SLOPE:** 110
HIGH SEASON: $50
P.O.Box 1469, Pinetop, AZ 85935
602-369-2461
3 miles south of Pinetop on Hwy 260 to Country Club Dr.

PINNACLE PEAK C.C.

TRADITIONAL, 18 HOLES, PRIVATE
M.PAR: 72   **M.RATING: 70.9**
M.YARDS: 6587   **M.SLOPE: 128**
HIGH SEASON: $60
8701 E. Pinnacle Peak Rd., Scottsdale, AZ 85255
602-585-0385
Go north on Pima Rd. to Pinnacle Peak Rd. Go east about a half mile untill you see the signs.

QUAIL CREEK C.C.

DESERT, 9 HOLES, PRIVATE
M.PAR: 36   **M.RATING: 69.5**
M.YARDS: 3174   **M.SLOPE: 124**
HIGH SEASON: $22
2010 E. Quail Crossing Blvd., Green Valley, AZ 85614
602-625-0133
1.5 miles east of Old Nogales Hwy and 2 miles south of Duval Mine Co.

QUAIL RUN G.C.

TRADITIONAL, 9 HOLES, PRIVATE
M.PAR: 31   **M.RATING: 58.9**
M.YARDS: 2902   **M.SLOPE: 90**
HIGH SEASON: $13
9774 Alabama Ave., Sun City, AZ 85351
602-876-3035
East of 99th Ave. and south of Grand Ave.

RIVERVIEW G.C. - SUN CITY

TRADITIONAL, 18 HOLES, PRIVATE
M.PAR: 72   **M.RATING: 70.0**
M.YARDS: 6379   **M.SLOPE: 120**
HIGH SEASON: $16
16401 N. Del Webb Blvd., Sun City, AZ 85351
602-876-3025
At Bell Rd. and 107th Ave, then go south on Del Webb for a half mile.

ROADHAVEN R. & G.C.

TRADITIONAL, 9 HOLES, PRIVATE
M.PAR: 27   **M.RATING: 24.8**
M.YARDS: 1022   **M.SLOPE: 40**
HIGH SEASON: $14
1000 S. Idaho Rd., Apache Junction, AZ 85220
602-982-GOLF
A half mile south of Broadway on Idaho Rd.

ROLLING HILLS G. C.

TRADITIONAL, 18 HOLES, PRIVATE
M.PAR: 63   **M.RATING: 58.4**
M.YARDS: 4146   **M.SLOPE: 84**
HIGH SEASON: $13
8900 E. 29th St., Tucson, AZ 85710
602-298-2401
Go north of Golf Links Rd. on Camino Seco & 29th St.

SKYLINE C.C.

TRADITIONAL, 18 HOLES, PRIVATE
M.PAR: 71   **M.RATING: 69.2**
M.YARDS: 6123   **M.SLOPE: 118**
HIGH SEASON: $60
5200 E. St. Andrews Dr., Tucson, AZ 85718
602-299-0464
.25 mile north of Skyline Dr. on N. Swan Dr.

STARDUST G.C.

TRADITIONAL, 18 HOLES, PRIVATE
M.PAR: 60   **M.RATING: 59.0**
M.YARDS: 4234   **M.SLOPE: 93**
HIGH SEASON: $22
12702 Stradust Blvd., Sun City West, AZ 85375
602-584-2916
Take Bell Rd. to R.H. Johnson Blvd., then go east on 128th Ave.

SUN CITY C.C.

TRADITIONAL, 18 HOLES, PRIVATE
M.PAR: 72   **M.RATING:** 68.9
M.YARDS: 6233   **M.SLOPE:** 113
HIGH SEASON: $16
9433 N. 107th Ave., SunCity, AZ 85351
602-933-1353
On 107th Ave., 4 blocks north of Olive.

SUN CITY NORTH G.C.

TRADITIONAL, 18 HOLES, PRIVATE
M.PAR: 72   **M.RATING:** 68.9
M.YARDS: 6434   **M.SLOPE:** 111
HIGH SEASON: $15
12650 N. 107th Ave, Sun City, AZ 85351
602-876-3010
.25 mile south of Grand Ave. on 107th Ave.

SUN CITY SOUTH G.C.

TRADITIONAL, 18 HOLES, PRIVATE
M.PAR: 72   **M.RATING:** 71.4
M.YARDS: 6953   **M.SLOPE:** 116
HIGH SEASON: $15
11000 N. 103rd Ave., Sun City, AZ 85351
602-876-3015
.25 mile south of Grand Ave. on 103rd Ave.

SUN LAKES C.C.

TRADITIONAL, 18 HOLES, PRIVATE
M.PAR: 60   **M.RATING:** N/A
M.YARDS: 3474   **M.SLOPE:** N/A
HIGH SEASON: $NA
25425 N. Sun Lakes Blvd., Sun Lakes, AZ 85248
602-895-9274
Exit I-10 at Riggs Rd., then go east for 3 miles to Sun Lakes Blvd.

SUNLAND VILLAGE EAST G.C.

TRADITIONAL, 18 HOLES, PRIVATE
M.PAR: 62   **M.RATING:** 56.4
M.YARDS: 3689   **M.SLOPE:** 80
HIGH SEASON: $15
2250 S. Buttercup, Mesa, AZ 85208
602-986-4079
1.5 miles east of Power Rd. on Baseline Rd.

TRAIL RIDGE G.C.

DESERT, 18 HOLES, PRIVATE
M.PAR: 72   **M.RATING:** 72.0
M.YARDS: 6605   **M.SLOPE:** 125
HIGH SEASON: $25
21021 N. 151st Ave., Sun City West, AZ 85375
602-546-0858
Go west on Grand Ave. and north to Meeker Ave., take Granite Valley Rd. west 1 mile to course.

TROON GOLF & C.C.

DESERT, 18 HOLES, PRIVATE
M.PAR: 72   **M.RATING:** 74.8
M.YARDS: 7041   **M.SLOPE:** 142
HIGH SEASON: $130
25000 N. Windy Walk Dr., Scottsdale, AZ 85255
602-585-0540
Take Pima Rd. north to happy Valley rd., go east 3 miles to Windy Walk Dr.

TUCSON C.C.

TRADITIONAL, 18 HOLES, PRIVATE
M.PAR: 72   **M.RATING:** 71.6
M.YARDS: 6809   **M.SLOPE:** 123
HIGH SEASON: $35
2950 N. Camino Principle, Tucson, AZ 85715
602-298-6769
A half mile east of Wilmot off Tanque Verde.

Tucson Estates G.C.

Desert, 18 Holes, Private
M.Par: 57   **M.Rating: N/A**
M.Yards: 2584   **M.Slope: N/A**
High Season: $10
2500 S. Western Way, Tucson, AZ 85713
602-883-5566
At Western Way & Kinney Rd.

Union Hills C.C.

Traditional, 18 Holes, Private
M.Par: 72   **M.Rating: 68.8**
M.Yards: 6293   **M.Slope: 110**
High Season: $25
9860 Lingren Ave., Sun City, AZ 85373
602-977-4281
Quarter mile south of Union Hills Dr. on 99th Ave.

White Mountain C.C.

Traditional, 18 Holes, Private
M.Par: 72   **M.Rating: 68.0**
M.Yards: 6523   **M.Slope: 108**
High Season: $58
P.O. Box 1489, Pinetop, AZ 85935
602-367-4913
Go east on State Rd. 260, 1 mile outside of Pinetop to the main gate.

Williams AFB G.C.

Traditional, 18 Holes, Private
M.Par: 72   **M.Rating: 70.1**
M.Yards: 6605   **M.Slope: 117**
High Season: $20
Bldg 90, Williams AFB, AZ 85240
602-988-5493
Take the Power Rd. exit off the Superstition Freeway for 5 miles to Power Rd. & Chandler Blvd.

Willowbrook G.C.

Traditional, 18 Holes, Private
M.Par: 60   **M.Rating: 59.5**
M.Yards: 3767   **M.Slope: 92**
High Season: $13
10600 Boswell Blvd., Sun City, AZ 85351
602-876-3033
Go north on Del Webb Blvd. off Bell Rd. to Boswell, go west.

Willowcreek G.C.

Traditional, 18 Holes, Private
M.Par: 72   **M.Rating: 69.3**
M.Yards: 6466   **M.Slope: 116**
High Season: $15
10600 Boswell Blvd., Sun City, AZ 85351
602-876-3030
Half mile north on Del Webb Blvd. off Bell Rd. to Boswell, go west.

Yuma Golf & C.C.

Traditional, 18 Holes, Private
M.Par: 72   **M.Rating: 69.8**
M.Yards: 6332   **M.Slope: 115**
High Season: $60
P.O. Box 2048, Yuma, AZ 85364
602-726-1104
At Hwy. 80 and Fortuna Ave.

ARIZONA COURSE INDEX

ALPHABETICAL BY NAME

CONT.

CONT.

CONT.

CONT.

ALPHABETICAL BY CITY

CONT.

CONT.

CONT.

ALPHABETICAL BY ACCESS

PAGE #	COURSE NAME	PAGE #	COURSE NAME

PUBLIC

<table>
<tr><td>4</td><td>500 CLUB</td><td>250</td><td>FRANCISCO GRANDE R. & G.C.</td></tr>
<tr><td>8</td><td>AHWATUKEE LAKES G.C.</td><td>82</td><td>FRED ENKE G.C.</td></tr>
<tr><td>10</td><td>ANTELOPE HILLS NORTH G.C.</td><td>250</td><td>GLEN CANYON G.C.</td></tr>
<tr><td>12</td><td>ANTELOPE HILLS SOUTH G.C.</td><td>94</td><td>GLEN LAKES G.C.</td></tr>
<tr><td>14</td><td>APACHE SUN G.C.</td><td>96</td><td>GOLD CANYON G.C.</td></tr>
<tr><td>18</td><td>ARIZONA BILTMORE C.C.- ADOBE COURSE</td><td>98</td><td>HAPPY TRAILS G.R.</td></tr>
<tr><td>20</td><td>ARIZONA BILTMORE C.C.- LINKS COURSE</td><td>250</td><td>HAVEN G.C.</td></tr>
<tr><td>22</td><td>ARIZONA CITY G.C.</td><td>250</td><td>HAYDEN MUNICIPAL G.C.</td></tr>
<tr><td>26</td><td>ARROYO DUNES MUNICIPAL G.C.</td><td>251</td><td>HIDDEN COVE G.C.</td></tr>
<tr><td>28</td><td>ARTHUR PACK DESERT G.C.</td><td>100</td><td>HILLCREST G.C.</td></tr>
<tr><td>30</td><td>BELLAIR G.C.</td><td>102</td><td>IRONWOOD G.C.</td></tr>
<tr><td>36</td><td>CAMELOT G.C. - 18</td><td>104</td><td>KARSTEN G.C. AT ASU</td></tr>
<tr><td>38</td><td>CAMELOT G.C. - 9</td><td>106</td><td>KEN MCDONALD G.C.</td></tr>
<tr><td>248</td><td>CANOA HILLS G.C.</td><td>251</td><td>KINGMAN MUNICIPAL G.C.</td></tr>
<tr><td>42</td><td>CAVE CREEK G.C</td><td>251</td><td>KINO SPRINGS C.C.</td></tr>
<tr><td>44</td><td>CLIFF VALLEY G.C.</td><td>114</td><td>LEGEND G.C.</td></tr>
<tr><td>46</td><td>COCOPAH BEND R.V. & G.R.</td><td>120</td><td>MARRIOTT'S MOUNTAIN SHADOWS G.C.</td></tr>
<tr><td>249</td><td>CONCHO VALLEY C.C.</td><td>122</td><td>MARYVALE G.C.</td></tr>
<tr><td>48</td><td>CONTINENTAL G.C.</td><td>124</td><td>MCCORMICK RANCH G.C. - PALM COURSE</td></tr>
<tr><td>50</td><td>CORONADO G.C.</td><td>126</td><td>MCCORMICK RANCH G.C. - PINE COURSE</td></tr>
<tr><td>249</td><td>COYOTE HILLS G.C.</td><td>251</td><td>MEADOW HILLS MUNI. G.C.</td></tr>
<tr><td>52</td><td>CYPRESS G.C.</td><td>128</td><td>MESA DEL SOL G.C.</td></tr>
<tr><td>249</td><td>DAVE WHITE REGIONAL MUNICPLE G.C.</td><td>252</td><td>MESA VIEW G.C.</td></tr>
<tr><td>249</td><td>DESERT FAIRWAYS G.C.</td><td>252</td><td>NAUTICAL INN G.C.</td></tr>
<tr><td>249</td><td>DESERT LAKES G.C.</td><td>134</td><td>OCOTILLO G.C. - BLUE/GOLD</td></tr>
<tr><td>56</td><td>DESERT HILLS MUNI. G.C.</td><td>136</td><td>OCOTILLO G.C. - BLUE/WHITE</td></tr>
<tr><td>58</td><td>DOBSON RANCH G.C.</td><td>138</td><td>OCOTILLO G.C. - GOLD/WHITE</td></tr>
<tr><td>60</td><td>DORADO G.C.</td><td>140</td><td>ORANGE TREE G.R.</td></tr>
<tr><td>249</td><td>DOUGLASS G.C.</td><td>252</td><td>PALO VERDE G.C.</td></tr>
<tr><td>250</td><td>DOVE VALLEY G.C.</td><td>142</td><td>PAPAGO G.C.</td></tr>
<tr><td>62</td><td>DREAMLAND VILLA G.C.</td><td>144</td><td>PARADISE VALLEY PARK G.C.</td></tr>
<tr><td>64</td><td>EL CARO G.C.</td><td>146</td><td>PAVILLION LAKES G.C.</td></tr>
<tr><td>68</td><td>EL RIO G.C.</td><td>252</td><td>PAYSON G.C.</td></tr>
<tr><td>250</td><td>ELEPHANT ROCKS G.C.</td><td>148</td><td>PEPPERWOOD G.C.</td></tr>
<tr><td>250</td><td>EMERALD CANYON G.C.</td><td>252</td><td>PINETOP LAKES G. & C.C.</td></tr>
<tr><td>70</td><td>ENCANTO G.C.</td><td>253</td><td>POCO DIABLO RESORT</td></tr>
<tr><td>72</td><td>ENCANTO NINE G.C.</td><td>152</td><td>POINTE HILTON G.C. AT LOOKOUT MTN.</td></tr>
<tr><td>74</td><td>ESTRELLA MOUNTAIN G.C.</td><td>154</td><td>POINTE HILTON G.C. ON SOUTH MTN.</td></tr>
<tr><td>76</td><td>FAIRFIELD FLAGSTAFF RESORT - ELDEN HILLS G.C.</td><td>253</td><td>PUEBLO DEL SOL G.C.</td></tr>
<tr><td>78</td><td>FIESTA LAKES G.C.</td><td>253</td><td>QUAILWOOD GREENS G.C.</td></tr>
<tr><td></td><td></td><td>253</td><td>QUEENS BAY C.C.</td></tr>
<tr><td></td><td></td><td>160</td><td>RANCHO DEL RAY G.C.   CONT.</td></tr>
</table>

CONT.

PRIVATE

CONT.

ALPHABETICAL BY LAYOUT

PAGE #	COURSE NAME

PAGE #	COURSE NAME

DESERT

CONT.

CONT.

CONT.

LINKS

COURSE HONOR'S & TOURNEY'S

TOP 50 TOUGHEST COURSES

ALL COURSES

	TOTAL	COURSE NAME
1	222.8	LA PALOMA C.C. - RIDGE/CANYON
2	218.7	DESERT FOREST G.C.
3	216.8	TROON GOLF & C.C.
4	214.6	DESERT MOUNTAIN G.C. - RENAGADE
5	213.9	DESERT MOUNTAIN G.C. - GERONIMO
6	212.9	LA PALOMA C.C. - CANYON/HILL
7	210.2	VENTANA CANYON G.C. - MTN. COURSE
8	209.8	DESERT MOUNTAIN G.C. - COCHISE
9	208.9	ALTA MESA C.C.
10	208.9	DESERT HIGHLANDS
11	208.7	LA PALOMA C.C. - HILL/RIDGE
12	207.5	ANCALA C.C.
13	207.1	FOREST HIGHLANDS
14	205.8	MOON VALLEY C.C.
15	204.9	SUN CITY VISTOSO G.C.
16	203.0	SUPERSTITION SPRINGS G.C.
17	201.0	TROON NORTH G.C.
18	200.8	GRANDVIEW G.C.
19	200.7	WIGWAM - GOLD COURSE
20	200.3	RIO RICO RESORT & C.C.
21	199.6	LOS CABALLEROS G.C.
22	199.6	OCOTILLO G.C. - BLUE/GOLD
23	199.4	FRED ENKE G.C.
24	199.0	EMERALD CANYON G.C.
25	198.9	PINNACLE PEAK C.C.
26	198.6	BOULDERS CLUB - NORTH
27	198.3	TPC AT STARPASS
28	198.1	ORO VALLEY C.C.
29	197.0	TRAIL RIDGE G.C.
30	196.9	McCORMICK RANCH G.C. - PALM COURSE
31	196.7	PHOENICIAN G.C.
32	196.7	PHOENIX C.C.
33	196.2	STONECREEK, THE G.C.
34	195.9	MESA C.C.
35	195.8	SAN IGNACIO G. C.
36	195.3	KARSTEN G.C. AT ASU
37	195.2	ARROWHEAD C.C.
38	195.1	POINTE HILTON G.C. AT LOOKOUT MTN.
39	195.0	TPC SCOTTSDALE - STADIUM COURSE
40	194.9	McCORMICK RANCH G.C. - PINE COURSE
41	194.7	GOLD CANYON G.C.
42	194.6	TUCSON C.C.
43	194.4	PRESCOTT C.C.
44	194.3	MARRIOT'S CAMELBACK G.C. - INDIAN BEND
45	194.0	TATUM RANCH G.C.
46	193.7	OCOTILLO G.C. - BLUE/WHITE
47	193.7	PAPAGO G.C.
48	193.5	QUAIL CREEK C.C.
49	193.2	COTTONWOOD C.C.
50	193.2	OCOTILLO G.C. - GOLD/WHITE

ALL COURSES OPEN TO PUBLIC

	TOTAL	COURSE NAME
1	222.8	LA PALOMA C.C. - RIDGE/CANYON
2	212.9	LA PALOMA C.C. - CANYON/HILL
3	208.7	LA PALOMA C.C. - HILL/RIDGE
4	204.9	SUN CITY VISTOSO G.C.
5	203.0	SUPERSTITION SPRINGS G.C.
6	201.0	TROON NORTH G.C.
7	200.7	WIGWAM - GOLD COURSE
8	200.3	RIO RICO RESORT & C.C.
9	199.6	LOS CABALLEROS G.C.
10	199.6	OCOTILLO G.C. - BLUE/GOLD
11	199.4	FRED ENKE G.C.
12	199.0	EMERALD CANYON G.C.
13	198.6	BOULDERS CLUB - NORTH
14	198.3	TPC AT STARPASS
15	196.9	McCORMICK RANCH G.C. - PALM COURSE
16	196.7	PHOENICIAN G.C.
17	196.2	STONECREEK, THE G.C.
18	195.8	SAN IGNACIO G. C.
19	195.3	KARSTEN G.C. AT ASU
20	195.2	ARROWHEAD C.C.
21	195.1	POINTE HILTON G.C. AT LOOKOUT MTN.
22	195.0	TPC SCOTTSDALE - STADIUM COURSE
23	194.9	McCORMICK RANCH G.C. - PINE COURSE
24	194.7	GOLD CANYON G.C.
25	194.4	PRESCOTT C.C.
26	194.3	MARRIOT'S CAMELBACK G.C. - INDIAN BEND
27	194.0	TATUM RANCH G.C.
28	193.7	OCOTILLO G.C. - BLUE/WHITE
29	193.7	PAPAGO G.C.
30	193.2	OCOTILLO G.C. - GOLD/WHITE
31	193.0	TUCSON NATIONAL - ORANGE/GOLD
32	192.7	RED MOUNTAIN RANCH C.C.
33	192.6	HILLCREST G.C.
34	191.0	RANDOLPH PARK G.C. - NORTH
35	190.9	TUCSON NATIONAL - GREEN/GOLD
36	190.7	FRANCISCO GRANDE R. & G.C.
37	190.5	ANTELOPE HILLS NORTH G.C.
38	190.4	KINGMAN MUNICIPAL G.C.
39	190.4	OAK CREEK C.C.
40	190.2	TUBAC G.R.
41	190.2	TUCSON NATIONAL - GREEN/ORANGE
42	190.0	GAINEY RANCH G.C. - ARROYO/LAKES
43	189.8	FAIRFIELD FLAGSTAFF RESORT - ELDEN HILLS G.C.
44	189.6	BOULDERS CLUB - SOUTH
45	189.5	LONDON BRIDGE G.C.
46	189.2	SADDLEBROOKE C.C.
47	188.8	SEDONA G.R.
48	188.7	HAPPY TRAILS G.R.
49	188.0	PUEBLO DEL SOL G.C.
50	187.2	SILVER CREEK G.C.

Based on "Mens" rating + slope

TOP 50 EASIEST COURSES

	ALL COURSES		ALL COURSES OPEN TO PUBLIC
TOTAL	**COURSE NAME**	**TOTAL**	**COURSE NAME**
1 64.8	ROADHAVEN R. & G.C.	1 112.2	QUEENS BAY C.C.
2 112.2	QUEENS BAY C.C.	2 124.7	CANYON MESA C.C.
3 124.7	CANYON MESA C.C.	3 127.7	EL CARO G.C.
4 127.7	EL CARO G.C.	4 128.3	ROLLING HILLS G.C.
5 128.3	ROLLING HILLS G.C.	5 129.3	PALO VERDE G.C.
6 129.3	PALO VERDE G.C.	6 130.4	MESA VIEW G.C.
7 130.4	MESA VIEW G.C.	7 136.0	PARADISE VALLEY PARK G.C.
8 132.3	LAKES EAST G.C.	8 136.4	NAUTICAL INN G.C.
9 136.0	PARADISE VALLEY PARK G.C.	9 136.6	SUNLAND VILLAGE G.C.
10 136.4	NAUTICAL INN G.C.	10 136.7	ENCANTO NINE G.C.
11 136.4	SUNLAND VILLAGE EAST G.C.	11 137.0	PEPPERWOOD G.C.
12 136.6	SUNLAND VILLAGE G.C.	12 137.7	VILLA MONTEREY G.C.
13 136.7	ENCANTO NINE G.C.	13 140.7	MARRIOTT'S MOUNTAIN SHADOWS G.C.
14 137.0	PEPPERWOOD G.C.	14 142.3	DORADO G.C.
15 137.7	VILLA MONTEREY G.C.	15 143.4	CONTINENTAL G.C.
16 140.7	MARRIOTT'S MOUNTAIN SHADOWS G.C.	16 144.8	BELLAIR G.C.
17 142.3	DORADO G.C.	17 147.4	COUNTRY MEADOWS G.C.
18 142.4	ROLLING HILLS G.C.	18 148.7	CORONADO G.C.
19 143.4	CONTINENTAL G.C.	19 148.8	VIEWPOINT R.V. & G.R.
20 143.7	PALO VERDE C.C.	20 149.3	SUNBIRD G.R.
21 144.8	BELLAIR G.C.	21 150.4	AHWATUKEE LAKES G.C.
22 147.4	COUNTRY MEADOWS G.C.	22 152.0	SHALIMAR C.C.
23 148.3	FOUNTAIN OF THE SUN C.C.	23 154.3	RIO SALADO G.C.
24 148.7	CORONADO G.C.	24 154.6	PINETOP LAKES G. & C.C.
25 148.8	VIEWPOINT R.V. & G.R.	25 155.5	QUEEN VALLEY G.C.
26 148.9	QUAIL RUN G.C.	26 156.6	CAMELOT G.C. - 18
27 149.3	SUNBIRD G.R.	27 160.7	COYOTE HILLS G.C.
28 150.4	AHWATUKEE LAKES G.C.	28 161.0	COCOPAH BEND R.V. & G.R.
29 151.2	ECHO MESA G.C.	29 164.4	APACHE WELLS C.C.
30 151.5	WILLOWBROOK G.C.	30 165.5	RANDOLPH PARK G.C. - SOUTH
31 151.6	LEISURE WORLD C.C. - EXEC.	31 166.5	POINTE HILTON G.C. ON SOUTH MTN.
32 152.0	SHALIMAR C.C.	32 169.2	SHOW LOW C.C.
33 152.0	STARDUST G.C.	33 169.6	RIVERVIEW G.C. - MESA
34 154.3	RIO SALADO G.C.	34 170.7	SHERATON EL CONQUISTADOR G.C.
35 154.6	PINETOP LAKES G. & C.C.	35 171.2	SNOWFLAKE MUNI. G.C.
36 155.5	QUEEN VALLEY G.C.	36 172.7	ALPINE C.C.
37 156.6	CAMELOT G.C. - 18	37 173.1	PAVILLION LAKES G.C.
38 160.7	COYOTE HILLS G.C.	38 174.0	WESTBROOK VILLAGE C.C.
39 161.0	COCOPAH BEND R.V. & G.R.	39 175.3	ELEPHANT ROCKS G.C.
40 164.4	APACHE WELLS C.C.	40 175.5	DESERT LAKES G.C.
41 165.5	RANDOLPH PARK G.C. - SOUTH	41 175.5	PAYSON G.C.
42 166.5	POINTE HILTON G.C. ON SOUTH MTN.	42 175.8	STONE BRIDGE G.C.
43 169.2	SHOW LOW C.C.	43 175.9	THUNDERBIRD C.C.
44 169.6	RIVERVIEW G.C. - MESA	44 176.4	GENERAL WILLIAM BLANCHARD G.C.
45 170.7	SHERATON EL CONQUISTADOR G.C.	45 176.4	TPC SCOTTSDALE - DESERT COURSE
46 171.2	SNOWFLAKE MUNI. G.C.	46 176.6	CONCHO VALLEY C.C.
47 172.7	ALPINE C.C.	47 176.6	EL RIO G.C.
48 173.1	PAVILLION LAKES G.C.	48 177.2	500 CLUB
49 174.0	WESTBROOK VILLAGE C.C.	49 177.3	SAN MANUEL G.C.
50 175.3	ELEPHANT ROCKS G.C.	50 177.4	PINE MEADOWS C.C.

Based on "Mens" rating + slope

TOP 50 LONGEST COURSES

	ALL COURSES			ALL COURSES OPEN TO PUBLIC	
	TOTAL	COURSE NAME		TOTAL	COURSE NAME
1	7515	DESERT MOUNTAIN G.C. - RENAGADE	1	7119	RIO RICO RESORT & C.C.
2	7437	DESERT MOUNTAIN G.C. - GERONIMO	2	7088	LA PALOMA C.C. - RIDGE/CANYON
3	7298	MOON VALLEY C.C.	3	7017	LA PALOMA C.C. - HILL/RIDGE
4	7132	ALTA MESA C.C.	4	6997	LA PALOMA C.C. - CANYON/HILL
5	7119	RIO RICO RESORT & C.C.	5	6975	FRANCISCO GRANDE R. & G.C.
6	7099	DESERT HIGHLANDS	6	6783	PRESCOTT C.C.
7	7088	LA PALOMA C.C. - RIDGE/CANYON	7	6730	TURQUOISE VALLEY G.C.
8	7051	FOREST HIGHLANDS	8	6657	EMERALD CANYON G.C.
9	7045	DESERT MOUNTAIN G.C. - COCHISE	9	6641	COBRE VALLEY C.C.
10	7041	TROON GOLF & C.C.	10	6600	CANOA HILLS G.C.
11	7017	LA PALOMA C.C. - HILL/RIDGE	11	6600	HILLCREST G.C.
12	6997	LA PALOMA C.C. - CANYON/HILL	12	6599	PUEBLO DEL SOL G.C.
13	6981	DESERT FOREST G.C.	13	6590	PAPAGO G.C.
14	6975	FRANCISCO GRANDE R. & G.C.	14	6554	LOS CABALLEROS G.C.
15	6964	ORO VALLEY C.C.	15	6549	TUCSON NATIONAL - ORANGE/GOLD
16	6961	ANCALA C.C.	16	6539	ANTELOPE HILLS NORTH G.C.
17	6953	SUN CITY SOUTH G.C.	17	6537	DESERT LAKES G.C.
18	6862	GRANDVIEW G.C.	18	6508	TPC SCOTTSDALE - STADIUM COURSE
19	6809	TUCSON C.C.	19	6504	WIGWAM - GOLD COURSE
20	6783	PRESCOTT C.C.	20	6500	SAN MANUEL G.C.
21	6742	PHOENIX C.C.	21	6494	SADDLEBROOKE C.C.
22	6737	COTTONWOOD C.C.	22	6486	MARRIOT'S CAMELBACK G.C. - INDIAN BEND
23	6730	TURQUOISE VALLEY G.C.	23	6474	TROON NORTH G.C.
24	6680	PARADISE VALLEY C.C.	24	6455	ARIZONA BILTMORE C.C.- ADOBE COURSE
25	6657	EMERALD CANYON G.C.	25	6440	ARIZONA CITY G.C.
26	6641	COBRE VALLEY C.C.	26	6436	RANDOLPH PARK G.C. - NORTH
27	6605	TRAIL RIDGE G.C.	27	6434	PINEWOOD C.C.
28	6605	WILLIAMS AFB G.C.	28	6423	ANTELOPE HILLS SOUTH G.C.
29	6600	CANOA HILLS G.C.	29	6415	ESTRELLA MOUNTAIN G.C.
30	6600	HILLCREST G.C.	30	6408	TUBAC G.R.
31	6599	MESA C.C.	31	6406	TOM WEISKOPF'S FOOTHILLS G.C.
32	6599	PUEBLO DEL SOL G.C.	32	6405	SUPERSTITION SPRINGS G.C.
33	6590	PAPAGO G.C.	33	6398	ORANGE TREE G.R.
34	6587	PINNACLE PEAK C.C.	34	6388	TUCSON NATIONAL - GREEN/GOLD
35	6579	FAIRFIELD FLAGSTAFF RESORT - ASPEN VALLEY	35	6386	BEAVER CREEK G.R.
36	6554	LOS CABALLEROS G.C.	36	6386	WICKENBURG C.C.
37	6549	TUCSON NATIONAL - ORANGE/GOLD	37	6384	ARTHUR PACK DESERT G.C.
38	6545	LEISURE WORLD C.C. - CHAMP.	38	6384	TWIN LAKES G. C.
39	6539	ANTELOPE HILLS NORTH G.C.	39	6383	TPC AT STARPASS
40	6537	DESERT LAKES G.C.	40	6379	OCOTILLO G.C. - BLUE/GOLD
41	6529	PALMBROOK C.C.	41	6372	DESRT HILLS MUNI. G.C.
42	6523	WHITE MOUNTAIN C.C.	42	6363	FRED ENKE G.C.
43	6508	TPC SCOTTSDALE - STADIUM COURSE	43	6357	TATUM RANCH G.C.
44	6504	WIGWAM - GOLD COURSE	44	6354	MOUNT GRAHAM G.C.
45	6500	SAN MANUEL G.C.	45	6346	MCCORMICK RANCH G.C. - PINE COURSE
46	6494	SADDLEBROOKE C.C.	46	6336	HAVEN G.C.
47	6486	MARRIOT'S CAMELBACK G.C. - INDIAN BEND	47	6336	KEARNY G.C.
48	6474	TROON NORTH G.C.	48	6324	ARIZONA SUNSITES C.C.
49	6466	WILLOWCREEK G.C.	49	6316	DAVE WHITE REGIONAL MUNICPLE G.C.
50	6455	ARIZONA BILTMORE C.C.- ADOBE COURSE	50	6316	KEN MCDONALD G.C.

Based on "Mens" tees

TOP 50 SHORTEST COURSES

	ALL COURSES	
	TOTAL	COURSE NAME
1	720	POCO DIABLO RESORT
2	1022	ROADHAVEN R. & G.C.
3	1123	ARROYO DUNES MUNICIPAL G.C.
4	1300	CANYON MESA C.C.
5	1373	QUEENS BAY C.C.
6	1437	PARADISE PEAK WEST
7	1460	IRONWOOD G.C.
8	1501	ROYAL PALMS G. C.
9	1503	FIESTA LAKES G.C.
10	1730	ENCANTO NINE G.C.
11	1742	CAMELOT G.C. - 9
12	1820	PALO VERDE G.C.
13	1850	CORONADO G.C.
14	1876	SUN VILLAGE RESORT & G.C.
15	1950	DREAMLAND VILLA G.C.
16	2010	PEPPERWOOD G.C.
17	2083	QUAILWOOD GREENS G.C.
18	2100	SHALIMAR C.C.
19	2100	VILLA MONTEREY G.C.
20	2217	VIEWPOINT R.V. & G. R.
21	2261	CLIFF VALLEY G.C.
22	2386	DESERT FAIRWAYS G.C.
23	2396	GLEN LAKES G.C.
24	2530	APACHE SUN G.C.
25	2536	RIO SALADO G.C.
26	2552	SHERATON EL CONQUISTADOR G.C.
27	2584	TUCSON ESTATES G.C.
28	2606	MARRIOTT'S MOUNTAIN SHADOWS G.C.
29	2631	PINE MEADOWS C.C.
30	2790	RIVERVIEW G.C. - MESA
31	2845	COYOTE HILLS G.C.
32	2902	QUAIL RUN G.C.
33	3000	DOVE VALLEY G.C.
34	3014	CONCHO VALLEY C.C.
35	3070	DOUGLASS G.C.
36	3096	AJO C.C.
37	3112	SNOWFLAKE MUNI. G.C.
38	3174	QUAIL CREEK C.C.
39	3200	RIO VERDE G.C. - WHITE WING
40	3214	WINSLOW MUNI. G.C.
41	3244	LAKES EAST G.C.
42	3259	GLEN CANYON G.C.
43	3318	MESA VIEW G.C.
44	3330	EL CARO G.C.
45	3400	GREENLEE C.C.
46	3412	BELLAIR G.C.
47	3441	MEADOW HILLS MUNI. G.C.
48	3474	SUN LAKES G.C.
49	3509	ROLLING HILLS G.C.
50	3579	SUNLAND VILLAGE G.C.

	ALL COURSES OPEN TO PUBLIC	
	TOTAL	COURSE NAME
1	720	POCO DIABLO RESORT
2	1123	ARROYO DUNES MUNICIPAL G.C.
3	1300	CANYON MESA C.C.
4	1373	QUEENS BAY C.C.
5	1460	IRONWOOD G.C.
6	1501	ROYAL PALMS G. C.
7	1503	FIESTA LAKES G.C.
8	1730	ENCANTO NINE G.C.
9	1742	CAMELOT G.C. - 9
10	1820	PALO VERDE G.C.
11	1850	CORONADO G.C.
12	1876	SUN VILLAGE RESORT & G.C.
13	1950	DREAMLAND VILLA G.C.
14	2010	PEPPERWOOD G.C.
15	2083	QUAILWOOD GREENS G.C.
16	2100	SHALIMAR C.C.
17	2100	VILLA MONTEREY G.C.
18	2217	VIEWPOINT R.V. & G. R.
19	2261	CLIFF VALLEY G.C.
20	2386	DESERT FAIRWAYS G.C.
21	2396	GLEN LAKES G.C.
22	2530	APACHE SUN G.C.
23	2536	RIO SALADO G.C.
24	2552	SHERATON EL CONQUISTADOR G.C.
25	2606	MARRIOTT'S MOUNTAIN SHADOWS G.C.
26	2631	PINE MEADOWS C.C.
27	2790	RIVERVIEW G.C. - MESA
28	2845	COYOTE HILLS G.C.
29	3000	DOVE VALLEY G.C.
30	3014	CONCHO VALLEY C.C.
31	3070	DOUGLASS G.C.
32	3096	AJO C.C.
33	3112	SNOWFLAKE MUNI. G.C.
34	3200	RIO VERDE G.C. - WHITE WING
35	3214	WINSLOW MUNI. G.C.
36	3259	GLEN CANYON G.C.
37	3318	MESA VIEW G.C.
38	3330	EL CARO G.C.
39	3400	GREENLEE C.C.
40	3412	BELLAIR G.C.
41	3441	MEADOW HILLS MUNI. G.C.
42	3509	ROLLING HILLS G.C.
43	3579	SUNLAND VILLAGE G.C.
44	3660	AHWATUKEE LAKES G.C.
45	3751	DORADO G.C.
46	3766	CONTINENTAL G.C.
47	3794	PARADISE VALLEY PARK G.C.
48	3820	SUNBIRD G.R.
49	3914	DESERT SANDS G.C.
50	4012	NAUTICAL INN G.C.

Based on "Mens" tees

TOP 50 MOST EXPENSIVE COURSES

ALL COURSES

	$ COST	COURSE NAME
1	150.00	DESERT MOUNTAIN G.C. - COCHISE
2	150.00	DESERT MOUNTAIN G.C. - GERONIMO
3	150.00	DESERT MOUNTAIN G.C. - RENAGADE
4	135.00	BOULDERS CLUB - NORTH
5	135.00	BOULDERS CLUB - SOUTH
6	130.00	TROON GOLF & C.C.
7	115.00	TROON NORTH G.C.
8	110.00	PHOENICIAN G.C.
9	99.00	GAINEY RANCH G.C. - ARROYO/LAKES
10	99.00	GAINEY RANCH G.C. - DUNES/ARROYO
11	99.00	GAINEY RANCH G.C. - LAKES/DUNES
12	99.00	RED MOUNTAIN RANCH C.C.
13	98.00	POINTE HILTON G.C. AT LOOKOUT MTN.
14	95.00	EL CONQUISTADOR C.C.-SUNRISE COURSE
15	95.00	LA PALOMA C.C. - CANYON/HILL
16	95.00	LA PALOMA C.C. - HILL/RIDGE
17	95.00	LA PALOMA C.C. - RIDGE/CANYON
18	95.00	TUCSON NATIONAL - GREEN/GOLD
19	95.00	TUCSON NATIONAL - GREEN/ORANGE
20	95.00	TUCSON NATIONAL - ORANGE/GOLD
21	95.00	WIGWAM - GOLD COURSE
22	89.00	VENTANA CANYON G.C. - MTN. COURSE
23	87.00	TPC SCOTTSDALE - STADIUM COURSE
24	85.00	STONECREEK, THE G.C.
25	80.00	ARIZONA BILTMORE C.C.- ADOBE COURSE
26	80.00	ARIZONA BILTMORE C.C.- LINKS COURSE
27	80.00	MARRIOT'S CAMELBACK G.C. - INDIAN BEND
28	80.00	MARRIOTT'S CAMELBACK G.C. - PADRE
29	80.00	WIGWAM - BLUE COURSE
30	80.00	WIGWAM - WEST COURSE
31	79.00	TPC AT STARPASS
32	75.00	ARIZONA C.C.
33	75.00	LOS CABALLEROS G.C.
34	75.00	McCORMICK RANCH G.C. - PALM COURSE
35	75.00	McCORMICK RANCH G.C. - PINE COURSE
36	75.00	ORANGE TREE G.R.
37	75.00	PHOENIX C.C.
38	75.00	RIO VERDE G.C. - QUAIL RUN
39	75.00	RIO VERDE G.C. - WHITE WING
40	75.00	SCOTTSDALE C. C. - NE
41	75.00	SCOTTSDALE C.C. - NS
42	75.00	SCOTTSDALE C.C. - SE
43	72.00	POINTE HILTON G.C. ON SOUTH MTN.
44	70.00	SHERATON SAN MARCOS G.R.
45	70.00	TATUM RANCH G.C.
46	69.00	SUPERSTITION SPRINGS G.C.
47	69.00	TOM WEISKOPF'S FOOTHILLS G.C.
48	66.00	LEGEND G.C.
49	65.00	FOUNTAIN HILLS G.C.
50	65.00	G.C. OF RANCHO MANANA
50	65.00	GOLD CANYON G.C.
50	65.00	OCOTILLO G.C. - ALL THREE

ALL COURSES OPEN TO PUBLIC

	$ COST	COURSE NAME
1	115.00	TROON NORTH G.C.
2	110.00	PHOENICIAN G.C.
3	99.00	GAINEY RANCH G.C. - ARROYO/LAKES
4	99.00	GAINEY RANCH G.C. - DUNES/ARROYO
5	99.00	GAINEY RANCH G.C. - LAKES/DUNES
6	99.00	RED MOUNTAIN RANCH C.C.
7	98.00	POINTE HILTON G.C. AT LOOKOUT MTN.
8	95.00	EL CONQUISTADOR C.C.-SUNRISE COURSE
9	95.00	LA PALOMA C.C. - CANYON/HILL
10	95.00	LA PALOMA C.C. - HILL/RIDGE
11	95.00	LA PALOMA C.C. - RIDGE/CANYON
12	95.00	TUCSON NATIONAL - GREEN/GOLD
13	95.00	TUCSON NATIONAL - GREEN/ORANGE
14	95.00	TUCSON NATIONAL - ORANGE/GOLD
15	95.00	WIGWAM - GOLD COURSE
16	87.00	TPC SCOTTSDALE - STADIUM COURSE
17	85.00	STONECREEK, THE G.C.
18	80.00	ARIZONA BILTMORE C.C. - ADOBE COURSE
19	80.00	ARIZONA BILTMORE C.C.- LINKS COURSE
20	80.00	MARRIOT'S CAMELBACK G.C. - INDIAN BEND
21	80.00	MARRIOTT'S CAMELBACK G.C. - PADRE
22	80.00	WIGWAM - BLUE COURSE
23	80.00	WIGWAM - WEST COURSE
24	79.00	TPC AT STARPASS
25	75.00	LOS CABALLEROS G.C.
26	75.00	McCORMICK RANCH G.C. - PALM COURSE
27	75.00	McCORMICK RANCH G.C. - PINE COURSE
28	75.00	ORANGE TREE G.R.
29	75.00	RIO VERDE G.C. - QUAIL RUN
30	75.00	RIO VERDE G.C. - WHITE WING
31	75.00	SCOTTSDALE C. C. - NE
32	75.00	SCOTTSDALE C.C. - NS
33	75.00	SCOTTSDALE C.C. - SE
34	72.00	POINTE HILTON G.C. ON SOUTH MTN.
35	70.00	SHERATON SAN MARCOS G.R.
36	70.00	TATUM RANCH G.C.
37	69.00	SUPERSTITION SPRINGS G.C.
38	69.00	TOM WEISKOPF'S FOOTHILLS G.C.
39	66.00	LEGEND G.C.
40	65.00	FOUNTAIN HILLS G.C.
41	65.00	G.C. OF RANCHO MANANA
42	65.00	GOLD CANYON G.C.
43	65.00	OCOTILLO G.C. - BLUE/GOLD
44	65.00	OCOTILLO G.C. - BLUE/WHITE
45	65.00	OCOTILLO G.C. - GOLD/WHITE
46	60.00	AHWATUKEE C.C.
47	59.00	ANCALA C.C.
48	58.00	ARROWHEAD C.C.
49	58.00	BEAVER CREEK G.R.
50	58.00	SUN CITY VISTOSO G.C.

Based on "High Season" green fees

TOP 50 LEAST EXPENSIVE COURSES

	ALL COURSES			ALL COURSES OPEN TO PUBLIC	
	$ TOTAL	**COURSE NAME**		**$ TOTAL**	**COURSE NAME**
1	5.00	ENCANTO NINE G.C.	1	5.00	ENCANTO NINE G.C.
2	6.00	COYOTE HILLS G.C.	2	6.00	COYOTE HILLS G.C.
3	6.50	PALO VERDE G.C.	3	6.50	PALO VERDE G.C.
4	7.00	GLEN LAKES G.C.	4	7.00	GLEN LAKES G.C.
5	8.00	FIESTA LAKES G.C.	5	8.00	FIESTA LAKES G.C.
6	8.00	MEADOW HILLS MUNI. G.C.	6	8.00	MEADOW HILLS MUNI. G.C.
7	8.00	PARADISE PEAK WEST	7	8.00	ROYAL PALMS G. C.
8	8.00	ROYAL PALMS G. C.	8	8.00	VALLEY CLUB G.C.
9	8.00	VALLEY CLUB G.C.	9	8.00	VIEWPOINT R.V. & G. R.
10	8.00	VIEWPOINT R.V. & G. R.	10	8.50	CLIFF VALLEY G.C.
11	8.50	CLIFF VALLEY G.C.	11	9.00	DOUGLASS G.C.
12	9.00	DOUGLASS G.C.	12	9.00	DOVE VALLEY G.C.
13	9.00	DOVE VALLEY G.C.	13	9.00	DREAMLAND VILLA G.C.
14	9.00	DREAMLAND VILLA G.C.	14	9.00	HAYDEN MUNICIPAL G.C.
15	9.00	HAYDEN MUNICIPAL G.C.	15	9.00	PEPPERWOOD G.C.
16	9.00	PEPPERWOOD G.C.	16	9.00	VILLA MONTEREY G.C.
17	9.00	VILLA MONTEREY G.C.	17	9.50	ARROYO DUNES MUNICIPAL G.C.
18	9.50	ARROYO DUNES MUNICIPAL G.C.	18	9.50	IRONWOOD G.C.
19	9.50	IRONWOOD G.C.	19	9.60	CORONADO G.C.
20	9.60	CORONADO G.C.	20	10.00	APACHE SUN G.C.
21	10.00	APACHE SUN G.C.	21	10.00	CAMELOT G.C. - 9
22	10.00	CAMELOT G.C. - 9	22	10.00	DESERT LAKES G.C.
23	10.00	DESERT LAKES G.C.	23	10.00	HIDDEN COVE G.C.
24	10.00	HIDDEN COVE G.C.	24	10.00	KEARNY G.C.
25	10.00	KEARNY G.C.	25	10.00	QUEENS BAY C.C.
26	10.00	QUEENS BAY C.C.	26	10.00	RIO SALADO G.C.
27	10.00	RIO SALADO G.C.	27	10.00	SAN MANUEL G.C.
28	10.00	SAN MANUEL G.C.	28	10.00	SHALIMAR C.C.
29	10.00	SHALIMAR C.C.	29	10.00	TWIN LAKES G. C.
30	10.00	TUCSON ESTATES G.C.	30	10.00	VALLE VISTA C.C.
31	10.00	TWIN LAKES G. C.	31	10.50	MOUNT GRAHAM G.C.
32	10.00	VALLE VISTA C.C.	32	11.00	GLEN CANYON G.C.
33	10.50	MOUNT GRAHAM G.C.	33	11.00	RIVERVIEW G.C. - MESA
34	11.00	GLEN CANYON G.C.	34	12.00	CONCHO VALLEY C.C.
35	11.00	RIVERVIEW G.C. - MESA	35	12.00	DESERT FAIRWAYS G.C.
36	12.00	CONCHO VALLEY C.C.	36	12.00	GREENLEE C.C.
37	12.00	DESERT FAIRWAYS G.C.	37	12.00	MESA VIEW G.C.
38	12.00	FORT HUACHUCA G.C.	38	12.00	POCO DIABLO RESORT
39	12.00	GREENLEE C.C.	39	12.00	TURQUOISE VALLEY G.C.
40	12.00	MESA VIEW G.C.	40	12.00	WINSLOW MUNI. G.C.
41	12.00	POCO DIABLO RESORT	41	13.00	ALPINE C.C.
42	12.00	TURQUOISE VALLEY G.C.	42	13.00	SNOWFLAKE MUNI. G.C.
43	12.00	WINSLOW MUNI. G.C.	43	14.00	DESERT SANDS G.C.
44	13.00	ALPINE C.C.	44	15.00	AJO C.C.
45	13.00	QUAIL RUN G.C.	45	15.00	BELLAIR G.C.
46	13.00	ROLLING HILLS G. C.	46	15.00	CANYON MESA C.C.
47	13.00	SNOWFLAKE MUNI. G.C.	47	15.00	CHAPARRAL C.C.
48	13.00	WILLOWBROOK G.C.	48	15.00	COBRE VALLEY C.C.
49	14.00	DESERT SANDS G.C.	49	15.00	DORADO G.C.
50	14.00	ROADHAVEN R. & G.C.	50	15.00	GENERAL WILLIAM BLANCHARD G.C.

Based on "High Season" green fees

NOTABLE COURSE DESIGNERS

Resort Courses

Course Name	Page #

COMPREHENSIVE GOLF COURSE GUIDES ™

ORDER FORM
FOR INDIVIDUAL SALES

**TEEBOX'S ARIZONA GOLF GUIDE IS WHAT EVERY GOLFER IN ARIZONA NEEDS.
WHETHER YOUR'E A RESIDENT OR VISITOR, THIS GUIDE WILL SHOW YOU
EVERYTHING YOU NEED TO KNOW ABOUT
ARIZONA'S GREAT GOLF COURSES.**

SEND TO	PHONE ORDER	FAX ORDER
TEEBOX	**(602) 494-2779**	**(602) 953-1552**

**3241 E. SHEA BLVD. SUITE #7
PHOENIX, AZ 85028**

Shipping & Handling **Standard UPS,** $4/first book and $2/book thereafter. Call for bulk order.
Two-day Priority Mail, $5/first book and $2/book thereafter. Call for bulk order
For Canada, $6/book. Call for multiple order.

Arizona Residents add 6.7% sales tax

No. of copies: [   ] x **$16.95=** [   ] **+ S/H=** [   ] **=Total** [   ]

☐ Payment Enclosed (check or money order, no cash please)

☐ Visa ☐ Mastercard Acct. # _____

Exp. Date _____

Name _____

Address _____

City _____

State _____

Zip _____ Phone # (___) _____ Signature _____